# THE
# MILITANT
# SOUTH

# THE
# MILITANT
# SOUTH

## 1800–1861

### John Hope Franklin

THE BELKNAP PRESS OF
HARVARD UNIVERSITY PRESS
Cambridge, Massachusetts

F
2/3
.F75
1970

For MOZELLA ANNE BUCK (*In Memoriam*)

## Preface to the Second Printing

When I began to do research for *The Militant South* more than twenty years ago, I was searching for answers to the question of why the South invariably reacted violently to crisis situations. I had in mind, of course, her responses to her many difficulties during the two generations preceding the Civil War. I was not unmindful, however, of the possible illumination that such answers might provide for much later, even recent, periods in Southern history. I made reference to that possibility in the original preface. Meanwhile, I disclaimed for the South any monopoly on bellicosity; and the history of violence in the country as a whole makes it abundantly clear how pervasive the tradition of violence has been.

If America in general has been a land of violence, it was the South that institutionalized it and bestowed on it an aura of respectability. It was a part of the section's social and cultural heritage, sanctified by such time-honored institutions as the code duello, the militia muster, the military academy, the ring tournament, and the lynching party. Thus, it could hardly have been regarded as entirely uncivilized. And if one could find such institutions and practices in other parts of the country — as, indeed, one could — they could hardly be branded as peculiarly Southern. But the role of the South in developing, maintaining, and commending such activities has been a large one. Throughout their history, many Southerners have continued to invoke the rule of personal judgment as to what the law was, long after the raw frontier had passed their region by. In no other part of the country was it so necessary that every white man decide for himself whether and how the law applied to him as in the region where it was so important to make certain that the blacks should not enjoy equal protection of the laws.

Long after the duels, the military academies, and the ring tournaments had become rather pleasant and innocuous relics of a distant past, the South's fundamental attitude toward the law — especially where the former slaves were concerned — remained essentially what it had been before the Civil War. And an important manifestation of that attitude was the militant defiance of unpopular law, whether enacted by a legislature or made by a judge. No other section of the country had ever responded so violently to legislation as the Southern whites responded to the laws passed by Congress and the state assemblies between 1867 and 1875. At no other time in the nation's history was the judgment of the law based so much on who the lawmakers were rather than on what the laws were. And the antipathy toward the Reconstruction lawmakers and their supporters revitalized and made even more respectable the militance that had been a part of the antebellum tradition.

Keeping this tradition alive and making it a part of the apparatus for maintaining white supremacy became a way of life in the South. Indeed, as Ulrich B. Phillips pointed out, it became the "central theme of Southern history." The man, white or black, who challenged what came to be regarded as the racial orthodoxy of the South learned by bitter experience what it cost to make the challenge. In 1898 it would cost Alex Manly, the Negro editor of Wilmington, North Carolina, his career as an editor, and it would cost four hundred of his fellow blacks any semblance of legal rights, including the right to remain in their homes. In 1954 it would cost the United States Supreme Court most of the respect and prestige it enjoyed in the South, when numerous prominent white Southerners, including a hundred Southern Congressmen, denounced bitterly the highest tribunal in the country for declaring segregation in public schools unconstitutional. In 1956 it would cost Nat "King" Cole bodily harm and untold indignities in Birmingham, presumably because of his virtuosity as a pianist and singer, even before an all-white audience.

When they were unsuccessful in securing their rights under the Constitution, Negro Americans took a page from the white Southerners' book and began to defy local segregation laws and discriminatory practices. In time, the militant defiance of the law that was as old as the South itself became the watchword and practice of Southern blacks. Sit-ins and freedom rides and militant demonstrations were the answers that Negroes gave to the Ku Klux Klan and the White Citizens Councils who were determined to maintain segregation at all costs. The South had reaped a whirlwind, resulting in a breakdown of respect for law among Negro Americans not unlike that which had traditionally characterized the attitudes of Southern whites toward racial laws.

If the white people of the South could be militant in the defiance of the law and if the most submerged element of the population could take the law into its own hands to redress ancient grievances, it is not surprising that others were inspired to do likewise. The White Citizens Councils and the Minute Men of the present day are determined to protect the nation — by violence, if necessary — from its own racial heretics and political subverters. The "higher law" adherents among the student and racial activists are equally determined to press the nation into an acceptance of their own objectives — within the law if possible, outside the law if necessary. Meanwhile, a hundred groups, large and small, have taken up one cause or another, and their general posture can best be described as a fierce determination to achieve their objectives, with or without the sanction of the law. The climate has encouraged not only the hording of arms but a resort to their use. The result has been a general escalation of violence, tragically dramatized in the assassination, in recent years, of a President of the United States, a distinguished civil rights leader, and a United States Senator.

Surely the South cannot be held responsible for these unhappy consequences of militancy and violence. But when the nation, even on the frontier, was groping toward an existence under the rule of law, the South contributed heavily to the idea that law could be successfully defied. In making heroes out of those who, on the basis of personal judgment, decided that a law should be disregarded or defied, it helped to preserve a tradition that lends respectability to the open flaunting of the law. The way in which that tradition developed and the manner in which it influenced later sectional and national history would seem to make the subject of this work germane to an effort to understand the condition of our society today.

JOHN HOPE FRANKLIN

September 1, 1969

## Preface to the First Printing

When the Union fell apart in 1861, it was not possible for anyone to answer all the questions that arose in the troubled minds of Americans regarding that catastrophe. In searching for an explanation of the tragic dissolution, thoughtful observers looked at the political and philosophical bases of the nation's structure. They found that the controversial question of the autonomy of the states and the concept of liberty that had evolved offered a partial answer to the question. They examined the economic order and realized that between a commercial–industrial section and one that was predominantly agricultural there was basis for conflict. They looked into the structure of society in the two sections and concluded that there were inherent conflicts between that committed to the view that universal freedom was the proper foundation for improving the social order and the other that insisted that its half-free, half-slave society needed only to be left alone.

Questions of how and why the war came have continued to baffle the minds of men in the generations since 1861. A notable lack of agreement, except on the point of the almost hopeless complexity, and the remarkable accumulation of details regarding the course of events prior to 1861 have been the most impressive results.

While considerable attention has been given to the social, cultural, and psychological conditions of the South before 1861, certain aspects are yet incomplete. In the ante-bellum period, large numbers of observers, including Southerners, made more than passing reference to those phases of Southern life and culture that suggested a penchant for militancy which at times assumed excessive proportions. The persistence of the rural environment, the Indian danger, the fear of slaves, an old-world concept of honor, an increasing sensitivity, and an arrogant self-satisfaction with things as they were contributed. Reflected in the culture and conduct of Southerners, it militated against a calm, deliberate approach to their problems. Several years ago, the late Wilbur J. Cash, a distinguished Southern journalist, observed that the ante-bellum Southerner "did not think; he felt." Feeling or groping his way toward a solution of his increasingly complex problems, the Southerner not infrequently reacted militantly, indeed violently.

This volume seeks to identify and describe those phases of life that won for the ante-bellum South the reputation of being a land of violence. It is concerned, therefore, not merely with the formal and conspicuous revelations of bellicosity but also with those varied conditions of life which not only reflect, but explain this tendency. In the South, for example, militant race superiority evolved out of the defense of plantation slavery, to become an ingredient in the culture. The South's dread of real and fancied Indian scalpers kept many inhabitants trigger-happy, while the persistent fight for *Lebensraum* added to the flavor of militancy. Growing interest in military education, preoccupation with military activities, and many other phases of everyday life reflected a warm attachment to things of a militant nature.

This study implies at no point that all Southerners, or even almost all of them, were bellicose or militant. It is mindful of the existence of elements in the South that regarded violence and other forms of precipitate action as revolting. But these elements dominated neither thought nor action in the crucial generation preceding the Civil War. Like the anti-slavery elements, they lost most of their influence as the controversy between the North and South became intense. They were shouted down, voted down, and fought down by those Southerners who — though they might have been in the minority — subscribed to a code of conduct and a plan of action that was the antithesis of moderation and conciliation. These created the climate of militancy.

The atmosphere of conflict that came to characterize much of the South was transformed into aggressive militancy as intersectional tension increased. Southerners began to think in terms of preparing themselves for "any eventuality," especially if that eventuality involved conflict with the North. Feverish preparations for war during the decade before the election of Lincoln suggest a South that was not only willing, but determined to be ready to fight.

It would be absurd to suggest that the conditions of life herein described were the exclusive possession of the South. The North had its problems of law and order, the West its Indian dangers and more than its share of violence, and almost everywhere in "Young America" rugged individualism pushed men dangerously close to an obnoxious imperiousness. In the North, however, these conditions were almost invariably to be found in the relatively new, sparsely settled regions close to the frontier and under its influences. As Northern areas increased in age and population, they also grew in maturity and responsibility; and they tended to shed their cruder frontier characteristics and take on new traits, sometimes no less violent, that were the product of change and increasing complexity. Meanwhile, in the South, even the older areas tended to retain the traits usually associated with the frontier, while the new areas of the cotton and sugar kingdoms nurtured a frontier militancy and violence that became almost as much a part of the scene as staple crops and Negro slaves. The excessive degree of these manifestations and their persistence throughout the ante-bellum period make the South worthy of special consideration in this regard.

It should be added that the tradition of a military spirit did not *drive* the South into an armed conflict with the North. But this tradition, together with the preparations to support and nourish it, gave the South a self-confidence that strengthened its determination to take the fatal step of secession. The martial spirit of the South helped it face the consequences of secession with confidence, if not with eagerness.

One should not draw the inference that, because this work is concerned primarily with the ante-bellum period, the manifestations of excessive belligerency disappeared with the Civil War. While that conflict may be regarded, in some respects and in some quarters, as the South's "finest hour" or the most dramatic and spirited defense of the concept of honor, it was by no means the final gesture. In the decades following the Civil War dueling was not altogether uncommon in the South. The record of the Klan, the night riders, and other self-constituted regulators is an impressive reminder of the resourcefulness and ingenuity of some Southerners in the area of violence. The fact that nearly 90 per cent of the 1,886 lynchings in the United States between 1900 and 1930 occurred in the South is further indication of this tendency. The assertion that the murder capital of the United States moves annually from one Southern city to another has considerable basis in fact and suggests a continuing indifference to violence. The persistence of these habits suggests the depth and tenacity of their hold and would also seem to suggest that an examination of their origins and early development is important in any effort to understand them.

This book is the result of the labor and cooperation of many generous persons. The endnotes and bibliographical notes indicate my indebtedness to those who have written on related subjects. The staffs of the Library of Congress, the National Archives, Duke University Library, the University of North Carolina Library, Harvard College Library, and the Howard University Library were helpful in numerous ways. The state librarians and archivists of North Carolina, South Carolina, Georgia, Tennessee, Mississippi, Alabama, and Louisiana were unfailing in their generous help. Rayford W. Logan and my other colleagues in the department of history at Howard University and numerous friends and associates, including Douglass Adair, the Joseph Mendelsons, the Henry F. Pringles, Alfred Kazin, Blake McKelvey, Carl Bridenbaugh, Merle Curti, Howard K. Beale, Arthur S. Link, Clement Eaton, and Charles G. Sellers, offered suggestions that place me under heavy obligation to them. The research and writing were made possible through generous grants from the Social Science Research Council and the John Simon Guggenheim Memorial Foundation. To all these persons and institutions I am deeply grateful. I assume full responsibility, however, for any errors or deficiencies in this work. I can never fully express my gratitude to my wife for her understanding patience and valuable assistance.

Washington, D. C.                    JOHN HOPE FRANKLIN

# Contents

# THE
# MILITANT
# SOUTH

# Background of Violence

In 1857, Edmund Ruffin, Virginia's perennial defender of Southern rights, was on the warpath. This time he had good reason to indulge in more than his usual amount of vituperation against the North. There was enough irresponsible talk about the "higher law" and the defiance of the Dred Scott Decision by Northern abolitionists to aggravate even a lukewarm Southerner, and the man who was to fire the first shot at Fort Sumter was not lukewarm. As an elder statesman of the Southern cause, he wrote a series of five articles for the Richmond *Enquirer* and *De Bow's Review*. He poured out his wrath against those who threatened the South and warned that such actions would lead to a disruption of the Union.

Why would the people of the North pursue a course involving such reckless disregard for the future of the nation, Ruffin asked. The answer was that they did so because they lacked respect for the military strength of the South. Consequently, they supposed that they could "vilify and wrong the South to any extent that interest or passion may invite without danger to the North." [1] A decade earlier, "Publicola" of Madison County, Mississippi, had warned Northerners that they "should know enough of Southern character to satisfy them that blustering and bravado are useless, and that the Southern people will at all times be ready to punish any invasion of their rights." [2]

Regarding the character of the Southerners, there was almost universal acknowledgment of their remarkable spirit and will to fight. Indeed, the reputation of the Southerner's readiness to fight was so well established that when Northerners spoke harshly and insultingly of Southern civilization, they could not have been unmindful of this trait. It might be said that the Southern hand rested nervously on its pistol, knife, or sword; and most visitors eyed this threatening posture with proper respect. Even before the War for Independence a British traveler in South Carolina and Georgia observed that the rural life and the constant use of arms promoted a kind of martial spirit among the people, "and the great dangers to which they were always exposed, habituated them to face an enemy with resolution." [3] In 1846, the Scot, Alexander Mackay, described the "fiery blood of the South." [4] A decade later James Stirling was disturbed by the proneness to violence and the readiness to fight which he observed in the Southern states where "wild justice easily degenerates into lawless violence, and a bloodthirsty ferocity is developed among the ruder members of the community." [5]

While the Southern reputation for militancy was viewed with interest and apprehension by some, it aroused considerable criticism and contempt on the part of others. William H. Russell, correspondent for the London *Times*, conceded that Southern gentlemen "travel and read, love field-sports, racing, hunting, and fishing, are bold horsemen and good shots. But after all," he concluded, "their state is a modern Sparta — an aristocracy resting on a helotry, and with nothing else to rest upon. . . They entertain very exaggerated ideas of the military strength of their little community, although one may do full justice to its military spirit." [6] In the practical application of this militancy it was distressing to Joseph Holt Ingraham to find violence so completely accepted that no youngster was entitled to the claims of manhood "until made the mark of an adversary's bullet." [7] This reputation for fighting did not always command respect, nor even serious consideration; but it came to be identified as an important ingredient of Southern civilization.[8]

Southerners disagreed with many judgments of their way of life, but they never resented the assertion that the martial spirit was a significant feature of their character. Thus William Ellery Channing's comment on the South's impetuousness was praised as a "finely drawn picture" that displayed "the hand of the master." [9] Articulate Southerners promoted the idea of their ferocity, if not bloodthirstiness. Edward B. Bryan thought the prospect for successful secession bright because the Southern fighting spirit was distinctly superior to the Northern. "As to the natural military spirit and predilection of the two people" he said, "we believe that there can be but little difficulty in reaching a definite conclusion." The pursuits and mode of life of the Southerners, "joined to their proverbial love of country, create a spirit within them, which once aroused, never could be conquered." [10]

What Bryan was saying in 1850, others had already said and would continue to say for another decade. Experience in everyday life had made the Southerner a kind of fighter unique in the world. His ordinary amusement was the chase, and as a hunter, horseman, and rifleman, he was almost naturally trained to war. In a military struggle the South would surely win, one writer predicted, for it had "more aptitude and genius for war" than the North.[11] And, having won the war, Southerners would display great qualities in their control of the Northern people. "Naturally generous," another admitted, "Southerners exercise much forbearance, till the question of honor is raised, and then they rush to the sword . . . fierce and fearless in a contest, yet just, generous and gentle in command, they possess every quality necessary to rule the Northern people . . ." [12] Inheritance was the chief explanation offered by this writer for the military and political superiority of the South. Those who settled the North were

"Disaffected religionists," who continued to "carry out the peculiarities of their religion and race." But "the Southern States were settled and governed by persons belonging to the blood and race of the reigning family . . . The Cavaliers directly descended from the Norman Barons of William" were "a race distinguished for . . . war-like and fearless character, a race . . . renowned for . . . gallantry . . . chivalry . . . gentleness, and intellect." That race ruled "the world over, whether the subject be African or Caucasian, Celt or Saxon." [13]

Even Southerners without a claim to cavalier ancestry did not suffer from lack of fighting spirit. Georgians could proudly point to an accumulated tradition of vigor in living and stearnness in their relations with their neighbors and with England that more than compensated for their humble origins.[14] The Scots and Scotch-Irish in the back country brought a tradition of pride, boastfulness, and vigor that found a congenial atmosphere in the frontier environment. The habit of war was ingrained in the Scots; usually their heroes were warriors and their admiration for the qualities of courage, endurance, and loyalty to leaders was almost unbounded.[15]

Thus, articulate Europeans, Northerners, and Southerners had contributed much to the idealization of the Southerner as one of the very fearful characters of the nineteenth century. He enjoyed the reputation of being sensitive, quick to defend his honor, adept and skilled in the use of weapons, and with an inherited capacity to rule the conquered with enviable effectiveness.

The Southerner's reputation as a fighting man rested not only on what others said about him, or even on what he said about himself, but also on what he had *done*. There had been a time when few people were convinced of the South's capacity or will to fight. During the War for Independence, for example, New England patriots feared that their Southern comrades would be derelict in shouldering arms against England.[16] Washington did not exclude the South when he complained of the "dearth of public spirit" in the colonies,[17] and General Charles Lee, in early 1776, was distressed over the lack of enthusiasm and decisiveness in the South.[18] So, too, General Gage anticipated little difficulty with the South. The people in the South "talk very high . . . but they can do nothing. Their numerous slaves in the bowells of their country and the Indians at their backs will always keep them quiet." [19] Few Southerners wrote histories of the War for Independence in the years immediately after the struggle,[20] and Northern writers emphasized the contributions of their section. Southerners remained indifferent to the matter until the intersectional struggle became bitter. In the 1840's, however, they sought not only to establish the unquestioned military superiority of the contemporary Southerner, but also to rehabilitate the gallant Southern fighter for independence.

In *American Loyalists*, Lorenzo Sabine noted this effort to glorify the martial South. "South Carolina," he charged, "with a Northern army to assist her could not, or would not, even preserve her own capital . . ." [21] Southerners who read the book were furious. Outraged, one said that "the claims of Carolina to the distinction which her public men assert may be slurred over by ingenious misrepresentation, but she cannot be defrauded of them . . . We cannot allow that her fame is to be smutched because there were many within her territories with whom her champions were hourly doing battle." [22] In 1850, that eloquent and ubiquitous champion of Southern rights, J. D. B. De Bow, vigorously defended the Southern fighter in the War for Independence. In an address in New York, he asserted that the South, never wanting in chivalrous devotion to the cause, supplied fully one-third of the yearly enlistments for the war.[23]

From many quarters came defenders of the South's role. William Martin recalled that England's defeat in South Carolina resulted from the heroic sacrifices of the men and wom-

en of that state.[24] Colonel Lawrence M. Keitt insisted that
the Revolution in South Carolina had been "conceived and
organized by the native population." There might have been
some division, he admitted, "but the constituted authorities
of the State committed her, from the first, to the Revolutionary movement, and she neither wavered nor faltered throughout its progress." [25] The argument over the South's valor in
the War for Independence found its way to the floor of the
United States Senate in 1856. In a debate on slavery, Charles
Sumner asserted that the institution had long been a burden
to the country, and taunted Senator Andrew P. Butler of South
Carolina for his state's dereliction during this war. South
Carolina had betrayed a "shameful imbecility" as a result of
slavery.[26] The following month Butler, who had been absent
when Sumner spoke, rose to answer.[27] "I challenge him to the
truth of history," he asserted. "There was not a battle fought
south of the Potomac which was not fought by southern
troops and southern slave holders . . ." Indeed, South Carolina had given as much to the cause as Massachusetts.[28]

In the 1850's, the Mecklenburg Declaration, Moore's Creek,
Camden, Eutaw Springs, Kings Mountain, and Yorktown became major Southern triumphs. In Southern eyes these land-
marks in the achievement of independence had been secured
primarily, if not exclusively, by Southern men. Doubtless
these experiences had stimulated the South's martial spirit.
The sheer inadequacy of its defenses at the outbreak of the
war with England had been terrifying to contemplate. Just
before the war an Englishman said that Charleston, the most
fortified town in the South, had only three "apologies for
Fortifications," and that the "Common Town Militia if possible make a worse Figure than the Train Bands of London." [29] Later, Southern writers were to speak of the lack of
defenses in their section, the inadequacy of the support from
Philadelphia, and the "severity and frequency of her fields
of fight." Indeed, the bitter experiences during the siege of

Charleston and the ignominious defeat at Camden were not soon to be forgotten. Southerners could well have decided that thereafter they should keep their powder dry and keep plenty of it.

In the War of 1812 the South's fighting reputation made substantial headway. The promoters of the war were, for the most part, Southerners, and nowhere was there more enthusiastic support of the war than in the South.[30] Southern militia were early placed on a war footing, while New England's governors were defying the federal government's call for men.[31] To one Virginian this seemed the blackest of crimes and in his remonstrance he cried:

O! Good people of New England! Pause! Pause! for heaven's sake, pause! Stand a moment on the brink and look at the great ocean of trouble before you embark or you may be lost amidst the storms of the deep. . .[32]

Meanwhile, in Baltimore, where an editor dared to criticize the war, a mob sacked and virtually destroyed his offices.[33] Southerners easily possessed the greater will and anxiety to fight. David Campbell of Richmond expressed the views of many when he said that he had a most "prodigious fever to put on the armour of a soldier . . . to bear a part in a glorious and honorable war waged for the liberty and happiness of man . . ."[34]

The Mexican War gave Southerners an opportunity to display their gallantry in battle and to advance their economic and political interests. As early as 1845, this "magnificent dream of sport, glory and opulence seemed to be on the point of realization, and the war spirit flamed high."[35] The Richmond Enquirer, its ardor for war overflowing, asked, "What more inspiring strain can strike the ears of freemen than the trumpet note which summons our people to the punishment of tyrants?"[36] The New Orleans Picayune observed that wherever one went in that city the talk was of "War and nothing but war." [37] When war came, the enthusiastic support of the Southern states completely eclipsed the rather feeble martial activity in other parts of the country. Thomas R. R. Cobb of Athens, Georgia, wrote his brother Howell, in Congress, that he "never saw the people more excited. A volunteer company could be raised in every county in Georgia." [38] Tennessee answered the call for 3,000 men with 30,000. North Carolina offered more than three times her quota. In Savannah, so many volunteer companies sought to represent the city that had been asked to send one company that it was deemed necessary to decide by lot which organization should be accorded the honor. [39]

The gallant men of Mississippi thought that Governor Albert G. Brown was much too slow in puttting the state on a war footing. The Natchez Fencibles marched to Jackson and burned the governor in effigy before his mansion. A fighting bard, who might have been motivated by political considerations, expressed the same feeling in a local paper:

> Our Gov'ner has betrayed his trust
> He has disgraced our name
> And for his treacherous acts we have
> Condemned him to the flame.
>
> Alas! let this hereafter be
> A warning to the rest
> We love a brave and valiant man
> A coward we detest. [40]

The war's impact on the South was remarkable, and the fighting zeal of the Southern people was incomparable. Almost everywhere men deserted peaceful pursuits for the battlefield. Charles Lanman said that many households in the Allegheny region had been "rendered very desolate by the Mexican War." When the call was issued for volunteers, the men of the Southern mountains "poured into the valley almost without bidding their mothers, and wives, and sisters a final adieu . . ." [41] The men of Mississippi were outraged when three regiments from Tennessee, "whose people were neither braver nor better," received a call while Mississippi men still waited.[42] One planter viewed the great enthusiasm for war as having, ironically enough, a real social significance. "The war," he wrote, "will serve one good purpose — thin out loafers. In Natchez there is quite a patriotic spirit amongst such folk." [43]

The victories gave the South an excellent opportunity to claim a superior will to fight, and it missed no opportunity to do so. After the battle of Buena Vista, Charles Dabney, a student at the College of William and Mary, wrote his parents, "we may all be proud to say that we are Mississipians. Look at the veteran coolness with which they received the charge of the Mexican cavalry. Look at the Southern impetuosity with which they threw themselves into every dangerous position." [44] To illustrate the South's superior military strength, James De Bow published a summary of the contribution of the North and the South to the war: 43,000 Southerners and 22,000 Northerners took part in the struggle. Louisiana contributed seven times as many men as Massachusetts; Tennessee sent more than 5,000 men, while New York sent less than 1,700.[45]

When Thomas Nichols made his first visit to New Orleans, he saw the returning heroes thrilling the crowds. In the Place D'Armes a military band was playing. The artillery company, going through its evolutions, was a further demonstration of the "pomp and circumstances of glorious war." [46] In 1859 the Mississippians were still praising the valor of their men in the war. "As long as American arms and valour shall be honored, or the American name be known," William Crane pronounced, "so long will the First Mississippi Regiment and Jefferson Davis be remembered and admired by every chivalric son of Mississippi." [47]

Some Southerners discerned a far-reaching significance growing out of their performance in the Mexican War. One thought that it proved the Southerners competent to engage in foreign conquest. "It has shown that, in foreign invasion we are wanting in none of the elements which enable us to maintain our liberties at home." The really significant thing, however, was the way in which the war enhanced the South's military reputation.

As a military people, none can deny that we are fully equal, perhaps superior, to any other. Our renown for skill, courage, and indomitable energy in battle, humanity and moderation after victory, has overspread the world . . . and the storm of war which shook Mexico to her foundations, roused not the slightest ripple upon the smooth waters of our internal repose.[48]

By 1860 the South claimed to be the fountainhead of martial spirit in the United States. It argued that it had turned the tide of battle in the nation's wars and had been the training ground for the soldiers of the country. America's soldiers had even been schooled in the art and science of war by treatises written by Southerners. Major D. H. Hill boasted that the Southern scholar had evinced the section's military spirit just as forcefully as had the soldier. "The books on Infantry Tactics we use, were prepared by Scott, of Virginia and Hardee, of Georgia. The Manual of Artillery Tactics in use is by Anderson, of Kentucky. The only works in this country on the Science of Artillery, written in the English language are by Kingsbury and Gibbon of North Carolina." Mordecai of South Carolina was the leading authority on gunpowder, while Mahan of Virginia had published the best works in military engineering. "These gentlemen are all graduates of West Point and are officers in the Army, but the South claims them as her own." [49]

The South's reputation for fighting — and winning — was secure. This reputation was more firmly established in the minds of Southerners than anywhere else, to be sure; but people in other places took cognizance of the South's claims and were willing to make some concessions regarding its military spirit.

Wars, however, had their limitations in strengthening the military reputation of Southern men, for there were years in which there was no resort to arms against the British, Indians, or Mexicans. But day-to-day experiences kept them in practice. Many were hot-headed and high-tempered, and, in personal relations, conducted themselves as though each were a one-man army exercising and defending its sovereignty. Duels were as "plenty as blackberries" in Mississippi in 1844.[50] Traveling in the Southwest in the 1830's, Ingraham saw and heard about much violence. In New Orleans, "the rage for duelling is at such a pitch that a jest or smart repartee is sufficient excuse for a challenge . . ." What manner of men were these who could refer to an appointment for a duel "with the *nonchalance* of an invitation to a dinner or supper party?" [51]

When there was not dueling, there was fighting. The public walks were arenas for sport among the rustics, most of whom carried weapons and "counted on the chance of getting into difficulty." [52] This violence was described with a mixture of jest and disgust by an Alabama editor:

The Summer Sports of the South, as Major Noah calls them, have already commenced in Huntsville. On Monday last, in the Court Square, and during the session of Court, too, a man by the name of Taylor stabbed another by the name of Ware in such a shocking manner that his life is despaired of . . . this stabbing and dirking business has become so common and fashionable, that it has lost all the horror and detestation among . . . our population . . .[53]

In Florida, Bishop Henry Whipple found the fighting spirit prevalent even among the community's more responsible members. On one occasion a member of the grand jury went outside where he found his son of eight or nine years of age fighting with another boy. "The father looked coolly on until it was ended and then said, 'now you little devil, if you catch him down again bite him, chaw his lip or you never'll be a man.' " The Bishop said that the father's attitude was "only one of the numerous specimens of this fighting spirit only to be found in the South." [54]

The fighting spirit was no respector of class or race, and the willingness of Negroes to resort to violence shows the extent to which such conduct pervaded the entire community. Free Negroes fought slaves, whites, and each other. Fearful of losing the few privileges that freedom accorded them and dogged by the vicissitudes that the struggle of such an anomalous position involved, they frequently outdid other members of the community in manifesting a proclivity to fight.[55] There were fights among slaves and revolts and rumors of revolts. Owners and overseers, moreover, occasionally met foul play as they undertook to supervise and punish their slaves. The people of Louisiana were excited in 1845 over the murder of a Caddo Parish mill superintendent by a Negro whom he sought to chastise. What was more, the *New Orleans Bee* complained, "instances of this kind are becoming quite numerous. It was only a few months since that a Negro was hanged in Greenwood for attempting the life of his overseer; and but a few weeks or so since in the . . . County of Harrison, Texas a Mr. Wilson met with the most distressing death by the hands of his own slaves." [56]

Southerners could have done no better job of establishing a reputation for violence and fighting had they sought to do so by formal dramatization. Visitors from the North and from Europe did much to spread the South's reputation for militancy. But the alacrity with which Southerners displayed their bellicosity and the boastful pride with which they discussed it contributed significantly to the general impression that Southerners were a pugnacious lot. They were not being merely theatrical, although they had their moments of sheer acting. The flow of blood and the grief produced suggest a deep, pervading quality that could not be overlooked. Violence was inextricably woven into the most fundamental aspects of life in the South and constituted an important phase of the total experience of its people.

Fighting became a code by which men lived. Southerners themselves were apt to explain their dueling and other fighting propensities by pointing to the aristocratic character of their society; but this explanation seems somewhat flattering. The aristocratic element was much too inconsequential to give a tone of manners to the whole community; and the widespread existence of violence, even where there was no semblance of aristocratic traditions, suggests influences other than those of the select. The prevalence of violence was due, in part at least, to the section's peculiar social and economic institutions and to the imperfect state of its political organization. The passions that developed in the intercourse of superiors and inferiors showed themselves in the intercourse with equals, for, observed Stirling, "the hand of the violent man is turned against itself." [57] Far from loathing violence, the man of the South was the product of his experiences as a frontiersman, Indian fighter, slaveholder, self-sufficient yeoman, poor white, and Negro. He gladly fought, even if only to preserve his reputation as a fighter.

# Fighters' Fatherland

When Gustave Beauregard was ten years old, he missed his own birthday party. His father was, in part, responsible. Before the arrival of the guests, he had presented Gustave with the prized family relic, an old muzzle loader "that had picked off its quota of Englishmen at the battle of New Orleans." The child, from infancy a lover of guns and all military trappings, promptly went into the woods to see what he could "pick off" with his cherished musket, and tarried for the rest of the day.[1] Even at ten years, young Beauregard was at home in the woods of St. Bernard Parish, Louisiana; and a horse and a gun were infinitely more exciting than a birthday party. Gustave's love for military things continued. At times he fancied himself a soldier guarding a rampart; at others a general leading his men to battle. At all times he was determined to be a *real* soldier; and when his father sensed his earnestness, he sent him to a semi-military school in New York. It was operated by the Peugent brothers, former captains in Napoleon's army and soldiers through and through. Here was additional inspiration which led Beauregard to West Point and a career in the United States and Confederate armies.

In Abingdon, Virginia, the story was essentially the same. Young Joseph Johnston wanted to be a soldier before he was ten years old. Although Joseph was next to the youngest son, the father presented him the sword he had used in the War for Independence. Young Joseph soon "burned to emulate his father's revolutionary record and the deeds of his neighbors and relatives at Kings Mountain." [2] After West Point he, too, could be a soldier in earnest. So could Stephen D. Ramseur, growing up under the influence of Major D. H. Hill in rural Lincolnton, North Carolina, and Richard Anderson, nurtured in Statesburg, South Carolina, on the traditions, relics, and mementoes of the heroic past of the Anderson family.

There is no way of knowing how many times such cases could be multiplied. And the realization of the dreams of many young Southerners can certainly be more than matched by the frustrations and disappointments suffered by others. It was not unusual, of course, to find youngsters in many parts of the world who had notions of growing up to become gallant soldiers and win the plaudits of the crowds. There was something rather singular, however, in the way the dream of military glory remained alive in the minds of young Southerners as they progressed toward manhood, while young Northerners tended to turn to other pursuits upon reaching maturity. At the first opportunity, which they not infrequently sought, they were off to win their spurs in battles, hoping that a military career would unfold itself.

If they were lucky, fame and fortune would be theirs forever. Consequently, some type of military experience — indeed, any type — presented an exciting prospect to young Southerners. Recruiters for the United States Army seldom experienced difficulty in filling their quotas in Southern communities. In 1833, Philip Cooke, member of a prominent Virginia family, went into western Tennessee to recruit a regiment of cavalry for use against the Indians. It was a prospect, "that did not fail to excite the enterprising and roving dispositions of many fine young men in that military State."

Indeed, they were so inflamed with the thoughts of "scouring the far prairies on fine horses, amid buffalo and strange Indians . . . that they scarce listened to any discouraging particulars." [3] To get into the army was a good thing for those whose prospects in other endeavors were none too bright. In 1836, James L. Petigru of South Carolina commented to his sister that if a friend and neighbor accepted an army captaincy that had been offered him it was "the best thing decidedly that the poor young man can do." [4]

There were those who felt that the army was the only career. John C. Simkins persuaded his influential brother-in-law, Lt. Francis W. Pickens of Edgewood, South Carolina, to enlist the support of a friend in Congress in his effort to remain in the army. Fearful of being discharged at the close of the Mexican War, Simkins, who had risen from Sergeant to First Lieutenant, implored his relative to help him. Pickens consequently wrote Representative Armstead Burt, "He writes so urgently about geting [sic] an appointment, if his regiment is discharged that I am induced to write you to know if all of the ten regiments will be discharged. . . If they are discharged is there any prospect of geting [sic] him an appointment of the same grade . . . in any branch of the service to be retained . . . He has tasted the sweets of war and seems so delighted that I fear he will never relish a common life again." [5]

When the future Confederate general Dick Ewell graduated from West Point in 1840, he expressed the view that there was no future for him outside the army. He told his mother that he had nearly as much aversion to army life as she had; but, he continued, "you know that the education that we get here does not qualify us for any other than a military life, and unless a man has money, he is forced to enter the army to keep from starving." [6] Perhaps Mrs. Ewell was convinced by the argument, but Cadet Ewell should have known better, and perhaps did. Other West Point graduates had entered fields where little or no capital was needed. New York's George W. Morrell of the class of 1835 had already become a successful railroad construction engineer by the time that Ewell graduated.[7] Morrell's classmate, Arnoldus V. Brumby from North Carolina, resigned from the army a year after graduating and became a distinguished civil engineer and professor of military science within a few years.[8]

To be sure, there were opportunities, and other young Americans were taking advantage of them. But the young Southerner was attracted, first of all, to the life of a planter. If he lacked the necessary capital to purchase land, he turned to politics or to a military career. While Northern men interested themselves in commerce, manufacturing, and the like, Southerners interested themselves, as Daniel Hundley accurately observed, in "agriculture mainly, political economy, and the nurture of an adventurous and military race." [9] The larger and more varied opportunities the average Southerner could not see; and some simply would not see. Instead, they dreamed of the day when they would take their places among the heroes of the ages either in defense of country, state, or, at least, their own honor.

While they were young, the everyday life of Southerners — the life that produced the dreams — was quite like that of Beauregard and his comrades in arms. At an early age they developed strong proclivities to fight and acquired its needed skills. An early experience of the young Southerner was learning to handle firearms and other weapons with proficiency. Ingraham was rather surprised to find that his Mississippi host's younger sons, ages eleven and thirteen, were studying boxing, fencing, and rifle and pistol shooting. He was completely amazed at the skill of a nineteen-year-old son who, with a double barreled shotgun, "hit two oranges, which he threw in the air together, firing right and left, and putting balls through both before they touched the ground." With an old gun, which he called "sharp's rifle," the lad then shot "a vulture that was flying so high, it seemed no bigger than a sparrow . . ."[10]

Not a few Southerners associated good marksmanship with the better attributes of manhood. A young Southerner who wanted to get anywhere would be well-advised to become skilled in the use of arms; at least his fellows would respect him. When Judge Augustus B. Longstreet made this point in one of his tales, the humorous vein did not detract from its importance. The Judge placed second in a shooting match of experts, and a group of onlookers was so impressed with his prowess that they inquired of him regarding the public office for which he was presumed to be running. When he assured them that he was not a candidate, one member of the delegation said, "If ever you come up for anything . . . just let the boys in Upper Hogthief know it, and they'll go for you to the hilt, against creation . . ."[11]

Even if the young Southerner never got into a war or a military outfit, he might need his fighting skills in everyday life. Many were undisciplined; even at school they frequently did as they pleased. In Savannah many carried sticks and canes, and some affected "the bravo by carrying bowie knives," which they were not averse to using. In a Louisiana town Frederick Olmsted was somewhat startled to see two boys running from another, "who was pursuing them with a large, open dirk-knife in his hand, and every appearance of ungovernable rage in his face."[12]

Even youngsters had exaggerated notions of personal honor and were quick to defend it. At South Carolina College "two boys encouraged by grown men as seconds . . . fought a duel because they had disputed about a dish of fish at the table. One was killed, and the other was crippled."[13] In 1852, James A. Walker, a senior at the Virginia Military Institute, challenged Professor T. J. Jackson to a duel because he claimed to have been insulted by a remark made to him by the professor. The court martial and dismissal of Walker relieved the professor of having to make the decision to accept or reject the challenge.[14] The Confederacy might not have had its "Stonewall" had the teacher accepted.

Even those who sought careers in politics, agriculture, or elsewhere found it difficult to pursue the paths of peace. A fledgling lawyer might, and frequently did, carry a brace of pistols in his portfolio. A planter, however absorbed in his crops and Negroes, did not lose his early acquired skills with knives and pistols. A young editor, daily running the risk of offending someone with his pen, was most unwise if he neglected any of the honorable means of self-defense. These and others, moreover, displayed an interest in the formal military organizations, where they could enhance their social and political standings, while preparing for some unforeseen eventuality. Stephen Miller tells of two young Georgia lawyers, one of whom although "almost beardless . . . was colonel of the Wilkinson County regiment, and the other was a member of Major General Wimberly's staff — appointments most gratifying to their ambition." Miller said that these young men were taking no chances with their future. If peace continued, they could be certain of success at the bar and even in politics. "And should war come, what a pair of chiefs they would make! Yorktown and New Orleans would be eclipsed by their strategy!" [15]

The apparent anxiety of Southern men to do battle, whether on the barroom floor, on the streets, or in more "honorable" places, may be explained largely by the conditions of life that developed and persisted in the South. The nature of the Southern economy discouraged the growth of compact communities which could provide diverse social experiences and where a sense of group interdependence could take root. Staple crop plantation agriculture could flourish only if one had large holdings; and the most prosperous planter was frequently the one who was separated from others by miles and miles of his own holdings. Living in splendid isolation, he and the members of his family developed little or no appreciation for social and civic responsibility unless the planter was also some public official. Consequently they were compelled by circumstances to evolve machinery for their own protection, diversion, and general welfare. Those without broad acres were frequently pushed back into relative isolation by the inexorable march of the plantation, thereby forming other islands of habitation, less prosperous, perhaps, but hardly less isolated.

The growth of the South's population and the development of its economic system did not substantially modify the conditions of life that prevailed from the beginning. There persisted, down to the Civil War, a remarkable number of the elements of the most rudimentary frontier existence, including long stretches of uninhabited land, inadequate roads and means of transportation, and few towns of any considerable size. Visitors always noted these primitive aspects, and many saw in them an explanation for the South's distinctive features. From Macon, Georgia, in 1857, Stirling wrote that, despite the South's rapid prosperity during the preceding twenty years, "the Gulf States . . . have, on the whole, a very wild appearance." He traveled some 2,000 miles down the Cumberland and Mississippi rivers, up the Alabama and across by rail from Montgomery to Macon, and, for the most part, had been "in sight of the primeval forest of the continent." During the journey of 430 miles up the Alabama River, he hardly saw a single village and he concluded that the whole picture was one of "impressive desolateness." [16]

This feature of the Southern scene made a great impression on James Silk Buckingham as he traveled through Georgia in 1839. The road from Warrenton to Sparta lay almost entirely through dense pine forests; and the constant succession of these trees made the way "gloomy and monotonous." As he moved west from Columbus "the woods . . . seemed more wild, the road being a mere pathway through and around standing trees . . ." With considerable depression of spirit, he remarked, "for miles in succession, we saw neither a human being, a fence, a road of cleared land, nor anything indeed that could indicate the presence of man, or the trace of civilization, so that we felt the solitude of the woods in all its fulness." [17] When Francis and Theresa Pulszky went up the Alabama River from Mobile to Montgomery in 1851, they felt that they were "amidst primitive nature, almost without any trace of culture . . . On the long tracts, no human abode meets the eye; distant smoke alone shows the presence of man; everything around is silent." [18]

The Virginia countryside was virtually the same. David Mitchell, whose ten years in the United States were spent largely in Richmond, got the impression that in the 1850's three-fourths of Virginia was still in the forest and that the bulk of the population was scattered in the remote corners of the state, out of communication with the rest of the world a goodly portion of the time.[19] When Frederick Olmsted was trying to get to a plantation not far from Petersburg he became almost hopelessly lost after going only a few miles. The roads had become mere trails and the whole countryside seemed deserted. "Of living creatures, for miles, not one was to be seen . . . except hogs," Olmsted complained. "Once I saw a house across a large new old-field, but it was far off, and there was no distinct path leading towards it out of the wagontrack we were following; so we did not go to it, but continued walking steadily on through the old-fields and pine woods for more than an hour longer." [20]

In such an environment, skill at arms and excellence in horsemanship were highly desirable, even necessary. A Southerner might be called upon to defend his life against some beast of the forest or some intractable human being. If this did not happen, it was always within the realm of possibility; and it was best to be prepared. The program of preparation was as exciting an experience as a rural Southern youth could hope to have. His existence, drab and monotonous as the countryside around him, was brightened considerably as he acquired skills in the shooting of rifles, the wielding of knives, and the riding of horses.

The lack of cities of any considerable importance contributed to the persistence of the primitive nature of the antebellum South. There was neither sufficient industry nor commerce to support a dynamic, urban civilization; with the exception of centers such as New Orleans, Charleston, and Baltimore, no Southern community deserved to be called a city. The center of power, the basis of the entire economic structure, rested on the land and on the people who owned the land. Where towns emerged, they were for the purpose of serving the peculiar and relatively simple needs of the agricultural interests. Most, therefore, remained agrarian in their contacts and provincial in their outlook. Seldom did they exert any extensive civilizing influence over the outlying regions. Instead, they remained under the influence of the rural areas; even after years of growth, they frequently resembled, in looseness of structure and simplicity of services, frontier trading posts.[21] It would be difficult for any individual or group living in such an environment to develop a point of view and a way of life attuned to the complexities of modern civilization.

In the decade before the Civil War, the physical features of the Southern towns reflected their primitive state. New Orleans had only open gutters for sewerage as late as 1857. At the same time Mobile, Montgomery, Columbus, and Macon were almost without paving of any description. There was only one paved street in Savannah, which no doubt influenced Olmsted to describe it as having a "curiously rural and modest aspect," despite its population and commerce.[22] Charleston, venerated by a century and a half of existence, had some well-constructed buildings; but to James Stirling the shops were, with few exceptions, "singularly mean, and many of them such as would be thought shabby in an ordinary Scotch village." [23]

In most towns there was almost a complete absence of diversions usually associated with urban communities. Norfolk, a bustling seaport in 1853, had no "lyceum or public libraries, no public gardens, no galleries of art . . . no public resorts of healthful and refining amusement, no place better than a filthy, tobacco-impregnated bar-room or a licentious dance cellar . . ." [24] Dozens of older Southern towns could have been described similarly. In the newer towns it was even worse. Life in Columbus, Georgia, was so uninspiring that its residents found the arrival of the stage one of their really exciting activities; many would get up at four o'clock in the morning to witness the event. This was much too mild, however, for some of the inhabitants of Columbus and other communities. In towns where speculators, ruffians, gamblers, and sharpers thrived, the diversion was more likely to be drinking, gambling, dueling, fighting, and other kinds of "affrays." In Columbus, druggists sold dirks, bowie knives, and "Arkansas toothpicks" over the same counter whence they dispensed arsenic and hemlock.[25] A citizen of Little Rock told Featherstonhaugh that "he did not suppose there were *twelve* inhabitants of the place who ever went into the streets without — from some motive or other — being armed with pistols or large hunting knives about a foot long . . ." [26]

New Orleans was full of suspicious characters who provided in their own activities the excitement and diversion that were lacking in other more peaceful pursuits. Ingraham said that nearly every gentleman carried a sword cane; he was convinced that most of them also carried concealed weapons. "Occasionally the bright hilt of a Spanish knife, or dirk, would gleam for an instant in the moonlight from the open bosom of its possessor, as with lowering brow, and active tread of wary suspicion, he moved rapidly by us . . ." [27]

Small wonder that in less than two years the New Orleans chief of police arrested 62 for murder, 146 for stabbing, and 734 for assault.[28] From New Orleans these ruffians spread into other towns on the Mississippi River — Natchez, Vicksburg, and Memphis — and continued to "play the bully towards all who ventured to take the least notice of their misconduct . . ."[29]

This was the atmosphere in which spirited Southern boys grew up. Whether in the desolate country or in the backwoods town, circumstances peculiar to the section fostered the fighting spirit. Southern life was not only rough and primitive from the beginning, but, for the most part, it remained so throughout the ante-bellum period. Despite the infusion of the so-called aristocratic element into Southern life and the emergence of the country-gentlemen ideal, the South was essentially an agricultural frontier. As Craven has pointed out: "The process of evolution from simplicity to complexity which Turner described [in his frontier hypothesis] never got beyond the agricultural stage in the South. The country-gentleman ideal, the development of peculiar marketing arrangements, the presence of Negro slavery on plantations, checked the development of towns, factories, and industrial captains. The Old South and the lower South, in spite of efforts to alter the situation, formed a rural–agricultural interest to the outbreak of the war. . ."[30]

Since the South retained many of the essential characteristics of frontier life, those attracted to the borderline zones of civilization tarried there, preserving the frontier flavor in Southern civilization. It was only natural that into the newly settled areas would flock fugitives from justice and rascals of every description. But a generation later those miscreants, or their descendants, had not moved on. The backward parts of the South continued to be an attractive place to perpetrate their mischief. Roads remained lonely and undeveloped for decades; and robbers found them a choice place for operations. The towns, lacking effective political institutions and a sense of civic responsibility, were a happy hunting ground for rowdies, dandies, and gamblers. The stable element of the population, therefore, found it necessary to organize vigilance committees and other extralegal, semi-military groups to strengthen the regular law enforcement agencies of the community.[31]

Where such conditions existed, they produced, not a civilized, refined society, characterized by restraint and order, but a positive, aggressive reckless one where disorder and irresponsibility were outstanding features. Some Southern spokesmen made extravagant professions of the refinement and advancement of their society; but its very appearance and actions denied such claims. As long as the plantation system so completely dominated every aspect of life in the South and as long as the essential characteristics of a frontier environment prevailed, the crudeness, violence, and other conditions which nurtured a fighting spirit would also flourish.

The proximity of Indian tribes to Southern settlements gave the section an additional flavor of frontier living. It also aroused grave apprehensions regarding the safety of the settlers from hostile attacks. From the beginning of the century down to the Civil War, Southerners in one quarter or another were crying out against Indian outrages or threats of them. They were constantly calling on the federal government to provide a greater measure of protection against possible depredations. There was the general feeling that the federal authorities were "singularly indifferent to the defense of the Southern frontier" and that their "apathy and ignorance, if carefully traced, would cast a deep stain" on the history of the country.[32] In the face of this presumed indifference, much of the defense of this frontier was carried on without any cooperation or authorization from the government in Washington.

In 1813 the governor of the territory of Mississippi authorized the mustering of local volunteers against the Creeks.
He found himself acting without the aid requested from the
federal government. But the people of Tennessee recognized
the Indian problem, and in 1813 the legislature authorized
the raising of 3,500 men, "in such proportions of Infantry,
Riflemen, Cavalry, Artillery, and Mounted Infantry as the
Governor and Commanding General deem proper, for public service, to any place in the Creek Nation of Indians or in
the Mississippi Territory where said troops may give relief
to the citizens of said territory, and repel the invasion of the
State of Tennessee by said Indians and their allies." The act
further provided that if the government of the United States
did not pay the troops, the State of Tennessee would.[33] This,
then, came to be the pattern of thought and action in some
parts of the South with respect to Indians: fear was ever present; adequate protection by the federal government was un-
likely; state and local military groups were obliged to provide protection. While land greed was, perhaps, the most
powerful factor in the South's determination to remove the
Indians, fear of them played an important part in strengthening the arguments for removal.

Southerner's forgot, rather soon, the "cruelty, hypocrisy,
and broken faith" [34] of the removal policy of the United
States. They did not soon forget, however, the stout resistance
put up by the Seminoles and the various ways in which the
other tribes registered their objections to removal between
1825 and 1845. Having assumed responsibility in the program of protecting their frontier from Indian depredations,
the warriors of the South proudly rushed forward to assist
in the removal of the Indians. Even before the outbreak of
the second Seminole War in 1836, General Duncan L. Clinch
anticipated some real difficulty in removing the Seminoles
from Florida, and suggested the use of Southern volunteers,
arguing that Southern troops, "being well mounted, and all

of them good woodsmen and good riders and well acquainted with every part of the country" would be the most efficient and least expensive soldiers to employ. The fact that the men of the South were "deeply interested" in the protection of their homes was an additional important argument for their use.[35]

With the outbreak of war with the Seminoles many rushed to take up arms. An Alabama newspaper reported, in February 1836, that there were already more than a thousand Georgia volunteers in Florida. Hundreds had gone from Charleston and Columbia.[36] By April a group of Louisiana volunteers, having seen action, were returning home.[37] Before the fighting was over there were considerable numbers of volunteers from almost every Southern state, and more seemed willing to go. One Tennessean offered to raise one thousand emigrants in the eastern part of his state for the armed occupation of Florida. The prospective fighters were "hardy — laborious — virtuous and efficient men" who would keep the territory free of Indian outrages.[38]

Throughout the war, volunteers primarily from Georgia, South Carolina, Alabama, Mississippi, and Louisiana went to Florida, ostensibly for the purpose of assisting in the defeat and removal of the Seminoles. They doubtless had more enthusiasm than ability, for the complaints against their ineptitude and cowardice were widespread. After three bitter battles in 1838, one army officer said that in all "the regulars have done the fighting — in all the irregulars have been false — leaving the honor and loss chiefly to the army . . . However delicate this subject may be in the ears of the politicians, it ought to be known that henceforth we may trust more to what will sustain us in the field and less to rapacious men who come for plunder, for Negroes, and run as soon as an Indian fires a rifle at them." [39]

Indeed, there were those who suggested that the bungling and irresponsible conduct of the volunteers had caused the prolongation of the war in Florida. One Army Major complained that the white men who had gone to Florida under the pretense of assisting in the war were "doing more to keep it up than the Indians themselves." He said that he believed that two-thirds of the recent murders had been committed "by the Whites themselves in order to keep up the excitement." [40]

This condemnation of the Southern fighters in the war against the Seminoles was not universal, however. The Louisiana Regiment of Volunteers "nobly did their duty," according to a general order in 1836. The men of Augusta, when mustered out, were told that "no troops . . . exhibited more obedience, promptness, and discipline," while Major Cooper's battalion of Georgia volunteers "maintained their post gallantly for seventeen days, twelve of which they were closely invested by the enemy." [41]

When the men returned home from the Indian wars they were received as conquering heroes. Whether they deserved it or not, they were honored not only for having served gallantly against an intrepid foe, but also for having successfully protected the lives and property of their fellows. The combination of glory, honor, and service that had earlier been identified with the careers of warriors like Andrew Jackson was now, in the minds of many Southerners, associated with thousands of volunteers who had seen service against the Indians. The prestige of the military was greatly enhanced in every community that witnessed the return of local men who had participated in the enterprise that was regarded as successful by 1842.

If the successful conclusion of the Seminole War had the effect of strengthening the position of the military, the persistence of the Indian danger was ample justification for the continued support of local military organizations in the South. By 1840 more than 60,000 Indians of the five civilized tribes had been removed to the plains beyond Arkansas and

Missouri; and some whites breathed a premature sigh of relief. Hundreds of Indians, however, did not go; and their
very presence seemed to be a source of genuine apprehension
among some Southerners down to the Civil War. As late as
1855, the Seminoles of Florida were engaged in activities
that caused the governor to call out a state force for the protection of the frontier. The federal government provided
some men and equipment, but this was deemed insufficient.
Florida sold $500,000 worth of bonds to finance the protec-
tion of the frontier; and in his next annual message to the
legislature the governor asked for additional support.[42] It
seemed that as long as there were even a few Seminoles in
Florida, lives were in grave danger and elaborate military
preparations were justified.

Whites on the Southern frontier not only lived under the
constant fear of Indian attacks, but also were distressed by
the presence of fugitive slaves among the Indians. For many
years Negroes had been running away from their masters
to the Seminoles, Creeks, or others. Some became slaves;
others, called maroons, lived in loosely organized communities, and enjoyed the status of free people. The presence of
Indian tribes near the plantations created an aggravating
situation which the planters were determined to eradicate.
This constituted an important motive of their support of
the federal government's removal policy.[43]

In other areas Southerners continued to have trouble with
Indians. In 1841, a citizen of Opelousas, Louisiana, urgently
requested the Secretary of War to establish a military post in
his district because of the outrages committed by Indians
and white outlaws in the vicinity.[44] In 1845, a writer observed
that Georgia's backward condition was the result, in part,
of many years of struggle against the "perfidious, marauding,
and revengeful savage tribes within her chartered limits."
The struggle had subsided, but it was not entirely over.[45]
In 1858, Charles Mackay said that Alabama was not totally

free of Indians and their very presence recalled the horrible incidents of the former warfare between the white and red men.[46]

When, in 1842, the War Department abolished the grand military geographical divisions, citizens of Memphis, Tennessee, were alarmed. They insisted that the absence of any intermediate authority between local commanders and Washington officials would prevent "the most effective use of the scanty supply of arms and munitions vouchsafed to this widely extended but important section of our country." It was conceiveable that an Indian disturbance on the frontier might get out of hand, while waiting on orders from Washington, and have grave consequences throughout that area. "As citizens of the great valley of the Mississippi . . . interested in the safety of our brethern on the frontier, and the preservation from pillage of our commercial emporium, we remonstrate and protest against the abolition of the Western Military Division." [47]

The people of Arkansas and Texas felt that the danger of Indian attacks was ever present. When the Seminole War caused the withdrawal of some of the regular troops from the West for use in Florida, Governor Fulton of Arkansas called out the militia to protect the citizens against possible Indian attacks.[48] In 1842 Governor Yell was greatly disturbed by the "numerous outrages" by Indians on the Arkansas frontier. He ascribed the acts of terror to the weakness of the military posts and asked that they be strengthened. The Indians, he said, were boastful of their power and asserted that the government of the United States was too weak and timid to protect its citizens. In a spirit of defiance the governor told the Secretary of War that if the federal government was too weak and inefficient to give them protection, they could and would protect themselves. "The State of Arkansas has repeatedly appealed to the General Government for a sufficient force to be placed upon the frontier to keep the Indians in subjection, but all to no purpose. If we must, we can and will be able to protect ourselves." [49]

The following year more than a hundred citizens of Arkansas appealed to the President to establish another military post on the frontier. Their proximity to the Indian country made their section the "receptacle for swarms of villains . . . murderers, counterfiters [sic], thieves, fugitives from justice and rascals of every grade placing their persons and property in hourly and imminent peril." The petitioners told the President that the escape of many such characters to the frontier and their continued depredations among the Indians caused disaffections "thus increasing the by no means imaginary danger of a rupture between the Indians and ourselves." [50] In this and similar requests the prayers of the citizens in or near the Indian country were denied. Whenever the federal government withdrew troops or in some other way modified its policy with respect to the South and West, there were always objections from those quarters.[51]

Thus, the South remained nervous about the Indians. The danger of attacks by these first Americans was, in part, imaginary; but there were enough breaches of the peace to keep alive the fear that the red men constituted a real threat. The more fearful Southerners developed such a hostility toward Indians that they were willing to fight them wherever they were. Louisianians were anxious to fight Seminoles in Florida, and Tennesseans enthusiastically joined in battle against the Creeks in Alabama. In 1852, a citizen of Jackson, Mississippi, upon hearing of Indian "outrages" in California, assured his government in Washington that "a thousand young Mississippians enured to camp life are ready at a moment to obey your call" to suppress the outrages.[52] Indian fighting had become a sport for which the season was always open.

Youths growing up in such an environment were hard put to find either satisfactory economic pursuits or engrossing social pastimes. If fate smiled, they inherited plantations or went into law or politics; and could enjoy travel, the excitement of urban life in the North or abroad, or select the best that the South had to offer as diversion. But few Southerners had such opportunities, and few of the alternatives in a sluggish social and economic order were very attractive. As boys, even the average could hunt; as men they could join some local military outfit and seek the glory attached to successful forays against the Indians. A boy with such experiences might decide on a military career; even if he did not, the marks left by an early military or semi-military experience were lasting. From this frontier atmosphere, a combination of monotony and conflict, emerged a tense, sensitive fighting man.

**3**

# Personal Warfare

In an area where political institutions matured slowly and where personal danger was frequently imminent, it was natural that the individual would develop means of self-protection. In the South, it was impractical to rely on the rather feeble protective arm of the government; and the Southerner was too self-sufficient and too realistic to do so. Thus, he tended either to evolve some loosely organized, temporary protective machinery or to prepare to do battle alone for the protection of himself and his family. Makeshift agencies such as vigilance committees could not be depended upon any more than patrols or other "official" instrumentalities. It was most frequently left to the individual, therefore, to adopt a policy that would safeguard the lives and interests of those for whom he was responsible.

The individual's limited resources tended to create a sense of personal insecurity which induced an inclination to be alert to any and all threats and to employ hasty, even premature, action to gain the advantage in any anticipated struggle. This sense of insecurity, among men who already had a reputation for being hot-blooded and trigger-happy, doubtless had much to do with producing what was regarded as the peculiar temperament of the Southerner. Relying on his own resources for protection, the individual was not inclined to respect and obey the law which seemed more obstacle than protection. It was easy for such an attitude to ripen into contempt for control and to render the further development of law and government even more difficult. While this attitude never succeeded in completely destroying government, it did make for distrust of all authority beyond the barest minimum essential to the maintenance of the political and social organism. Cash has aptly observed that the South "never developed any such compact and effective unit of government as the New England town. Its very counties were merely huge, sprawling hunks of territory, with almost no internal principle of cohesion. And to the last day before the Civil War, the land remained by far the most poorly policed section of the nation." [1]

There were, moreover, certain concepts of chivalric conduct that were involved in the reaction of the Southerner to crisis situations. However seriously or lightly he may have taken other rules of life — such as religion and morality — the Southerner was convinced that life should be ordered by certain well-defined codes of conduct that were a part of the cult of chivalry. Horsemanship and skill in the use of arms, so indispensable to successful living in the South, fitted conveniently and prominently into the cult of chivalry. Respect for and protection of white women were aspects that seemed to increase in importance as the problem of sex and race became more complicated and as the maintenance of racial integrity became a part of the program. Other attributes and trappings of the chivalric cult ranged from flamboyant oratory to lavish hospitality.[2] But through them all, and affecting them all, ran a concept of honor that was of tremendous importance in regulating and determining the conduct of the individual.

While the concept of honor was an intangible thing, it was no less real to the Southerner than the most mundane commodity that he possessed. It was something inviolable and precious to the ego, to be protected at every cost. It promoted extravagance, because of the imputation of poverty which might follow retrenchment. It sanctioned prompt demand for the redress of grievance, because of the imputation of guilt that might follow a less precipitate policy. It countenanced great recklessness of life, because of the imputation of cowardice that might follow forgiveness of injuries. The honor of the Southerner caused him to defend with his life the slightest suggestion of irregularity in his honesty or integrity; and he was fiercely sensitive to any imputation that might cast a shadow on the character of the women of his family. To him nothing was more important than honor. Indeed, he placed it above wealth, art, learning, and the other "delicacies" of an urban civilization and regarded its protection as a continuing preoccupation.

This Southern concept of honor discouraged the growth of strong law enforcement agencies. The individual insisted on the right to defend his own honor. To him it was a peculiarly personal thing in which the rest of the community could have little more than a casual interest. And his peers upheld him, realizing that they might play a similar role. The community, going beyond mere acceptance of vigorous defense of honor, regarded such action with hearty approval. The man who killed his adversary in a personal quarrel (while showing some regard for the amenities), need not fear public disgrace. The chances were excellent that his conduct would be judged as self-defense. Only in the case of some flagrant violation of the rules of a fair fight might he expect an indictment and conviction.

The idea of honor contained certain elements that encouraged its excessive application. Whenever a difficulty arose in which there was a *possibility* that honor was involved, it was usually decided — just to be on the safe side — that it *was* involved. Alexander Mackay saw this phenomenon among the people of Richmond and was shocked at its consequences. "Their code of honour," he remarked, "is so exceedingly strict that it requires the greatest circumspection to escape its violation. An offence which elsewhere would be regarded as one of homeopathic proportions, is very apt to assume in Richmond the gravity of colossal dimensions; even a coolness between parties is dangerous as having a fatal tendency speedily to ripen into a deadly feud . . ." [3] It was only natural that such an atmosphere would lead to an excessive amount of violence in personal relations that caused a Southerner to "pop over an antagonist from a sense of duty much as he would a turkey, or a 'pa-atridge,' from a sense of pleasure." It has been suggested, with some reason, that these excesses in violence, growing out of the code of honor, actually created a "cult of murder" in the South from which sprang feuds between families as well as between individuals. [4]

The feeling of personal responsibility in defending himself, together with the deep appreciation for the idea of honor, created in each Southerner a sense of "personal sovereignty." Ruler of his own destiny, defender of his own person and honor, keeper and breaker of the peace, he approached a personal imperiousness that few modern men have achieved. Not since the days of the medieval barons, perhaps, had there been such individual sovereignty as was found in the antebellum South. Whenever a Southerner fought another, he was, in a very real sense, engaged in war. The honor and dignity at stake were no less important to the individual than they would be to an embattled nation.

No single class had a monopoly on these sentiments and attitudes. While the planters refined the notion of honor and set the pattern for adhering to certain rules of conduct in personal warfare, this concept and that of personal sovereignty descended to other groups as they assimilated the interests and points of view of the dominant element of the community. [5] The sense of personal insecurity in the absence of law and order was an important factor in the lives of *all* Southern whites, and violence was to be found at every level of the social scale. If there were distinctions, they were in the relative crudeness in the violence of the lower classes in contrast to the refinement in that of the upper.

The reckless disregard for life and the consequent violence in evidence throughout the South and Southwest greatly alarmed Harriet Martineau, who called it the most savage in the world. Where else, in the nineteenth century, she asked, were there such practices as "burning alive, cutting the heart out, and sticking it on the point of a stick, and other such diabolical deeds?" [6] The countryside and the towns vied in their production of violent incidents. Violence could be predicted whenever there was any considerable assemblage of persons for a militia muster, protracted meeting, or a similar gathering. On such occasions there were numerous fights, some to avenge an alleged wrong, others merely for sport. It was hardly possible to distinguish by observation between the sport and the "blood fight." Even if it began in good humor as a display of physical prowess, there was a good chance that it would end on a more serious and, sometimes, deadly note.

In some communities there were men who, by their own appointment or by popular consensus, where the champion fighters of their respective bailiwicks. Such champions "strutted, bragged, and issued challenges" that were frequently accepted.[7] These local heroes provided diversion for spectators and anxious moments for their opponents who felt compelled to defend not only their manhood but their lives. Bishop Whipple was disgusted to find that in Florida in 1843, people were witnessing public fights in which "those who ought to be gentlemen descend to the common bully" but admitted that there were moments of levity. At the trial of a judge he was quite amused to hear the details of how the defendant had whipped another judge; but he was "surprised to hear such scurrility and vulgarity allowed in a court of justice as was used by one of the parties." [8]

Longstreet's classic account of "The Fight" is presumably based on an actual incident, and the description of the blood-thirstiness of the crowd as well as the fighters indicates the importance of such events to the people. The two principals, each the champion fighter of his militia battalion, and on friendly terms, were literally forced into a bloody engagement by the continuous agitation of their friends and supporters. There was also an unimportant misunderstanding between their wives. A duel, with their massive hands and sharp teeth as weapons, was arranged by the seconds, five for each man. The ensuing fight was apparently satisfactory to all concerned, although one had lost an ear, a large piece from his left cheek, and a finger, and the other had lost a third of his nose and sustained numerous bruises and lacerations.[9] In commenting on this type of encounter a contemporary remarked that in such fights he had seen men "scratch, bite and gouge, bite fingers, nose, ears, gouge out eyes, blate like goats." Frequently the fight would spread to the supporters of the principals, and at the end one could pick up fingers, ears, and pieces of noses. After the blood was washed off the principals with a dash of water, they would "shake hands and take a drink of whiskey or peach brandy" and forget the whole affair.[10] If one's ears had been cut or bitten off, it would be well for him to have the fact entered on the court records to protect himself from the suspicion that his ears had been cropped for crime.[11]

No Southern state was more subservient to the "Bloody Code" than Mississippi. It was freely admitted in the 1850's that a man of talent seldom attained high political position if he had not demonstrated his manhood in some bloody affray. The proclivity to fight seemed contagious; and loafers, idle gentry, young and old, made the public walks mere arenas for sport. "Weapons were in everybody's bosom and everybody counted on getting into difficulty." [12] Even in 1861, William Russell said that when he reached Mississippi he felt that he was "indeed in the land of Lynch-law and bowie-knives, where the passions of men have not yet been subordinated to the influence of the tribunals of justice." [13] The most significant single contribution to Mississippi's reputation as a wild and bloody land was made by Alexander Keith McClung who has been dubbed "The Black Knight of the South." Born in Kentucky, McClung settled, as a young man, in Vicksburg and promptly became involved in a feud with a family, seven members of which he killed. Others likewise met death at his hands, while many more lived in mortal fear of incurring his wrath. A braggart, bully, and loafer, he engaged briefly in journalism and politics and served in the Mexican War. In 1855, with no more fields to conquer and poverty staring him in the face, the state's toughest man took his own life.[14]

In areas that were newly settled or where the law enforcement agencies were weak, organized brigandage of every description forced the victims to adopt cooperative measures to put a stop to the lawlessness. On the frontier traffickers in whiskey, unauthorized Indian traders, fugitives from justice, and rowdies from town and country unduly strained the patience of those settlers who had some appreciation for law and order. In Alabama, Louisiana, and other Southern states, citizens were compelled to take the law into their own hands to restore a semblance of order. In 1859, for example, more than 3,000 Louisiana vigilantes subdued a group of 150 vicious outlaws. After lashing them soundly, they banished them under threat of hanging. As the chastised persons left, various groups of "lawful men" pursued the fleeing bandits across the border. "In six months of bitter strife hundreds suffered death or exile at the hands of the vigilantes, who were exonerated and disbanded by the grand jury." [15]

The Southern town was, of course, the locale for the greatest amount of violence and bloodshed. It was the town that offered numerous opportunities for the clash of personalities and of arms and where the glaring inadequacies of law enforcement were so apparent. Here were to be found, also, the various trappings for waging personal warfare, including a large choice of weapons, suitable grounds on which to do battle, and an ever-enthusiastic group of spectators. The great agitator of violence, though not always a participant, was the bully. While he certainly existed outside the South, there was a type in that section that can indeed be regarded as indigenous. Hundley describes him as a "'Swearing, tobacco-chewing, brandy drinking Bully, whose chief delight is to hang about the doors of village groggeries and tavern tap rooms, to fight chicken cocks, to play Old Sledge . . . and the like, as well as to encourage dog fights and occasionally to get up a little raw-head-and-bloody-bones on his own account . . . This was the Southern Bully *par excellence,* and a valiant Southerner he was too! . . . No Giddings of the North, no fiery Greeley ever felt one half so able to thrash the trembling South into meek submission." [16] But the Southern bully's horizons usually did not extend beyond his immediate environment, except in the vaguest way; he was more interested in a fight in the local barroom than in one between the North and South. Hundley observed that in nine cases out of ten he was a loafing ex-overseer. But he might also be a disgraced drygoods clerk or a bankrupt groggery-keeper. Now and then he was a man of wealth, having accumulated money as a Negro trader or even as a planter.[17] Rich or poor, he was a constant menace to the peace of the community. His boorish manners and his love of a fight almost invariably produced an incident that would culminate in a bloody battle. All too frequently he was implicated in the local, personal warfare that was a part of the culture of the Southern town.

Much of the turbulence in the Southern towns occurred during the election canvass, on muster day, at patriotic celebrations, or simply whenever two or more men decided to treat the town to a hair-raising spectacle of violence. During the elections of 1832 the disorder in Charleston assumed the proportions of a riot, and only the prudence of some of the leaders prevented extensive bloodshed.[18] The following year the *Niles Register* remarked that violence during elections seemed all too common in Georgia. In consequence of some quarrel about politics, one Major Camp "was way-laid in the streets of Columbus, and instantly killed by deliberate discharges of a double-barrelled gun by Colonel Milton. The second shot, it is stated, was fired into Major Camp after he had been mortally wounded by the first." [19]

Vicksburg and other Mississippi towns were the scenes of some of the most violent displays of distemper and disorder to be found in the South. When one of the Vicksburg military companies was going through its evolutions on Independence Day in 1835, a drunken bully, acting like a "ruffian and blackguard," attempted to break up the performance. He was put under guard and later released. When the company returned to the courthouse he was there, heavily armed and ready to make trouble. The men seized and disarmed him, escorted him to the edge of town where they put a coat of tar and feathers on him and admonished him not to return. His friends were furious and vowed vengeance. By this time, however, the wrath of the responsible citizenry had been aroused. More than four hundred citizens, militiamen and others, went to every gambling house, dislodged the gambling effects, and burned them in the streets. One such place was barricaded and when entry was forced, a gambler shot one of the town's respected physicians. For this crime five gamblers were hanged immediately.[20]

A full-scale battle was barely avoided in Vicksburg in the winter of 1838, when several hundred men tied up their flatboats at the wharf and proceeded to compete with local dealers for the patronage of Vicksburg consumers. The city, regarding them as rowdy nuisances as well as serious competitors, decided to tax them so heavily that they would leave. The men paid the tax of $1.00 per month, then $2.00 per day. But when it was raised to $50.00 per day, the flatboat men said they would go to court and protest the outrageous charges. The citizens had no intention of permitting the matter to be settled by the courts. Consequently, two companies of the military, in full uniform, with muskets and bayonets and a piece of ordnance, intervened. In the company of the mayor and chief of police, they marched down to the levee to force payment. The flatboat men were equal to the occasion. They erected a breastwork of cotton bales and loaded their cannon. There seemed to be a few on either side, however, who were not quite ready to engage in deadly combat. After some wrangling they were able to persuade their fellows to let the court decide the issue. The court decided that the tax was unduly high, and the flatboat men were permitted to tie up at the usual nominal fee.[21]

No place in Mississippi, or in any other state, was the scene of more violence than the village of Clinton. The thirties were highlighted by numerous duels and fights. This was the town where "the sword hung all too loosely in its scabbard," and where a wife told her husband, as he left for the dueling grounds, that she would rather be "the widow of a brave man than the wife of a coward." In 1835 the Spring Hotel was the scene of many tragic events, including the killing of Robinson by Gibson at dinner, the shooting between Sam Marsh and several of his enemies, hand-to-hand fights with pistols, and the killing of Gilbert by Herring. In June of that year the people were terrified by the news that the infamous Murrell gang was approaching the town. The women and children crowded into the church which was surrounded by a heavy guard, while bands of organized regulators were stationed at every approach to the town. Perhaps the Murrell gang learned of Clinton's unusual preparations, for the town escaped a visit from the desperadoes.[22]

As younger sons of Eastern planters moved into the Memphis region to make their fortunes, they seemed to wear their honor "on their sleeves," as if to compensate for their lack of inheritance. From the middle thirties to the outbreak of the Civil War, affairs of honor were a common occurrence in the Tennessee city on the bluff. And the ritual of "genteel murder," as McIlwaine calls it, was not confined to the scions of the East. Others fought it out on the streets or on the wharf with knives, guns, or fists.[23]

The following account of the Memphis court proceedings, reported with a sense of humor, had its daily counterpart in many towns or cities:

Fighting — A. Dolan indulged in a fight. This is in direct opposition to Ecclesiastical and Civil Law — both of which tell us that little boys should not scratch *out* each others eyes . . . Capt. O'Haver marched him up, where he was fined $3.00 for his amusement.

Another Fight — Andrew Hartley indulged in another fight like the above mentioned gent. But his must have been carried to a greater extent. He invested his capital to the amount of $24.25, and left the office under the impression that it was a "sinking fund" sure enough . . .

Still Another Fight — B. D. (which may stand for "bad devilment," "bully driving," "barking dogs," or "baked dumplings," no matter which) had a fight. Fined $3.50.[24]

The day-to-day violence in New Orleans became so commonplace as hardly to deserve notice. Only when an incident generated unusual heat did it attract any considerable attention in the Crescent City. In 1858 the election was contested so bitterly that many feared extremely violent consequences.[25] A self-appointed vigilance committee took possession of the courthouse and state arsenal and set itself up in a headquarters, appropriately dubbed Fort Vigilance. The armed men numbered more than a thousand, and various field pieces were placed in Jackson Square and at other strategic points. The expected major breach did not occur and the battle was confined to relatively small skirmishes. Even so, eleven members of the vigilance committee were slain and others were wounded. The day of election passed quietly, and, for the moment, peace was restored.[26]

The most refined defense of honor found expression in dueling which was widespread throughout the ante-bellum South. In Prussia and other militaristic European countries the duel was based on the principle of self-regulation by which the military sought to protect itself from civilian intervention.[27] In the South it was the manner of settling personal disputes by which "gentlemen," reflecting the strong influence of the European military tradition, sought to draw some line of behavioral distinction between themselves and others. Men of any class could — and did — fight; but dueling should be confined to those who claimed to be "gentlemen." The practice was defended "on the ground that it tended to preserve the amenities of life, that it was an incentive to virtue, and a shield of personal honor . . ."[28]

While the duel was not an outgrowth of slavery, it was the most convenient and proper way for a slaveholder to settle a dispute involving honor. Accustomed to the use of firearms and the exercise of almost unlimited power over his dependents, "he could not endure contradiction, he would not brook opposition. When one lord ran against another in controversy, if the feelings were deeply engaged the final argument was the pistol."[29] Governor Hammond of South Carolina vigorously denied any connection between slavery and dueling. Admitting that "the point of honor is recognized throughout the slave region and that disputes of certain classes are frequently referred for adjustment to the 'trial by combat,'" it was not, he insisted, caused by slavery, "since the same custom prevails in France and England." But he failed to give a satisfactory explanation of its causes.[30]

It was fitting that a practice engaged in by the more refined elements of society should be a highly developed institution with agencies for the training of prospective duelists, an elaborate etiquette to govern participants, and regular places at which the grim events occurred. Generally, fathers taught sons the proper use of arms, while some academies and military schools offered courses in fencing and marksmanship.[31] Few towns could boast of the extensive facilities for the training of duelists that New Orleans had. Throughout the period, teachers, some of them gunsmiths and others fencing masters, sold their services to men who sought proficiency in the use of firearms and swords. In the 1840's there were Emile Cazére, who had an aristocratic clientele, Gilbert Rosiére, the most popular fencing master in the city, and several others, including the Negro, Basile Crokere, whose *salle d'armes* was visited by many.[32]

It is fairly clear that Major Dunn, who opened an academy in New Orleans in 1845, was setting up little more than a school for duelists. As a specialist in short courses, he offered the student "a perfect knowledge of the cane or 'Single Stick,'" as a part of a three-weeks' course on "The Infantry Sword or 'Cut and Thrust.'" The course could even be made shorter: an advertisement stated that "Gentlemen visiting the city, who cannot remain the aforesaid length of time, shall receive Two Lessons Daily — Morning and Evening." [33]

Etiquette was a very important factor in affairs of honor, and prospective duelists adhered to the rules of conduct, as they understood them, with a faithfulness equaled only by their meticulous regard for the concept of honor itself. Because of the general adherence throughout the South to dueling etiquette, in 1838, John Lyde Wilson thought it desirable to codify the various rules.[34] In this way he hoped to eliminate any conflicting practices that might exist and to insure a common understanding of the rules by all persons affected. If it seemed somewhat irregular for a former governor of South Carolina to publish an extensive work on dueling at a time when sentiment against it was increasing in many parts of the world, the author did not think so. While Wilson decried the practice of resorting to arms in trivial disputes, he insisted that there were situations in which it was "right and proper" to resort to the duel. "If an oppressed nation has a right to appeal to arms in defense of its liberty and the happiness of its people, there can be no argument used in support of such appeal, which will not apply with equal force to individuals," Wilson asserted. He then argued that there were many instances in which there were no courts to do justice to an oppressed and deeply wronged individual. If a person is subjected to insult and disgrace, the first law of nature points out the only remedy for his wrongs, and society should condone such measures.

The principle of self-preservation is co-extensive with creation, and when by education we make character and moral worth a part of ourselves, we guard these possessions with more watchful zeal than life itself, and would go farther for their protection. When one finds himself avoided in society, his friends shunning his approach, his substance wasting, his wife and children in want around him, and traces all his misfortune and misery to the slanderous tongue of the calumniator, who, by secret whisper or artful innuendo, has sapped and undermined his reputation, he must be more or less than man to submit in silence.

It was appropriate, therefore, to publish a work on dueling since it "will be persisted in as long as a manly independence and a lofty personal pride in all that dignifies and ennobles the human character, shall continue to exist." [35]

Wilson's *Code of Honor* is a carefully organized exposition on the conduct of all persons involved in a duel. There is a discussion of the preliminaries, in which the author admonishes an aggrieved person not to issue a challenge immediately, but to hold his temper and send a note, as a gentleman, making demands. There is advice for the recipient of the note and suggestions regarding a forthright and honorable reply. Presuming a breakdown in negotiations or the failure — through seconds, of course — to reach a satisfactory settlement, there follow lengthy instructions on the conduct of principals and seconds during and after the duel. All details are discussed, even such matters as who should be on the dueling ground and how the arms should be loaded and presented. The whole question of what constitutes "satisfaction" on the dueling ground is examined, and there are suggestions regarding the ways in which the seconds might reach a compromise at various points in the proceedings. For those who wished to make comparisons with practices elsewhere, Wilson reproduced the Irish Code of Honor in the appendix.

When the laws of their own state forbade such encounters, some duelists preferred to settle questions of honor at some point just outside its borders.[36] Notables of Washington retired to one of several points just across the Virginia or Maryland lines; a favorite spot was Bladensburg Heights between the District line and Beltsville.[37] North and South Carolinians accommodated each other by permitting out-of-state dueling.[38] Before the removal of the Cherokees, some Georgia duelists sought exemption from prosecution by retiring to territory under the jurisdiction of the Indians.[39] On the southern border the Georgians used Amelia Island on the Florida side of the St. Mary's River, while Floridians went to Cumberland Island on the Georgia side of the river's mouth.[40] The Vicksburg and Memphis dueling grounds, scene of many celebrated encounters, were on the western side of the Mississippi, while Arkansans crossed to the eastern banks to settle their disputes on Mississippi or Tennessee fields of honor.[41]

Of course many had no fear of their state's laws and, consequently, did not trouble to remove themselves from its jurisdiction when engaging in a duel. The tempers of some were so ungovernable that they had no time to make

even a short journey to a prearranged spot. Such persons
were hard put to maintain the barest amenities which the
Code of Honor required. For them the streets or the bar-
room were more likely to be the dueling grounds than some
secluded spot across the state line. In other communities,
moreover, dueling was so widely accepted that the likelihood
of a prosecution arising out of an encounter was practically
non-existent. The New Orleans dueling ground, "The Oaks,"
was perhaps the most celebrated field of honor in the New
World. Located just across the Bayou St. John, at the foot
of Esplanade Street, this magnificent little forest of giant
live oaks was the scene of almost all New Orleans duels from
1834 to the beginning of the Civil War. The contrasting
lights and shadows of the leafy arcades seemed to typify a
"state of society where tragedy and gayety walked side by
side in chivalrous converse." [42] "The Oaks," silent host to a
steady stream of spectators and participants, came to be
synonymous with dueling in New Orleans. A recent writer
observed that the words, "under the oaks," continue to have
a sinister significance in New Orleans "even to those who
have never heard of Allard [the owner of the oaks] and do
not know precisely what 'oaks' are meant." [43]

The fortunes of men in public life were invariably tied
up with their honor, and they knew full well that their future
would be seriously jeopardized if they did not preserve their
honor with scrupulous care. While this has been universally
true, only in the ante-bellum South did men in public life
persist in defending their honor by dueling. The shock that
the death of Alexander Hamilton at the hands of Aaron
Burr produced in the North had no counterpart in the
South. Institutions were too imperfect, society too unstable,
and men too intemperate to sanction the abolition of the
honorable practice of dueling. It not only continued in the
South in the nineteenth century, but, for a time, increased
in both frequency and respectability.

The South's turbulent men — and there were plenty of them — gave little consideration to the suggestion of abolishing dueling. Dueling was a means of displaying manhood and reflecting gentility. Rising young men, far from resisting opportunities to do formal battle with their opponents, seemed to welcome them. Louis T. Wigfall, Senator from Texas at the beginning of the Civil War, believed the duel a factor in the improvement of both the morals and manners of the community! He held that it "engendered courtesy of speech and demeanor — had a most restraining tendency on the errant fancy, and as a preservative of the domestic relations was without an equal." [44]

An enemy of Andrew Jackson asserted in 1828 that the hero of New Orleans had engaged in nearly one hundred duels, fights, and other altercations.[45] This was doubtless an exaggeration, but enough people recalled his duel with Dickinson in 1806 and his battle with the two Bentons in 1813 to know that he was a faithful adherent to the code and a deadly adversary on the field of honor.[46] The ambitious Southern gentleman who finally persuaded himself that he should not engage in duels frequently qualified his conclusions, as did Benjamin F. Perry in 1832. The South Carolina Unionist declared that he would pay no attention to abusive remarks that his editorial foes in Columbia might make about him. "I am not going to challenge any blackguard of an editor," he vowed. "The next man I fight or challenge shall be a man of distinction. I am done with lackeys. There is no honor to be acquired in a contest with such men, and I am unwilling to become their executioner. The practice of duelling is a bad one, but a necessary evil, and must some time be adopted in order to avoid a worse one." [47] It was indeed important, as Perry observed, that the duel should be with someone of distinction. The survivor of such an encounter would surely enhance his standing on his own account, and might even fall heir to some of the influence of his victim if they were competitors. After his arrival in Georgia in 1799, William H. Crawford made his first important step toward popularity and success on the dueling grounds. Indignant over an invitation to join a group of land speculators in 1804, Crawford insulted the group by the tenor and implications of his refusal. In a subsequent duel, Crawford killed Peter Van Alen, one of the speculators. His victory brought public approval and he began to rise steadily in public esteem.[48]

It was not necessary, however, to kill one's foe to win public acclaim. In March 1825, young Major Robert A. Beall of Augusta, Georgia, issued a challenge to Thomas D. Mitchell, who had made some remarks which Beall regarded as insulting. At the dueling grounds — on the Carolina side of the line — two shots were exchanged with no effect. Then, "on the mediation of Major Pace, who was recognized as an authority in such affairs, the combatants retired from the field without further hostilities." Major Beall's friends rejoiced upon his safe return and, while many had regretted that he had issued the challenge, all now regarded him with increased admiration. At twenty-five years of age he was elected to the state legislature. While a misunderstanding could sometimes be settled on the field without injury to the principals, there was the danger that in the process of negotiations other offenses might be made. Seconds, surgeons, and other participants took their roles fully as seriously as the principals. Aspersions regarding their functions might well lead to their becoming the principals in some later encounter. At the Beall-Mitchell duel some comments made by Dr. Ambrose Baber, who attended as the surgeon of Major Beall, called forth a public card from Mitchell. The statements in the card were offensive to Baber, who promptly sent a challenge which Mitchell accepted with equal promptness. They met at Hamburg, South Carolina, in March 1826; the weapons were rifles at ten paces. On the second fire

Mitchell was mortally wounded, "being shot through the lungs — and instantly expired." [49]

Some members, largely Southern, of the highest lawmaking body in the land were not averse to resorting to arms to settle a question of honor. When Armisted T. Mason was killed in a duel by his cousin, John M. McCarthy, he had already lost his seat in the Congress, but his greatly embittered feelings over his political misfortunes led to the duel in which he lost his life.[50] Sam Houston was in the Congress, as a representative from Tennessee, when he met General William White in a duel. White was struck in the groin and lay abed for four months. A Kentucky grand jury indicted Houston for assault, but he was not arrested. When Houston was praised at a political gathering for his prowess in dueling, he silenced the cheering crowd and told them he was opposed to the practice and was happy that General White was injured no worse.[51] The duel in 1826 between Henry Clay and John Randolph grew out of a criticism which Randolph made regarding the manner in which the Secretary of State had handled matters relating to the proposed Conference of Latin American Republics. Clay was furious and demanded satisfaction. Although he could have claimed immunity since he had made the remarks on the floor of the Senate, Randolph accepted the challenge, though with obvious reluctance. The two men met on the Virginia side of the Potomac, April 8, 1826. "On the first fire both discharged their pistols without effect. On the second Clay missed him, and Randolph reserving his pistol discharged it in the air," having been determined from the beginning not to harm Clay.[52] When the latter saw this unexpected display of magnanimity, he is said to have exclaimed, "I trust in God, my dear sir, you are untouched; after what has occurred, I would not have harmed you for a thousand worlds." [53]

Conclusions to duels were not always so pleasant. Ironically enough, the first member of Congress to be killed in a duel came, not from the South, but from the extreme Northern end of the country — Maine. His adversary, however, was a Southern gentleman. In 1838 Jonathan Cilley of Maine, while on the floor of the House, attacked Colonel J. Watson Webb, editor of a leading New York Whig paper, the *Courier and Enquirer*. Through his friend William Graves, a member of the House from Kentucky, Colonel Webb demanded satisfaction. Cilley rejected the demands on the grounds that he was not accountable for what he said on the floor of the House. Graves took offense and demanded satisfaction in his own name, which Cilley granted. On February 24, 1838, the men met near Marlboro, Maryland. The weapons were rifles at eighty yards. On the third exchange, and after considerable wrangling, Graves shot Cilley who died almost instantly.[54] News of the tragedy provoked widespread indignation. The death of the popular Maine representative seemed to confirm the view that dueling was a reckless, irresponsible, and illogical means of settling disputes. Many regarded Cilley as having been murdered. A full-scale investigation was ordered by the House.[55] Petitions to outlaw dueling poured into the Congress, and Samuel Prentiss of Vermont introduced a bill in the Senate to prohibit dueling in the District of Columbia. In pleading for its passage, he spoke of the "spirit of insubordination and lawless violence which is abroad in the land, infecting and pervading, it would seem entire communities, threatening the subversion of established institutions of the country, and which, if not checked and subdued, will, it is to be feared, sooner or later, overthrow all law and all government, and open the way to brutal anarchy and misrule . . ."[56] The bill, providing for five years' imprisonment for giving or accepting a challenge, became law in 1839. There were still the dueling grounds in Maryland and Virginia, however, to accommodate the overly sensitive residents of the nation's capital.

The death of Cilley was not without its effects, however,

even on Southern members of the Congress. There were, thereafter, fewer duels, and many disagreements were settled without resorting to the field of honor. In 1842, Edward Stanley, a member of the Congress from North Carolina, challenged Henry A. Wise of Virginia, but friends intervened and made the duel unnecessary. In the same year Representative Thomas Marshall of Kentucky met the New York editor, James Watson Webb, on the field of honor outside Wilmington, Delaware. The affair ended after the second fire in which Webb sustained a superficial leg wound.[57] One of the last significant duels involving members of the Congress was the 1845 encounter between Thomas L. Clingman of North Carolina and William L. Yancey of Alabama, both of whom were members of the House of Representatives. In the heated debate over the annexation of Texas, Yancey made remarks that were personally offensive to Clingman. After an unsatisfactory exchange of letters the matter was placed in the hands of their representatives who likewise had no success in settling it. Consequently, the Congressmen agreed to meet on January 13, 1845, at a spot between Beltsville, Maryland and the District of Columbia line on the Washington turnpike. An elaborate set of rules governing the encounter was drawn up. The word had leaked, and a force of police invaded a nearby hotel where some members of the party had spent the night. Arrangements were hastily made to complete the proceedings before they were interrupted, but just as the men exchanged the first, ineffectual, fire the police arrived. From that point the affair was settled by a consultation between the friends of the principals.[58]

Despite the increasing preoccupation of the South's leaders with the sectional controversy after 1850 — or perhaps because of it — dueling and other altercations remained a feature of their personal relations. Frequently, however, when offended by their Northern adversaries' severe criticisms, the aggrieved Southerners did not go through the formality of challenging them to a duel, which most Northerners would have declined. Instead, they promptly set out to chastise their critics by caning, pistol-whipping, or some other form of corporal punishment. In the contest over the House Speakership in the winter of 1855–1856, Horace Greeley went to Washington to support the candidacy of Nathaniel P. Banks. He criticized and probably helped to defeat a House resolution presented by Albert Rust of Arkansas calling for all candidates to withdraw. At their next encounter Rust and Greeley exchanged a few words, and Rust began to strike Greeley on the head with his cane. They were separated, but a few minutes later Rust met Greeley again and resumed the lashing. Once more they were separated by bystanders.[59]

In general, the South approved the summary chastisement of those who offended it or censured its leaders. When, in 1856, Representative Preston Brooks of South Carolina beat Charles Sumner into insensibility with a cane because of Sumner's severe strictures against South Carolina in his "Crime Against Kansas" speech, the South was delighted. Even the next day Brooks could write his brother that the "fragments of the stick are begged for as *sacred relics*." [60] Southern newspapers lavishly praised Brooks's deed and numerous groups, among them the student body of the University of Virginia, passed resolutions endorsing it.[61] A leading Richmond paper rejoiced that a Southern gentleman had the courage to register his objections to Sumner's "insults" and to "cow-hide bad manners *out* of him, or good manners *into* him." Later, when it was reported that a few Southern editors expressed disapproval of Brooks's action, the fiery Richmond editor called them "mealy mouthed pharisees of the press." [62] All over the South Brooks was praised by editors, student groups, and citizens' mass meetings. In Columbia, South Carolina, even the slaves collected a handsome purse for him, much to the disgust of a Charleston editor, who felt that the South did not need the assistance of its slaves to show the North the extent of its resentment as well as its unity.[63] When Brooks resigned and returned to South Carolina — to be triumphantly reelected — he was given a hero's welcome. In Columbia an enormous crowd greeted him, and the mayor presented him a silver pitcher, a goblet, and a "fine hickory cane," with a handsome gold head. In Charleston the citizens presented him a cane with the inscription, "Hit Him Again," while his constituents in the Fourth District gave him one that was inscribed, "Use Knock-Down Arguments." [64]

No class of Southerner, perhaps, went to the field of honor more frequently than newspaper editors.[65] Of course, there were some editors who never had the opportunity to settle their disputes with their readers in such a formal manner. If the offense was grave enough and the aggrieved person impulsive enough, the latter might well storm into the editor's office or meet him on the streets and start shooting. Editors enjoyed neither the immunity that a member of Congress could invoke — although no real gentleman would — nor the claim of misquotation that an oral purveyor could make. The written word by which he was compelled to stand made him especially vulnerable; and the occasions on which he was called to defend, by pistol or sword, his words are so numerous that it is not possible to make more than a brief reference to some of them.

The years following the 1836 establishment of the Vicksburg *Sentinel* as a daily newspaper were turbulent for its editors who showed considerable boldness in their writings. Their position led almost immediately to a series of street encounters and fatal duels. The first important editor, Dr. James Hagan, seemed especially bold. In 1837 and 1838 his condemnation of certain cotton speculators led to a duel with one of them. The editor of the rival paper, the *Vicksburg Whig,* began to attack Hagan, and bitter feeling developed between the two. After several desperate encounters on the streets, they engaged in a duel. Hagan was involved in so many encounters that he gave up the practice of carrying arms. In 1843, he was killed on the street by Daniel W. Adams, who took exception to an article in the *Sentinel* reflecting on his father, Judge George Adams of Jackson, Mississippi.[66]

In Louisiana, in 1843, the political campaign reached an unusually feverish pitch, and "personality and virulent criticism were never before carried to such a pitch" in the state. The daily *Tropic*, a New Orleans Whig sheet edited by Colonel W. H. McCardle, was especially belligerent and irresponsible in its attacks on the candidates for the Democratic party. Several personal conflicts and affairs of honor resulted from its bellicose articles. McCardle had his Baton Rouge counterpart in J. Hueston, editor of the *Gazette*. Hueston taunted the Democrats for nominating for Congress Alcee LaBranche whom he described as "destitute of spirit and manhood." This presumably was because LaBranche was one of the few men in public life in the state who had never engaged in a duel. LaBranche was insulted and, when Hueston visited New Orleans shortly thereafter, LaBranche came upon him in the St. Charles billiard room and demanded reparations for the "gross insult." Receiving a defiant reply, LaBranche struck Hueston with a cane or billiard cue, knocking him down and disabling him. A duel was hastily arranged for three days later, which Hueston insisted on going through with, although he had not fully recovered from his wounds. The weapons were double-barreled shotguns at forty yards. The place was, of course, The Oaks, from which they were forced to retire because of rumors of police interference. At a more remote point the affair proceeded. The first and second exchanges were ineffective; on the third Hueston's skull was grazed; on the fourth he was shot through the lungs and died instantly.[67]

It was almost inevitable that in Charleston the editors of

the powerful *Mercury* would have difficulties with readers, as they took a firm, partisan stand on various public questions. In September 1856, the *Mercury* published three articles reflecting, it was claimed, on the honor of Judge A. G. Magrath. The judge's brother Edward sent a challenge in his own name to W. R. Taber, one of the editors. They met on September 29. Neither was satisfied with the first ineffectual exchange of shots. After the second exchange, Taber's second suggested that both parties should be satisfied. Magrath and his second said that they would be satisfied only if Taber apologized for publishing the articles; this, of course, he would not do. On the third exchange Taber was killed.[68]

Dueling with editors was not confined to the lower South; Virginia had its share. In Portsmouth, in 1843, Melzer Gardner, editor of the *Chronicle*, bitterly condemned the employment of Negroes in the Norfolk Navy Yard. He was denounced for his stand by Mordecai Cook, a Portsmouth lawyer. Gardner replied in a strong article, reflecting severely on Cook. Each demanded a retraction and was equally adamant. When they met on the street, Cook assaulted Gardner with a cane. Gardner drew a revolver which Cook wrenched from his hands. After shooting Gardner through the heart, Cook is reported to have remarked, "Let him die there. I am satisfied." [69]

Perhaps the most exciting encounter in the history of American journalism was the duel between Thomas Ritchie, Jr., son of the distinguished editor of the Richmond *Enquirer* and John Hampden Pleasants, editor of the influential Richmond *Whig*. Early in 1846 an article appeared in the *Enquirer* accusing Pleasants of abolitionist leanings. This was a serious charge in Virginia; and although Pleasants was not a dueling enthusiast, he could not ignore such an accusation. Consequently he challenged Ritchie to meet him, equipped with side arms only. At Belle Isle in the James River, they advanced on each other, without the usual formalities, firing at will. Pleasants fell with several wounds, and died two days later. Ritchie, only slightly wounded, was arrested, tried, and acquitted.[70]

The persistence of dueling in the South was not due to a lack of legislation on the subject. Stringent laws were enacted rather early in all the states below the Potomac. The North Carolina law of 1802 banned all participants in duels from holding office and provided that the survivor of a fatal duel should suffer death as a convicted murderer.[71] In 1812 an act of the South Carolina legislature declared that all participants in a duel, including the seconds as well as the principals, should serve prison sentences of twelve months and pay fines of $2,000 each. They were also barred from holding public office, practicing law, medicine, or the ministry, "or any other trade or profession or calling whatever." Survivors of fatal duels were declared to be guilty of homicide and were to receive penalties regularly given for such offenses.[72] In the Louisiana law of 1818 the challenger in a non-fatal duel was to be fined $200 and imprisoned for two years, while the person accepting a challenge was to be fined $100 and imprisoned for one year. The survivor and the seconds in a fatal duel were to be dealt with as murderers.[73]

Some states required all members of the General Assembly, other public officials, and attorneys-at-law to subscribe to an oath disclaiming participation in any duel. Alabama's oath was as follows:

I . . . do solemnly swear . . . that I have, neither directly nor indirectly given, accepted or knowingly carried a challenge in writing, or otherwise, to any person or persons (being a citizen of this State) to fight in single combat or otherwise, with any deadly weapon, either in or out of this State, or aided or abetted in the same since the first day of January, 1826, and that I will, neither directly or indirectly, give, accept, or knowingly carry a challenge . . . to any person or persons . . . to fight in single combat or otherwise, with any deadly weapon . . . or in any manner . . . aid or abet the same, during the time for which I am elected, or during my continuance in office, or during my continuance in the discharge of any public function.[74]

Nor was there a lack of sentiment in certain respected quarters against dueling. In his baccalaureate address at the University of Nashville in 1827, President Phillip Lindsley declared that the law of honor requiring dueling was a European inheritance. Although the people of the United States acknowledge themselves neither nobility nor gentry, Lindsley argued, yet so ambitious are they of what "savours of *high life*, that, without family, or estate, or royal favour, or legal immunities," they have introduced all "the pompous phraseology and all the aristocratic usages of that very country whose right to govern them they have long since disclaimed and forever renounced." [75]

Others spoke out against dueling. In a sermon in Charleston in 1844, the Reverend William H. Barnwell referred to it as a "barbarous practice, still too common among us, which provokes Jehovah, and defies his law; disturbs the State, and spurns its enactments; destroys men, and afflicts their families; while it usually brings upon those that engage in it, certain misery both here and hereafter." Barnwell admitted that there had been some decrease, but said that in its persistence not even the professors of religion were exempt from the "Iron Law." It was, he said, "heathenish, impious, and absurd," and Christians should "detest and reprobate the practice." [76] But, as Bishop Whipple pointed out, most men admitted that dueling was "in every way contrary to the Christian religion." [77] They, nevertheless, felt that their position as gentlemen required them to defend their honor whenever it was questioned. The "Iron Law" was a higher law that transcended the laws of the state and of religion.

Anti-dueling associations became the means by which responsible citizens hoped to cope with the practice. Affairs of honor became so frequent in Savannah that a group of clergy and other prominent men met on December 26, 1826, and organized the Savannah Anti-Duelling Association. Its constitution was modeled after that of the recently organized Charleston Anti-Duelling Association.[78] The members asserted that they considered dueling to be "a violation of all law, both human and divine, as hostile to the peace and good order of society, and as destructive to the happiness of domestic life." A committee of seven was appointed to attempt to prevent any contemplated duel. The association planned an anti-dueling educational program to consist of public meetings, essay contests, and the issuance of pamphlets. By 1837, the association had become inactive; and it is not possible to evaluate the influence it may have exerted.[79]

There were those who took a dim view of anti-dueling societies. When such an organization was founded in Natchez in 1828, an Alabama editor doubted that any good would come of it. It was laudable and Christian, but would have little effect on "those false notions of honor entertained by our modern Fireeaters and would-be gentlemen, who think it a greater disgrace to bear an imaginary insult that to murder a fellow-being in cold blood, and render a whole family miserable." The editor was not without ideas as to what should be done. He continued:

A very different remedy should be pursued, and we would say that to all such testy touch-wood gentry, who are ready to draw a pistol if a cat should tread on their toe, the strong arm of the law should be applied. Let it be in all cases a crime of murder for one man to kill another in a duel, and let the law be rigidly executed in a few instances, and it will, in a short time, do more to suppress this odious practice than all the *Anti-Duelling Societies* that can be established from this time to the Millennium.[80]

It was not quite as simple as the editor seemed to believe, as the experience in his own state clearly showed. Alabama had a law against dueling, though perhaps not as stringent as the editor desired. And yet, four months after he made his suggestion a jury declined to enforce it.[81] Even the oath against dueling proved ineffective. In the 1841 session of the Alabama General Assembly, special acts were passed which excused thirteen citizens from taking a dueling oath covering their activities up to January 1, 1842![82] A similar piece of legislation in 1848 released five persons from the oath.[83]

In a section where laws were casually regarded and indifferently enforced, it was too much to expect that legislatures could merely write off dueling. Andrew Jackson realized this and made a significant remark regarding it shortly after he left the Presidency. Commenting, in 1837, on the Earl of Clarendon's strictures against dueling, Jackson said, "The views of the Earle are those of a Christian, but unless some mode is adopted to frown down by society the slanderer, who is worse than the murderer, all attempts to put down dueling will be vain." [84]

John Lyde Wilson, the eminent authority on dueling etiquette, believed, like Jackson, that the real offender was the person who sought to damage reputation and honor. He could not condone a "passive forbearance to insult and indignity"; instead, he would teach the rising generation that nothing was more derogatory to the honor of a gentleman than to wound the feelings of another, however humble. To eliminate dueling he "would strongly inculcate the propriety of being tender of the feelings as well as the failings of those around him. I would teach immutable integrity, and uniform urbanity of manners . . . Once let such a system of education be universal, and we should seldom hear, if ever of any more dueling." [85]

Here was the ambivalence that made any direct, effective attack impossible. Those opposed to it in principle, at times favored it, in practice. To Southern gentlemen, like slavery, it was a necessary evil. By the mid-nineteenth century, it had become sectional just as slavery had. And, although dueling and slavery have been described as the South's "two ill-favored sacred cows," [86] it must be admitted that, in contrast to opposition to slavery, one could condemn dueling without fear of recrimination. Perhaps there were relatively few duelists, as there were relatively few slaveholders, but dueling and other forms of violence had become acceptable, because of deficient political institutions and a highly refined sense of personal honor and integrity. Anti-duelists and other opponents of personal violence were to be tolerated as being harmless. Bent on waging personal warfare whenever he desired, the hot-blooded Southern knight of the 1850's would ignore them.

# 4

# A Militant Gentry

The English pioneer who settled in the South could hardly be called a utopian dreamer or reformer. He had little desire to build a community radically different from that which he had left behind. Unlike his Puritan compatriot, whose dream of an entirely new order obsessed him and provided motivation for his desertion of England, the prospective Virginian or Carolinian would regard his New World venture as highly successful if he could reproduce, on a grander scale perhaps, the way of life of the mother country. The social order he wanted to emulate was seventeenth-century England, which had not yet felt the full effects of the political upheavals at home or the important commercial undertakings abroad.[1] It was a way of life which retained much of the feudal spirit and which, consequently, rested on an agrarian social and economic system where ideas of fealty to the lord, of personal honor, and of obligations to codes of soldierly conduct predominated. The wildest dreams of the Southern settler involved his establishing himself as a country gentleman, living in noble splendor, receiving the services of his coterie of subordinates, and discharging the obligations that his "high position" imposed upon him.

If he failed to establish such an order, it was not because he did not try. In several places there was a conscious move toward building and maintaining a sort of feudal aristocracy in the South. There was the futile attempt by the founders of South Carolina to impose a prefabricated feudal system on the stubborn, uncongenial environment between the Ashley and Cooper rivers. And there were numerous individual attempts by would-be feudal lords, from Maryland to Georgia, to establish all or a part of the English system as they conceived it.

From the beginning there were several difficulties that had to be overcome in the effort to establish a feudal regime in the Southern colonies. One was trying to play the role of aristocrat, without any experience; for, unless he was a most unusual settler, the pioneer Virginian or Carolinian descended, not from the Cavaliers or the near-Cavaliers, but from ambitious, energetic common folk. He sought in the New World what he had failed to find in the Old. His notions about the kind of society in which he should like to be the central figure came, therefore, from what he could remember about English society rather than from experience in the New World or the Old. In Virginia, for example, he dreamed of a social system to which belonged "well-to-do proprietors, boasting of the title of gentleman, professional men . . . skilled artisans . . . [and] day laborers." In reality, however, the locale of his activities was a distinctly agricultural community of small farms, owned and worked by a sturdy class of English farmers who gradually came to learn the social and economic value of Negro slavery.[2] On the latter, they discovered that they could build a New World aristocracy.

Another difficulty sprang from the utter impracticability or impossibility of reproducing a European social and economic system in the New World wilderness. The struggle for existence was so preoccupying, at times, that even gestures in the direction of the "genteel" life had to give way to the stern realities of an unrefined environment. But, while there was no chance for the Southern settler to reproduce the English aristocratic tradition to which he seemed warmly attached, his efforts were not entirely barren. He early realized the futility of attempting to erect an elaborate social and political order that did not provide the economic strength to ensure its own survival. In the search for economic reinforcement, he embraced plantation agriculture and Negro slavery which, incidentally, gave him some of his desired status. As slavery grew, toward the end of the seventeenth century, the majority of the white farmers found it difficult to compete with the system. They either migrated to the West or remained to compete, against great odds, with those who owned slaves. Those wealthy few began to emerge as slaveholding planters; soon their position in the social scale corresponded roughly to that of the old aristocrats.[3]

Each community had its leading planter or planters, and on these devolved the responsibilities and privileges that added luster and attractiveness to their station. They dominated the legislative branch of the government, and some belonged to the council of state. One was designated commander of the military forces in his jurisdiction and given the title of "colonel"; another became country sheriff; others assumed other responsibilities. As working gentry they remained close to the soil; but they were coming to be regarded as members of the aristocracy, the dominant and domineering element in the local social order.

When the Southern planter emerged as an aristocrat, he did not seem to mind the contempt in which some quarters on this side of the Atlantic held the very idea of aristocracy. Fancying himself as adhering to the best traditions of his English models, he sought to incorporate them into his mode of living; this would give greater validity and acceptance to his status and way of life. Equalitarianism, an increasingly important attribute of American character, did not play an important role in his life. Freedom of the mind and body, rapidly becoming a watchword of the American heritage, was accepted with specific reservations by the Southern aristocrat. Meanwhile, his new station as planter, slaveholder, and arbiter of the political and social order, gave him ample opportunity to put into practice his concept of Old World aristocracy. It was like some musically inclined person attempting to play an instrument "by ear." He had the desire, perhaps even the talent, but not the training.

Planters in the tidewater South, proud of their historic memories and of the heritage of which they claimed to be a part, fancied themselves as feudal princes living in a kind of medieval splendor. In this reverie, with non-slaveholding whites and the great body of Negroes apparently loyal to the established system, they styled themselves as "high blooded, high minded" guardians of the best chivalric traditions. Viewing slavery as the cornerstone of their civilization, they rounded out their conception of what the New World feudal order should be, the specific roles of the various classes and races.

The slave was, or course, permanently at the botton of the scale, and it was believed that any and every measure should be taken to keep him there and to keep him docile. Even the non-slaveholding white was induced to support the system by the near-fiction that he could eventually move up into the planter-slaveholding class and by the argument that in a system based on the utter degradation of the blacks, even the most wretched white could be proud. Planters believed that, to preserve social and economic stability, the Negro must be kept at the bottom — by discipline, if possible, by force and violence, if necessary. Perhaps as much as the crude frontier and the ever-present Indian, the institution of slavery had a profound effect on Southern character. It was not only a central feature in commercial agriculture, but also a major factor in the development of the South's domineering spirit and will to fight to defend its position.

Thomas Jefferson recognized and deplored this condition as early as 1782. In his *Notes on Virginia* he observed that the whole relationship between master and slave was "a perpetual exercise of the most boisterous passions, the most unremitting despotism on the one part; and degrading submissions on the other." Even worse, the slaveowner's child imitates it. Seeing the parent storm, he "catches the lineaments of wrath, puts on the same airs in the circle of smaller slaves, gives loose to the worst of passions, and thus nursed, educated, and daily exercised in tyranny, cannot but be stamped by it with odious peculiarities." [4]

These views were not confined to the period of the Enlightenment. Observers of a later day noted what Jefferson had seen. They believed that slavery had a most deleterious effect on both owners and children. Captain Basil Hall reported in 1828 that the slaveowners themselves lamented the "evil influence" of slavery on their children's character. It was a curious and instructive fact, he asserted, that the slaves themselves delighted in "encouraging 'young master' or even 'young mistress' to play the tyrant over them!" [5] Tocqueville made some significant observations regarding the effect of slavery on the character of the master. In part, he said:

The citizen of the Southern states becomes a sort of domestic dictator from infancy; the first notion he acquires in life is, that he was born to command, and the first habit he contracts is that of ruling without resistance. His education tends, then, to give him the character of a haughty and hasty man, — irascible, violent, ardent in his desires, impatient of obstacles but easily discouraged if he cannot succeed upon his first attempt.[6]

James Buckingham noted the same thing in Columbia, South Carolina, in 1839. White children of four to seven years of age played about the streets under the care of Negro boys and girls slightly older than themselves. "But the little whites soon learn their own superiority, and make great progress in the art of tormenting and abusing their black guardian; laying thus, in their very first steps in life, the foundation of that irascible temper and ungovernable self-will, which characterize nearly all the white inhabitants of the Slaves States." [7]

Fanny Kemble, after marrying a Southern planter, was greatly disturbed by what her oldest child's superior position was doing. With dismay, she saw how the little girl's "swarthy worshiper . . . sprang to obey her little gestures of command. She said something about a swing, and in less than five minutes head man Frank had erected it for her, and a dozen young slaves were ready to swing little 'missus' — think of learning to rule despotically your fellow-creatures before the first lesson of self-government has been well spelt over!" Miss Kemble said that the habit of command, developed so early among Southerners, seemed to give them a certain self-possession and ease. This, she believed, was rather superficial, and upon closer observation the vices of the social system became apparent. The "haughty, overbearing irritability, effeminate indolence, reckless extravagance, and a union of profligacy and cruelty" of the slaveholders were the immediate result of their "irresponsible power over their dependents." These traits became apparent upon intimate acquaintance with Southern character, she asserted.[8]

That slavery tended to create tyranny in the South was not merely abolitionist prattle. For years it had been the considered judgment of some responsible white Southerners that a powerful socio-political absolutism was a significant consequence of the institution of slavery. In the debate on the question of the importation of slaves, Coloner George Mason of Virginia told the Federal Convention in 1787 that slaves produced "a most pernicious effect on manners" and that every master was a "born petty tyrant." [9] Ulrich B. Phillips said that the actual regime "was one of government not by laws but by men." In fact, he continued, each slave was under a paternalistic despotism, "a despotism in the majority of cases benevolent but in some cases harsh and oppressive, a despotism resented and resisted by some . . . but borne with lightheartedness, submission and affection by a huge number of blacks." [10]

The amount of benevolence, if any, in the despotism depended on the individual's relationship with his slaves. The system provided the despot with extensive prerogatives and ample opportunities for their abuse. The master had almost unlimited personal authority over his slaves as long as they were guilty of no flagrant violations of the rights of whites or of the feebly enforced state laws. For all practical purposes he was the source of law on the plantation; and, in the rare instances when he resorted to the law of the state to invoke his right over his human property, its interpretation and enforcement were in his control. If the government of the plantation was not by laws but by men, its stability rested on force or the threat of force. Believing that slavery could be sustained by force and violence exercised against the slave, or against the challenges of free men, owners had no qualms about resorting to force and violence.

The planter regarded arms as a necessary adjunct to the machinery of control. The lash was used generously or sparingly, depending on the temperament of the master and the tractability of the slave. If the slave resisted the "mild" discipline of the lash or undertook to return blow for blow, how else could the master maintain his complete authority except through the use of, or the threat to use, more deadly weapons whose possession was forever denied the slave? Arming themselves with knives and guns became habitual with some masters and overseers. In moments of anger, they sometimes turned their weapons against each other. This was to be expected among an aggregation of armed lords having no superimposed discipline. The rule of tyranny by which they lived fostered independence and self-sufficiency — almost an individual sovereignty — that occasionally burst out in their quarrels.

The relationship between master and slave was that of

superior and subordinate, despot and subject, or victor and vanquished. A spirit approaching the martial pervaded the entire plantation atmosphere. The conduct of the master toward the slave was determined by rules and considerations not unlike those of the military. Slaves enjoyed no well-defined rights: infractions brought summary punishment from which there was no appeal. A vigorous antislavery tract pointed out that the plantation was "the seat of a little camp, which over-awes and keeps in subjection the surrounding peasantry." The master could claim and exercise over his slaves all the rights of a victorious warrior over a vanquished foe.[11]

The connection between slavery and the martial spirit was almost universally recognized. If the observer were an implacable foe like Charles Sumner, he could see only its bad effects; to him the result was a criminal distortion of the values and notions regarding the fighting spirit. In the South, the swagger of the bully was called chivalry, a swiftness to quarrel was regarded as courage. The bludgeon was adopted as a substitute for argument; and assassination was lifted to a fine art.[12] If the observer were an apologetic friend, he could be proud of the fact that Southerners had been bred under the influences of an institution "which, with its admitted evils, was calculated to foster the martial spirit and give force of character." [13]

The slave was never so completely subjugated as to allay all fears that he would make a desperate, bloody attempt to destroy the institution which bound him. Slaveholders could never be quite certain that they had established unquestioned control; fear and apprehension were always present. Judgment insisted on the strictest vigilance with no relaxation — the only policy consistent with the maintenance of the institution. As one Southerner pointed out, a policy of carelessly widening the sphere of freedom for the slave "would have virtually destroyed the institution. The policy pursued by the slave states was consistent with the *fact* of slavery, and it was an inexorable necessity that the policy should be maintained." [14]

The fear that prevailed even in periods of relative calm greatly impressed Olmsted during his visit to the lower Mississippi Valley in 1856. At the place where he secured accommodations, his roomate, a Southerner, insisted on barricading the door of the rather small, windowless room, explaining that he would not feel safe if the door were unlocked. " 'You don't know,' said he; 'there may be runaways around.' He then drew two small revolvers, hitherto concealed under his clothing, and began to examine the caps. He was certainly a nervous man," Olmsted concluded, "perhaps a mad man . . ." [15]

The responsibility for maintaining control rested, first of all, with the owner and his staff. Neither the laws of the state nor those of the slaveholder were of any avail unless they were enforced by the plantation constabulary. The importance of the owner's role was indicated by Justice Thomas Ruffin of the North Carolina Supreme Court who said, "The power of the master must be absolute, to render the submission of the slave perfect . . ." [16] The owner, his overseer, if he had one, and other subordinates were dedicated to the task of maintaining the kind of discipline that would strengthen the institution. Such a policy called for action resembling a declaration of war on the slaves. An overseer told Olmsted that if a slave resisted a white man's chastisement, he should be killed. On one occasion a slave, whom he was about to whip, struck him in the head with a hoe. The overseer "parried the blow with his whip, and drawing a pistol tried to shoot him." When the pistol missed fire he "rushed in and knocked him down with the butt of it." [17] While deadly weapons might be used to discipline slaves only in extreme cases or by singularly cruel masters and overseers, they were, nevertheless, a part of the pattern of control

which even the most judicious owners did not entirely
overlook.

Despite the fact that the plantation sought to be self-
sufficient and that it succeeded in many respects, the maintenance of a stable institution of slavery was so important that
owners early sought the cooperation of the entire community.
This cooperation took the form of the patrol, which became
an established institution in most areas of the South at an
early date. There were many variations in its size and organization. The South Carolina law of 1690 provided that each
patrol detachment should be composed of ten men under
the captain of a militia company. The number was reduced
to five in 1721. All white men were eligible for patrol service
when the system was established. Between 1737 and 1819,
however, patrol service was limited to men of some affluence,
presumably slaveholders. In the latter year all white males
over eighteen were made liable for patrol duty; non-slaveholders, however, were excused from duty after reaching the
age of forty-five.[18] In Alabama the law of 1819 required not
less than three nor more than five owners of slaves for each
patrol detachment, while the Mississippi law called for four
men, slaveholders or non-slaveholders, for each detachment.[19]

The duties of the patrols were similar in all places. The
detachment was to ride its "beat" at night for the purpose of
apprehending any and all Negroes who were not in their
proper places. Alabama empowered its patrols to enter, in a
peaceable manner, upon any plantation; "to enter by force,
if necessary, all Negro cabins or quarters, kitchens and out-
houses, and to apprehend all slaves who may there be found,
not belonging to the plantation or household, without a pass
from their owner or overseer; or strolling from place to
place, without authority." [20] There were variations in the disposition of offenders taken up by patrols. If the violators
were free Negroes or runaways, they were to be taken before
a justice of the peace. If they were slaves, temporarily away

from their master's plantation, they were to be summarily punished by a whipping, not to exceed thirty-nine lashes.[21] There were, of course, abuses. On occasion, for example, members of the patrol whipped slaves who were legally away from their masters' premises or who were even "peaceably at home." [22]

The patrol system tended to strengthen the position of the military in the Southern community. In most instances there was a substantial connection between the patrol and the militia, either through the control of one by the other or through identity of personnel. In South Carolina the patrol system was early merged into the militia, "making it a part of the military system, and devolving upon the military authority its arrangement and maintenance." There the "Beat Company" was composed of a captain and four others of the regular militia, all of whom were to be excused from any other military service.[23] Sydnor has observed that in Mississippi the structure of the patrol was "but an adaptation of the militia to the control of slaves." In Alabama the infantry captains of the state militia completely dominated the selection of personnel for patrol duty and designated the officers.[24] Under such circumstances the patrol system was simply an arm of the military.

When the countryside was peaceful and the whites turned their attention to other matters, there was much neglect of the patrol system. It tended to lapse into disuse in towns where it was felt that there was adequate machinery for control or in rural areas whenever peace and contentment seemed to prevail among the slaves.[25] Complaints regarding its ineffectiveness arose whenever the whites had reason to feel that they were not adequately protected. The system continued, however, down to the Civil War. In some areas it was an effective deterrent to slave mischief. As late as 1858 it was operating in Virginia. While visiting a friend, Thomas C. Grattan was aroused during the night by noises which, his host informed him, were made by the patrol. He then remembered having heard how the "unfortunate, conscience haunted planters were obliged, in the midst of peace, in all times and seasons thus to keep watch and ward through each other's grounds, armed to the teeth, and never for one hour safely and soundly sleeping in their beds . . ." [26] Only quite infrequently was the situation this desperate; even so, the militia-controlled patrol system helped to create a warlike atmosphere in times of peace.

Nor was the military support of slavery confined to the plantations. In the towns and cities, where slaves frequently enjoyed a measure of freedom seldom accorded them in rural areas, there was considerable protection of the whites from possible dangers. When Captain Hall visited Richmond in 1828 he thought that the sentinel marching in front of the capital building was part of an honor guard for the legislature. His guide corrected him, pointing out that the soldier was part of a guard to keep order among the Negroes. "It is necessary," he told Hall, "or at all events it is customary in these States to have a small guard always under arms; — there are only fifty men here. It is in consequence of the nature of our coloured population." He explained that it was done more as a preventive check than anything else. "It keeps all thoughts of insurrection out of the heads of the slaves, and so gives confidence to those persons amongst us who may be timorous." [27] The sight of the armed guard at the capital "had almost the startling effect of an apparition" on William Chambers when he visited Richmond in 1853. It was the first time that he had seen a bayonet in the United States, and it "suggested the unpleasant reflection, that the large infusion of slaves in the composition of society was not unattended with danger." [28]

Charleston likewise felt the need for special guards to keep order among the slaves. In 1839, the city constructed a guardhouse for the military on the important corner of Meeting and Broad Streets. Strategically located across from the city hall, the courthouse, and St. Michael's Church, it housed soldiers whose chief duty was "to watch and crush any attempt at insurrection by the slaves!" [29] Benwell, the English traveler, arrived at the city several years later, during an Independence Day celebration. His first impression was that "a sense of happiness and security reigned in the assembled multitude." This he found "a notion quite fallacious" upon observing troops stationed at the guardhouse and sentinels pacing in front of the building, "as if in preparation or in expectation of a foe . . ." Each evening at about nine o'clock the roll of drums at the guardhouse announced the departure of the patrol, armed with muskets and bayonets, to make its rounds through the Negro quarters.[30] Kingsford said that the patrol went through the city at all hours in 1857. While, in part, these precautions increased due to the presence of a goodly number of thugs and seafarers, he believed that the slave population was their primary cause.[31]

By 1787, a Savannah militia company was performing police duties and patrolling the streets of the town. Composed of a commanding officer, a sergeant, a corporal, and fifteen privates, the company was under orders to mount guard each evening at 8 o'clock at the court house and patrol even the outskirts of the town. During the spring months they were to be on duty throughout the night. The guard was instructed to be particularly careful not to offend persons walking the streets in a peaceable manner, "but to challenge with Decency." Should any suspicious characters be taken, they were to be conducted to the officer of the guard, "who will examine and deal with them as his discretion shall direct." [32] Seventy years later, with the Mississippi Valley well populated, Natchez was facing a similar problem of law and order. The citizens of that growing town were pleased that the Christmas holidays of 1856 has passed off without incident. They were quick to credit the proper persons for this good fortune: the "careful and prescient mayor" who "had taken the precaution to double the night guard" and "the voluntary military companies" that had been unusually alert.[33]

The South's greatest nightmare was the fear of slave uprisings; and one of the most vigorous agitations of her martial spirit was evidenced whenever this fear was activated by even the slightest rumor of revolt. Fear easily and frequently mounted to uncontrollable alarm in which the conduct of some citizens could hardly be described as sober or responsible. "We regard our Negroes as JACOBINS" of the country, Edwin Clifford Holland declared. The whites should always be on their guard against them, and although there was no reason to fear any permanent effects from insurrectionary activities, the Negroes "should be watched with an eye of steady and unremitted observation . . . Let it never be forgotten, that our Negroes are freely the JACOBINS of the country; that they are the ANARCHISTS and the DOMESTIC ENEMY: the COMMON ENEMY OF CIVILIZED SOCIETY, and the BARBARIANS WHO WOULD, IF THEY COULD, BECOME THE DESTROYERS OF OUR RACE." [34]

A farmer's account of how the fear of revolts completely terrified some Alabama whites suggested to Olmsted both the extent of fear and the impact of fear upon the mind. The farmer said that when he was a boy "folks was dreadful frightened about the niggers. I remember they built pens in the woods," he continued, "where they could hide, and Christmas time they went and got into the pens, 'fraid the niggers was risin' . . . I remember the same thing where we was in South Carolina . . . we had all our things put up in bags, so we could tote 'em, if we heerd they was comin' our way." [35]

This was hardly the usual reaction to threats of slave insurrections. To be sure, such grave eventualities threw them into a veritable paroxysm of fear; but they moved swiftly to put up a defense against the foe. Committees of safety sprang into existence with little prior notice, and all available military resources were mobilized for immediate action. These were not the times to entrust the lives of the citizens to the ordinary protective agencies of civil government. If a community or a state had any effective military force, this was the time for its deployment. Military patrols and guards were alerted, and volunteer troops and the regular militia were called into service. It was a tense martial air that these groups created. For all practical purposes, moreover, even the civil law of the community tended to break down in the face of the emergency. Something akin to martial law, with its arbitrary searches and seizures and its summary trials and executions, prevailed until the danger had passed.

Instances when fears of uprisings were not followed by immediate militarization of a wide area of the Southern countryside are practically non-existent. When Gabriel attempted the revolt in Richmond in 1800, the Light Infantry Blues were called into immediate service, the public guard was organized and drilled to help avert the calamity, and Governor Monroe instructed every militia commander in the state to be ready to answer the call to duty.[36] In 1822, when Charleston was thrown into a panic by rumors of Vesey's plot, all kinds of military groups were called into service. A person unfamiliar with the problem doubtless would have thought that such extensive mobilization was for the purpose of meeting some powerful foreign foe. The Neck Rangers, the Charleston Riflemen, the Light Infantry, and the Corps of Hussars were some of the established military organizations called up. A special city guard of one hundred and fifty troops was provided for Charleston. The cry for reinforcement by federal troops was answered before the danger had completely subsided.[37] The attempted revolt of Nat Turner in 1831 brought military assistance, not only from the governor of the state, "acting with his characteristic energy," but from neighboring North Carolina counties, and from the federal government.[38] Indeed, more troops reached Southampton County than were needed or could be accommodated.[39] With artillery companies and a field piece from Fort Monroe, detachments of men from two warships, and hundreds of volunteers and militia men converging on the place, there was every suggestion of a large-scale impending battle.[40]

There was a strong show of military force not only when large-scale plots like those of Gabriel, Vesey, and Turner were uncovered, but also whenever there was any intimation of insurrection, however slight. Even a cursory glance at the accounts of insurrections and threats or rumors of insurrections reveals the role of the military.[41] The rumor of revolt in Louisiana in January 1811, caused Governor Claiborne to call out the militia: a contingent of four hundred militiamen and sixty federal troops left Baton Rouge for the reported scene of action.[42] Two years later the Virginia militia was ordered out to quell a suspected revolt in Lancaster.[43] In 1816 the South Carolina militia took summary action against a group of Negroes suspected of subversive activities.[44] The militia of Onslow County, North Carolina, was so tense during a "Negro hunt" in 1821 that its two detachments mistook each other for the Negro incendiaries and their exchange of fire caused several casualties.[45] Alabama pressed its militia into service in 1841 to search for slave outlaws and to put down rumored uprisings.[46]

Few ante-bellum years were completely free of at least rumors of slave revolts. Agitation for stronger defenses against slave depredations was almost constant, with some leaders advocating a state of continuous preparation for the dreaded day of insurrection. Governor Robert Hayne of South Carolina told the state legislature, "A state of military preparation must always be with us a state of perfect domestic security. A period of profound peace and consequent apathy may expose us to the danger of domestic insurrection." [47] A New

Orleans editor called for armed vigilance, adding that "The times are at least urgent for the exercise of the most watchful vigilance over the conduct of slaves and free colored persons." [48]

A Southerner seeking military activity did not have to wait for war with Britain, Mexico, or the North. He could find it in the almost continuous campaign against the subversion of slavery. He could go with General Youngblood to annihilate a group of suspected slave rebels in South Carolina, or with Brigadier General Wade Hampton in 1811 in the march from Baton Rouge to an infected plantation in St. John the Baptist Parish. The citadels, sentries, "Grapeshotted cannon," and alerted minute men became familiar and integral parts of the Southern scene and were regarded by many as indispensable for the preservation of the "cornerstone" of Southern civilization.

# 5

# Defending The Cornerstone

Slavery strengthened the military tradition in the South because owners found it desirable, even necessary, to build up a fighting force to keep the slaves under control. They also felt compelled to oppose outside attacks with a militant defense. They regarded the abolitionist attack as a war on their institutions. Calhoun called it "a war of religious and political fanaticism, mingled, on the part of the leaders, with ambition and the love of notoriety." The object being "to humble and debase us in our own estimation, and that of the world in general; to blast our reputation, while they overthrow our domestic institutions." [1] As they read anti-slavery literature, observed the establishment of organizations dedicated to the destruction of slavery, and felt the sting of "subversive" activities like the Underground Railroad, Southerners reasoned that they were the targets of an all-out offensive war.

In the early thirties the scope of the abolitionist offensive was felt. These years saw the establishment of numerous militant antislavery societies. This decade saw the appearance of Garrison's uncompromising *Liberator* and the revolt of the Negro Nat Turner in Virginia. Petitions against slavery began to pour into Congress, and abolitionist literature flowed in an ever-swelling stream. Calhoun admonished, "if we do not defend ourselves none will defend us; if we yield we will be more and more pressed as we recede; and if we submit we will be trampled underfoot . . ." [2] The editor of the *Southern Quarterly Review* took up the North's challenge in the first issue of that journal, saying, "all the south wants . . . is a fair field, fair weapons on both sides, and an opportunity to defend herself." [3] The people of the South would strike back with all the resources at their command. The assailants should be met, editor John Underwood cried, "and never suffered to enter the citadel till they walk over our prostrate bodies." [4]

These were more than rhetorical flourishes. As Garrison and his fellows forced the North to consider the danger of the ever increasing slave power, the Southern leaders asserted themselves. From dozens of pens came ardent defenses of a social structure by which they would live or die. In these "bloodless conquests of the pen" they hoped to surpass "in grandeur and extent the triumphs of war." [5] They evolved a defense of slavery that was as full of fight as a state militia called out to quell a slave uprising. Chancellor Harper, Professor Dew, Governor Hammond, Fitzhugh, and others seemed aware of the fact that, however sound or logical their proslavery arguments might be, they must infuse in them a fighting spirit. The successful defense of slavery, whether by argument or by force, depended on the development of a powerful justification based on race superiority that would bring to its support all — or almost all — white elements in the South. Thus they redefined the "facts" of history, the "teachings" of the Bible, the "principles" of economics.[6] Convinced that thought could not be free, they believed that there should be some positive modifications of the democratic principles enunciated by the founding fathers. They rejected the equalitarian teachings of Jefferson and asserted that the inequality of man was fundamental to all social organization. There were no rights that were natural or inalienable, they insisted. In his *Disquisition on Government,* Calhoun asserted that liberty was not the right of every man equally. Instead of being born free and equal, men "are born subject not only to parental authority, but to laws and institutions of the country where born, and under whose protection they draw their first breath." [7] Fiery Thomas Cooper stopped working on the South Carolina statutes long enough to observe wryly, "we talk a great deal of nonsense about the rights of man. We say that man is born free, and equal to every other man. Nothing can be more untrue: no human being ever was, now is, or ever will be born free." [8]

In the rejection of the principles of liberty and equality, political democracy was also rejected. "An unmixed democracy," said one Mississippian, "is capricious and unstable, and unless arrested by the hand of despotism, leads to anarchy . . ." There was too much talk about democracy and too little about the aristocratic tradition. "Too much liberty and equality beget a dissolute licentiousness and a contempt for law and order." Virginians and South Carolinians led the demand for a recognition of Southern honor because they were true to their ancient sentiments and "with constant pride they guard their unstained escutcheons." [9] Life, liberty, and the pursuit of happiness were not inalienable rights. Every government, South Carolina's Chancellor William Harper explained, deprives men of life and liberty for offenses against society, while "all the laws of society are intended for nothing else but to restrain men from the pursuit of happiness . . ." It followed, accordingly, that if the possession of a black skin was dangerous to society, then that society had the right to "protect itself by disfranchising the possessor of civil privileges and to continue the disability to his posterity . . ." [10]

It was left to George Fitzhugh, that shrewd professional Southerner, to crystallize and summarize Southern thinking on social organization. Free society was an abject failure, he said; and its frantic, but serious consideration of radical movements like socialism, communism, and anarchism was a clear admission of its failure. If slavery was more widely accepted, man would not need to resort to the "unnatural remedies of woman's rights, limited marriages, voluntary divorces, and free love, as proposed by the abolitionists." [11] Only in a slave society were there proper safeguards against unemployment and all the evils that follow as a country becomes densely settled and the supply of labor exceeds its demand. Fitzhugh, with a sneer at the North, observed that the "invention and use of the word Sociology in a free society and the science of which it treats, and the absence of such word and science in slave society shows that the former is afflicted with disease, the latter healthy." It was bad enough that free communities were failures, but it was intolerable that they should try to impose their impossible practices on the South. "For thirty years," he argued, "the South has been a field on which abolitionists, foreign and domestic, have carried on offensive warfare. Let us now, in turn, act on the offensive, transfer the seat of war, and invade the enemy's territory." [12]

The South's society was to rest on the inequality of men in law and economics. Social efficiency and economic success demanded organization; and organization inevitably meant the enslavement of the ignorant and unfortunate. *Slavery was a positive good.* It was regarded by James H. Hammond as "the greatest of all the great blessings which a kind providence has bestowed." It made possible the transformation of the South from a wilderness into a garden, and gave the owners the leisure in which to cultivate their minds and create a civilization rich in culture and gentility. More than that, it gave to the white man the only basis on which he could do something for a group of "hopelessly and permanently inferior" human beings.[13]

The idea of the inferiority of the Negro enjoyed wide acceptance among Southerners of all classes and was an important ingredient in the theory of society promulgated by Southern leaders. It was organized into a body of systematic thought by the scientists and social scientists of the South, out of which emerged a doctrine of racial superiority to justify any kind of control maintained over the slave. In 1826, Dr. Thomas Cooper had said that he had not the slightest doubt that Negroes were of an "inferior variety of the human species; and not capable of the same improvement as the whites";[14] but, while a mere chemist was apparently unable to elaborate the theory, the leading physicians of the South were. Dr. S. C. Cartwright of the University of Louisiana was only one of a number of physicians who set themselves up as authorities on the ethnological inferiority of the Negro. In his view, the capacities of the Negro adult for learning were equal to those of a white infant; and the Negro could properly perform certain physiological functions only when under the control of white men. For example, Negroes "under the compulsive power of the white man . . . are made to labor or exercise, which makes the lungs perform the duty of vitalizing the blood more perfectly than is done when they are left free to indulge in idleness. It is the red, vital blood sent to the brain that liberates their mind when under the white man's control; and it is the want of a sufficiency of red, vital blood that chains their mind to ignorance and barbarism when in freedom." Because of his inferiority, liberty and republican institutions were not only unsuited to the Negro, but actually poisonous to his happiness.[15] Variations on this theme were still being played by many Southern "men of science" when Sumter was bombarded. Like racists in other parts of the world, Southerners sought support for their militant racist ideology by developing a common bond with the less privileged. The obvious basis was race, and outside the white race there was to be found no favor from God, no honor or respect from man. Indeed, those beyond the pale were the objects of scorn from the multitudes of the elect.[16] By the time that

Europeans were reading Gobineau's *Inequality of Races,* Southerners were reading Cartwright's *Slavery in the Light of Ethnology.* In both cases the authors conceded "good race" to some, and withheld it from others. In admitting all whites into the pseudo-nobility of race, Cartwright won their enthusiastic support in the struggle to preserve the integrity and honor of *the* race.

While uniting the various economically divergent groups of whites, the concept of race also strengthened the ardor of most Southerners to fight for the preservation of slavery. All slaves belonged to a degraded, "inferior" race; and, by the same token, all whites, however wretched some of them might be, were superior. In a race-conscious society whites at the lowest rung could identify themselves with the most privileged and affluent of the community. Thomas R. Dew, Professor of Political Law at the College of William and Mary, made this point clear when he said that in the South "no white man feels such inferiority of rank as to be unworthy of association with those around him. Color alone is here the badge of distinction, the true mark of aristocracy, and all who are white are equal in spite of the variety of occupation." [17] De Bow asserted this even more vigorously in a widely circulated pamphlet published in 1860. At one point, he said that the non-slaveholding class was more deeply interested than any other in the maintenance of Southern institutions. He said that non-slaveholders were made up of two groups: those who desired slaves but were unable to purchase them; and those who were able but preferred to hire cheap white labor. He insisted that there was no group of whites in the South opposed to slavery. One of his principal arguments was that the non-slaveholder preserves the status of the white man "and is not regarded as an inferior or a dependent . . . No white man at the South serves another as a body servant, to clean his boots, wait on his table, and perform the menial services of his household. His blood revolts against this, and his necessities never drive him to it. He is a companion and an equal." [18]

Southern planters paid considerable attention to the nonslaveholding element whenever its support was needed in the intersectional struggle. Their common origins, at times involving actual kinship of planters and yeomen, gave them a basis for working together in a common cause. The opportunities for social mobility, however rare, provided the dreams of yeomen. These dreams strengthened their attachment to the planter class; while the fear of competition with a large group of freedmen was a nightmare. But *race* — the common membership in a superior order of beings of both planters and poorer whites — was apparently the strongest point in the argument that the enslavement of the Negro was as good for small farmers as it was for large planters. The passion of the Southern planter and politician for oratory found ample release in the program to persuade Southern whites that theirs was a glorious civilization to be defended at all costs. In the absence of active and bitter class antagonisms, it was possible for the various white groups to cooperate especially against outside attacks and in behalf of slavery.[19]

Most Southerners were not satisfied merely to have their leaders restate the theory of Southern society and argue with abolitionists in Congress and other respectable places; they wanted to give effective and tangible support to their cause. Chancellor Harper had told them that, in the South as in Athens, "every citizen should be a soldier, and qualified to discharge efficiently the duties of a soldier." [20] In *De Bow's Review* "A Virginian" advised his fellows that *"without ceasing to be free citizens, they must cultivate the virtues, the sentiments, nay, the habits and manners of soldiers."* [21] They should be ready for vigorous, militant action to protect and defend the South's institutions. James Buckingham believed that they were determined to do exactly that. In 1839, he remarked, "Here in Georgia . . . as everywhere throughout the South, slavery is a topic upon which no man, and, above all, a foreigner, can open his lips without imminent personal danger, unless it is to defend and uphold the system." He stated further that the violence of the measures taken against the few who ventured to speak in favor of abolition was such as to strike terror in others.[22]

There was no strong antislavery sentiment in the Southern states after 1830. Moreover, Northern antislavery organizations were doing little to incite the slaves to revolt or, except for sporadic underground railroad activities, to engage in other subversive activities. It was enough, however, for Southerners to believe either that abolitionists were active or that there was a possibility of their becoming active. This belief, running very strong at times, placed under suspicion everything Northern, including persons and ideas. "Upon a mere vague report, or bare suspicion," Harriet Martineau observed, "persons travelling through the South have been arrested, imprisoned, and, in some cases, flogged or otherwise tortured, on pretence that such persons desired to cause insurrection among the slaves. More than one innocent person has been hanged . . . She reported with horror that, after William Ellery Channing published his attack on slavery, several South Carolinians vowed that, should he visit their state with a bodyguard of 20,000 men, he would not come out alive.[23]

After 1830, the South increased its vigilance over outside subversion, and pursued the elusive, at times wholly imaginary, abolitionist with an ardor born of desperation. When they could not lay hands on him they seized the incendiary publications that were the products of his "fiendish" mind. In the summer of 1835, overpowering the city guard, they stormed the post office in Charleston and burned a bag of abolitionist literature. According to the postmaster, this act was not perpetrated by any "ignorant or infuriated rabble." [24] In the same year, citizens of Fairfax County, Virginia, formed local vigilance committees in each militia district "to detect and bring to speedy punishment all persons circulating abolitionist literature." A correspondence committee of twenty was to keep in touch with developments in other parts of the South.[25]

It was in 1835 that Sergeant S. Prentiss, rising to prominence in Mississippi, wrote his mother who had remained at their Maine home, that fifteen Negroes and six whites had been hanged in connection with an insurrection plot that never materialized.[26] He added, "It certainly ought to serve as a warning to the abolitionists, not only of their own danger but of the great injury they are doing the slaves themselves by meddling with them." [27] The hunt was on. In the last decade before the Civil War, mobs and vigilance committees arrested Northern "peddlers, book agents, traveling salesmen, and . . . school teachers." [28] William Lloyd Garrison, indeed no impartial reporter of events, gathered enough information on the violent treatment of Northerners in the South to publish two tracts on the subject.[29] He reported that in one Alabama town the militia was called out to eject an agent who was selling Fleetwood's *Life of Christ*.[30] In Virginia "a company of brave and chivalrous militia was assembled, with muskets and bayonets in hand," to escort out of the community a Shaker who was peddling garden seeds.[31] He also reported that twenty-five vigilance committees had been set up in four Virginia counties to keep a strict eye on all suspicious persons "whose business is not known to be harmless or . . . who may express sentiments of sympathy . . . with abolitionists." [32]

These incidents were, of course, excellent grist for Garrison's mill; and allowance should be made for any exaggeration that might have come from his zeal in reporting such incidents. They bear a striking resemblance, however, to those reported by more disinterested sources. When John C. Underwood of Clark County, Virginia, went to the Republican

National Convention in 1856, his neighbors were outraged. In a mass meeting they passed resolutions condemning him of moral treason and threatening him with violence if he ever returned to Virginia. He moved out of the state and remained away until 1864.

In the middle fifties a Texas legislator who had lived in the North expressed views on slavery that some of his fellows regarded as heretical. When it was announced that he was to speak in Galveston, a group of prominent citizens composed a letter to him which contained the following instructions:

That your views . . . on slavery are unsound and dangerous is the fixed belief of this community . . . You are, therefore, explicitly and peremptorily notified that, in your speech you will not be permitted to touch in any manner on the subject of slavery . . . Your introduction of it in any manner will be the prompt signal for consequences to which we need not allude. . . This communication will be read to the assembled public before you proceed with your speech.[33]

All over the South mob action began to replace orderly judicial procedure, as the feeling against abolitionists mounted and as Southern views on race became crystallized. Even in North Carolina, where one citizen felt that there should be some distinction between that "civilized state and Mississippi and some other Western states," the fear of abolitionists caused many of its citizens to resort to drastic measures.[34] In 1850, two missionaries, Adam Crooks and Jesse McBride, came into the state from Ohio, ostensibly to preach to those North Carolina Methodists who had not joined the newly organized Methodist Episcopal Church, South.[35] Soon they were suspected of abolitionist activities, and McBride was convicted of distributing incendiary publications. According to one source they were "mobed and drove out of Gulford." Ten years later a vigilance committee threatened to deal violently with one John Stafford whose crime had been to give food and shelter to Crooks and McBride during their sojourn in the state.[36] This was the kind of activity that Professor Benjamin S. Hedrick, dismissed from the University of North Carolina for his free-soil views, deprecated. Safe in New York City he asked Thomas Ruffin, Chief Justice of the North Carolina Supreme Court, to use his influence "to arrest the terrorism and fanaticism" that was rampant in the South. "If the same spirit of terror, mobs, arrests and violence continue," he declared, "it will not be long before civil war will rage at the South." [37]

As the people of the South went about the grim task of exterminating persons and ideas hostile to their way of life, they began to give serious consideration to the relationship of slavery to their military strength. Since Revolutionary days critics had argued that slaves were a burden during periods of armed conflict. Despite Madison's warm attachment to the South he was convinced that slavery was a military liability. In the 1797 debates on the question of increasing the duty on imported slaves, he insisted that it was as much in the interest of Georgia and South Carolina as of the free states to end the slave trade altogether. "Every addition they receive to their number of slaves," he said, "tends to weaken and render them less capable of self-defense. In case of hostilities with foreign nations, they will be the means of inviting attack instead of repelling invasion." [38]

John Randolph of Roanoke, with his characteristic flair for the dramatic, made it clear that he regarded slaves as a liability in peace or in war. During the debates in Congress preceding the outbreak of the war of 1812 he declared that during the preceding ten years slaves had become more dangerous and that the equalitarian doctrines of the French Revolution had trickled down even to them. "God forbid," he said to his colleagues, "that the Southern states should ever see an enemy on their shores, with these infernal principles of French fraternity in the van . . . the night-bell never tolled for fires in Richmond, that the mother does not hug the infant more closely to her bosom." [39] Randolph, who was in Richmond at the time of the aborted Gabriel uprising in 1800, looked at slavery with an objectivity which few of his contemporaries possessed. He was convinced that slaves would strike for freedom whenever any crisis gave them the opportunity.

Few Southerners after Madison and Randolph entertained similar views regarding the military liability of slaves. But as these views lost favor in the South they found articulate supporters in the North. In 1840, Hildreth asserted that, in the hour of danger, slaves would "be regarded with more dread and terror even than the invaders themselves." In case of a threatened invasion they would "far from aiding in the defense of the country . . . create a powerful diversion in favor of the enemy." Slavery was clearly a military liability, for:

> Should the slaveholding states become involved in a war, which it would be necessary for them to prosecute from their own resources, they would be obliged to depend upon a standing army levied from among the dregs of the population. Such an army would be likely to become quite as much an object of terror to those for whose defence it would be levied, as to those against whom it would be raised.[40]

To Olmsted there was no question of the deleterious effect of slavery on the South's military strength. How could it be otherwise when so large a portion of the working force in the South "is the offspring of a subjected foreign people, itself held to labor without stipulated wages, not connected by marriage with the citizens, owning nothing of the property, having no voice in the state, in the lowest degree ignorant, and yet half barbarous in disposition and habits. . ." In a war the slave would, at the very first opportunity, strike for his freedom. Any other view was ridiculous.

> To suppose that in case of a war, either foreign or civil, the slave would be an element of strength to the South . . . seems to me, to be, on the face of it, a foundation upon which only the maddest theorist or the most impracticable of abstractionists

could found a policy. Whether . . . in case of a civil war . . . northern men are likely to be more influenced by the cost of extra hazardous insurance policies on their manufactures and stores than southern gentlemen by the dread of losing the services of their slaves, we can best judge by the past.[41]

From the slaveholder's point of view it became necessary to nail such claims as lies. Regardless of how much the abolition- ists wished it, slaves were not a military liability. Why should they be when the vast majority were happy and the whites had no fear of them? Indeed, Southerners protested almost too much that they had no fear of slaves. Hammond said that Randolph's description of the white mother clinging to her infant while fearing insurrection was "all a flourish." Of course, he admitted, "there may be nervous men and timid women, whose imaginations are haunted with unwonted fears . . . as there are in all communities on earth, but in no part of the world have men of ordinary firmness less fear of danger from their own operatives than we have." In his cele- brated letter to the English humanitarian Thomas Clarkson in 1845, Hammond made another concession to possible ap- prehension. He explained that "the habitual vigilance" of the South, "with its small guards in . . . cities and occasional patrols in the country" was responsible for the repose and security which the South enjoyed.[42] Two years later, a writer refused to make even these slight concessions regarding the possible danger of slaves. He said that the slaves had no dis- position to violence. The security of the Southern states from a general revolt did not depend on a police force or military organization "or upon any measures of severity, but upon the general feeling that prevails between the two classes."[43] Ed- ward Bryan added that as to any danger arising out of slavery, the South was "as safe as man can be."[44]

If slaves were not to be feared, the argument ran, there was no reason to look upon them as a military liability. A. P. Upshur, the Virginia publicist and jurist, put the proposition firmly but modestly when he said that if slavery added nothing to the owners' strength in war, it certainly took nothing from their power of resistance. Upshur went on to claim that in time of war slaves could, under the proper guidance, be turned into a distinct asset, for their diligent labor at home could release the entire white population for use in the struggle against the enemy. After surveying the whole sweep of history he was able to conclude that "those republics which have been most distinguished for their power, both in defensive and aggressive war, were, without exception, holders of slaves." [45]

History was frequently quoted by Southerners who wanted to prove that slavery did not undermine military strength. Hammond reminded Clarkson that slavery was not a source of weakness to Sparta, Athens, or Rome. What was more, their slaves were comparatively far more numerous than those of the South, "of the same color for the most part with themselves, and large numbers of them familiar with the use of arms." [46] Ruffin reminded critics that slavery had actually increased the military efficiency of the Greeks and Romans. He concluded that "History has nowhere shown that the holding of slaves was deemed a national weakness in war." [47] Another Southerner insisted that the slave system as a source of military weakness for the South existed only in the imagination of the abolitionist. "As we read history," he continued, "the slave institution has never been a source of weakness, and is in reality, one of strength. It has never enfeebled us in any foreign contest." [48]

Southern leaders argued so vehemently against the very idea of the slave as a military liability that they tended to hold him up as a distinct military asset. As wartime laborers their value was undeniable.

Judging from what we all know ourselves of the character of the African in America . . . the idea that our slaves would embarrass and weaken us in time of war — even in a contest conducted for the express purpose of giving them liberty, appears to us to be wholly groundless. . . On the contrary, the proofs are conclusive that they would add vastly to our strength — that under the superintendence of a few they would cultivate the soil as diligently as they do now and maintain our agricultural resources undiminished, while the great body of our adult males would be fighting in the field . . .[49]

The suggestion was even made that slaves might be enlisted in military organizations to do battle for the cause of the South. Chancellor Harper seriously entertained that idea. He noted that some in the North and in Europe believed that, in the event that the South was engaged in a war, insurrection could be organized among the slaves and they could be used as a fighting force against their masters; this he stoutly denied. Because of their attachment to their masters, slaves were a "hundred fold" more available to the South than to any invading foe.

They are already in our possession, and we might at will arm and organize them in any number that we might think proper. . . Thoroughly acquainted with their characters, and accustomed to command them, we might use any strictness of discipline which would be necessary to render them effective. . . Though morally most timid, they are by no means wanting in physical strength or nerve. . . With white officers and accompanied by a strong white cavalry, there are no troops in the world from whom there would be so little reason to apprehend insubordination or mutiny.[50]

Even the entertainment of such an idea reflects the extremes to which Southern thinking could go and the measures which desperation might force. While Harper recognized the dangers inherent in such a suggestion, he seems not to have realized that such action repudiated much which the South stood for. The South was more closely attached to the concepts of military service in feudal Europe than to those in ancient Sparta. Military service, like planting, was the pursuit of the gentleman. The term "gentleman" had been so loosely construed, at least for certain purposes, as to include most white men. To move to the point of including Negro slaves was to move dangerously close to nullifying the entire Southern social order.

In the eyes of Southerners, Negro slavery had become not only a positive economic and social good, but also a positive military good. Slaves would work in the fields while their masters went to do battle against the enemy. If the masters needed help, the slaves might shoulder arms and save the day. In still another somewhat negative way, the institution of slavery was a positive military good: it could have a salutary effect on the nature of wars to come; it could eliminate aggressive warfare. One Southerner pointed out that, since it was unwise and inexpedient for masters to go away on expeditions of foreign conquest leaving their slaves undisciplined for long periods, aggressive warfare would be virtually eliminated as slavery spread over the world.[51]

Slavery might even help to prevent war or, at least, to mitigate its horrors, President Dew claimed. By fixing the wanderer to the soil and establishing an interest in private property, slavery would moderate the savage temper of man and direct his attention toward establishing a society governed by law and dominated by civil institutions. Then the horrors and lawlessness of war would disappear.[52] Slavery could, therefore, be made to serve the interests of the pacifists or warmongers, depending on the point of view of the advocate. On the whole, however, there seems to be no doubt that it strengthened the military tradition, if not the hand, of the South.

# 6

# Militant Expansionism

From the beginning, the Southern half of the United States seemed destined for agriculture. There were no prosperous industrial and commercial classes, few bustling towns, and no dynamic and diversified economic life to give exciting hope to English investors or their later American counterparts. Whether in Virginia, the Carolinas, or Alabama, farming was not only the way of making a living; it was also the way of life. Land assumed an importance surpassed by no other single factor. When in the 1850's Southerners vowed that they would fight to preserve their institutions and way of life, land and slavery loomed large in the picture.

Very early in the movement of whites from the older regions of the South to the newer ones in the Southwest, there developed the notion that expansion was essential to the existence of slavery. The wastefulness of the plantation system necessitated the constant accession of virgin lands. It was felt that without new lands the institution would be doomed. To employ slave labor on poor land merely added to the already mounting cost of cultivating the staple crops and brought nothing but economic ruin.

There was a strong feeling, moreover, that it was necessary to extend the institution of slavery into new territories "in order to lighten its burden on the old slave communities."

The well-being of the latter could best be guaranteed by providing a "safety valve through which the excess Negro-population would flow to the western territories," one observer declared.[1] The delegates to the Tennessee Constitutional Convention of 1834 expressed a similar view. They said that "while slavery exists in the United States, it is expedient, both for the benefit of the slave and the free man, that the slaves should be distributed over as large territory as possible; as thereby the slave receives better treatment, and the free man is rendered more secure."[2]

Some Southerners insisted that they were not advocating the extension of slavery, as the abolitionists claimed; they were merely promoting the "diffusion" of the institution. Diffusion was important for two reasons, A. S. Roane, a prominent publicist, asserted. In the first place, restriction touched the South's honor and degraded its status by depriving it of full equality under the Constitution. In the second place, the continued equilibrium in the Senate demanded the creation of new slave states if free states were to be formed. Roane continued, "When the evil day comes . . . when an increased North will be represented in the Senate by abolitionists, it will then become the duty of the South to provide for its own safety, by dissolving the bond which will no longer connect states with reciprocal interests."[3]

In 1849, a group of Mississippians argued that the extension of slavery into new areas would even facilitate emancipation! Various efforts to confine slavery to narrow limits would "tend to render it always unsafe and forever impossible to emancipate slaves in the slave States." If slaves should be scattered over half the territory of the United States, the time will come when "they will be surrounded with and in the midst of an overwhelming superiority in numbers of free whites, among whom they will find an abundance of employment in such menial offices as would yield to emancipated slaves an easy support, and slavery may disappear as silently and as unnoticed as in its character of vassalage it has done in England." [4]

The body of rationalization developed regarding slavery did not interfere with expansionist views. Since the slaveholder was arguing that his humanitarian instincts supported slavery because it gave new opportunities to a benighted people, the extension of the South's institutions into other areas could have none other than good results. Thus, he could speak of extending slavery and of diffusing democracy without sensing the slightest incompatibility in the two propositions. In the planter's view, religion and natural law made the Negro a "necessary exception to the principle of political equality." [5] Furthermore, the crystallization of the views on race provided a rationale for the southward extension of the system. If they should overrun Cuba, Mexico, and Central America, they would merely be repeating on a grander scale what other superior peoples had previously done to further the progress of humanity. As one writer explained:

Conquest, extension, appropriation, assimilation, and even the extermination of inferior races has been and must be the course pursued in the development of civilization. Woe may be unto those by whom the offence comes, when there is a real offence — but such is unquestionably the plan prescribed for the progressive amelioration of the world. [6]

The South's expansionist sentiment was doubtless connected with its martial spirit. The conviction that the South had the greatest institutions in the New World was an aggressive conviction. While the desire for new agricultural lands was a dominant motivation, the same spirit that urged the section to a hasty, almost precipitate defense of its honor also imposed on it the responsibility to push back the frontiers and bring new areas under its beneficent influence. This spirit forced an enthusiastic participation in every expansionist scheme, and supported sectional programs of expansion when there were none on the national agenda.

It is no mere accident that most of the leading filibusters were southerners.[7] In a land where men resorted to the duel in the defense of their honor and the honor of their white women and where the chivalric ideals of an earlier age prevailed, an important manifestation of the martial spirit was the strong interest in the conquest of new lands. J. D. B. De Bow gave eloquent expression to this interest. He said that the field before the South was boundless, and "the power that broods over it, grows every day in energy, in resources and in magnitude, and will be as restless, in time, as the whirlwind." At some future date armed bands would sally forth from Southern ports, as they had previously done from Northern ports, "in the service of every power that shall offer emolument and glory. . . We have a destiny to perform, a manifest destiny over all Mexico, over South America, over the West Indies and Canada." [8]

Political as well as economic and social considerations in the South's urgent demands for new lands strengthened the planters' determination to expand, even against the sternest opposition. The remarkable expansion of plantation slavery after the close of the War of 1812 had astonished and distressed the opponents of slavery. Consequently, they sought to evolve a policy of containment which, slaveowners feared, might conceivably lead to the extinction of the institution. The North's policy of containment threw the South into a panic that was second in intensity only to that created by slave insurrections or rumors of them. It was first demonstrated in the Tallmadge Amendment to Missouri's application for admission into the Union. The proposal to prohibit further extension of slavery into the Louisiana Territory and to free, upon reaching the age of twenty-five, all slave children born in Missouri after its admission was regarded by Southerners as an attempt to strike a lethal blow at slavery.

Peace was not restored by the 1821 compromise on the Missouri question. There came from the Southern press a veritable barrage of defenses of slavery and militant attacks on the North's policy of containment. Speeches and articles sought to deflect the attacks on slavery by calling attention to its worth and to the necessity for its protection and extension. In 1822, Edwin C. Holland, agitated not only by the Missouri question but also by the slave uprising recently attempted by Denmark Vesey, felt compelled to give vent to his views. This he did in a ringing *Refutation of the Calumnies Circulated Against the Southern and Western States Respecting Slavery.* He condemned Northern leaders for their attempts to prevent the expansion of slavery, and said that the people of the South and West would not surrender their cherished constitutional rights. "If they are to be sacrificed by a system of legislation that strikes at the root of all their interests, the safety of their lives and the prosperity of their fortunes, they will not be sacrificed without a struggle." [9]

Among the steps taken by the leaders of the antislavery movement to contain slavery, the defenders of slavery ranked the "infamous" Wilmot Proviso with the Tallmadge Amendment. Coming as it did during the Mexican War, this attempt to prohibit slavery in the territory to be acquired from Mexico was regarded as the most desperate move yet made to contain and destroy slavery. Calhoun's fury was controlled only by the remarkable discipline to which he could subject himself. Even so, he regarded the Proviso as little short of a declaration of war, as he told his Charleston friends in 1847.[10] He asked the people of the South to unite as one party, a request that was repeated by a caucus of Southern Congressmen in 1849. The following year the Nashville Convention passed resolutions affirming the equal rights of states in the territories and declaring the Wilmot Proviso unconstitutional. This group of business and political leaders also asserted that the spectacle of the states "involved in quarrels over the fruits of war, in which the American arms were crowned with glory" was humiliating. The Proviso, the delegates said, was regarded as disparaging and dishonorable by fourteen states and its incorporation in any offer of settlement was "degrading to the country." [11]

The South's position with regard to the expansion of slavery was not merely one of opposing the policy of containment. There was also an active program to extend the area of the United States, especially in those directions that would serve the economic and political interests of the slave states. Expansionism always had strong support in the South. Men of the section were among the most enthusiastic expansionists in 1812. They were eager to overrun the entire Southern border, and "war with England seemed a perfectly clear occasion for doing so." [12] Felix Grundy of Tennessee, John Calhoun and William Lowndes of South Carolina, Governor W. C. C. Claiborne of Louisiana, and Nathaniel Macon of North Carolina were among those who confidently expected important territorial acquisitions to result from the war with England.

During the war, Southern groups engaged in expansionist programs which had little or nothing to do with the struggle with England. In August 1812, several hundred men from around Natchez permitted José Bernardo Guitierrez de Lara to lure them off on a poorly planned, unsuccessful expedition against Mexico.[13] A few months later, William Shaler, who had been advising Guitierrez, wrote from Natchitoches that the "business of volunteering for New Spain has become a perfect mania" in the lower Mississippi Valley. "I hear of parties proceeding thither from all quarters, and they are constantly passing thro' this village from Natchez. . ." [14] During the second year of the war, another group of Natchez adventurers organized themselves into the "Friends of Mexican Emancipation." They were no more successful than their predecessors.[15] Later, another independent expansionist scheme — this time originating in New Orleans — was attempted. The pressing necessity on the part of everyone to prepare for the defense of New Orleans thwarted it, however.[16]

Attempts to acquire land through conquest were wholly unsuccessful during the War of 1812 and the Mexican Revolution, but the Southern adventurers were not dismayed. In the following decade, the men of Natchez and New Orleans continued to probe points along the frontier to see if Texas and other areas of the Southwest were ripe for acquisition. Despite President Madison's proclamation of September 1, 1815, forbidding citizens of the United States to participate in expeditions against Spanish possessions, they continued to do so. In the fall of 1815, Colonel Henry Perry of Connecticut crossed the Sabine with a band of adventurers recruited from several Southern communities. Nothing resulted, but such activities kept Luis de Onís, the Spanish envoy to the United States, busy. In 1816, he complained that 1,500 men from Kentucky and Tennessee were plotting a Texas invasion and that filibuster activities were being openly conducted in New Orleans.[17]

While the acquisition of Florida in 1819 momentarily quieted expansionist schemes in the Southeast, it did not stifle the general expansionist tendencies in the South. The following decades witnessed some of the most extensive efforts yet made to expand toward the Southwest.

Texas, the objective of some adventurers during the Mexican Revolution, continued to appear especially attractive to Southerners. When slavery was abolished throughout Mexico in 1829, the howl of resentment from the Southern press made it clear that slavery was an important factor in the desire for Texas.[18] United States support of the Texas Revolution — coming largely from the slave states — was doubtless moved, in part, by a strong impulse to support the movement for independence; but the planters' desire to win the area for slavery was also a strong motivation. New Orleans became a center of enthusiastic support of the Texas Revolution. As early as November 1835, the Mexican envoy to the United States complained that the insurgents in Texas were receiving daily assistance of all kinds, including "munitions and arms . . . silver and soldiers, who publicly enlist, in the city and carry with them arms against a friendly nation." [19] The minister had good reason to complain. One military outfit, the New Orleans Grays, had already offered its services, and two companies had sailed for Texas before the protests were made.[20]

John A. Quitman, organizer of the Natchez Fencibles, could not resist the temptation of the Texas Revolution. He requested leave from his duties as captain of the company, which was graciously given, "so long as he may deem his presence necessary to the glorious cause he has espoused, and may the God of battles speed and protect him." Some of the Fencibles said farewell to their beloved captain; others accepted his offer to take along any who had "a good horse, rifle or musket, and pistols." The action they saw was relatively inconsequential, but the venture is said to have cost Quitman $10,000. His gallant men, who were supposed to go at their own expense, had far more zeal than financial resources.[21] From other parts of the South, fighters poured into Texas. A company of volunteers left Courtland, Alabama, in December 1835. Early in the following month two companies of volunteers from Huntsville, Alabama, and Louisville, Kentucky, arrived.[22] If Southerners could win Texas for independence or annexation, they felt certain that they would also be winning it for slavery. At the same time, the struggle would give Southern warriors and would-be heroes an opportunity to prove their mettle.

By the 1850's, the tradition of fighting for land was well established in the slave states. Perhaps a wealthy romantic like John A. Quitman did regard himself as a "knight errant of old" taking up arms "to redress the wrongs of the weak and helpless." [23] For most, however, the struggle was more directly connected with economic and political problems. Planters saw in Florida, Texas, Mexico, and Cuba opportunities to extend the agricultural system to which they had become committed. Others hoped that new accessions would give them an opportunity to achieve dreamed-of opulence. The Montgomery citizen who suggested that the banner of the Georgia troops en route to Texas be changed from "Texas and Liberty" to "Texas, Liberty, and Land," was merely taking cognizance of an important motivating factor of much widespread interest in Texas.[24] Southern political leaders, moreover, wanted the advantage that new slave states would give them in the race for power in national politics.

As the debate over slavery became more heated and as the South sought to prevent its containment, the political aspects of expansion assumed greater importance. Indeed, they seemed to dominate the expansionist movement between 1850 and 1860. This is not to say that planters no longer believed that there was economic value in extending the plantation system. As late as 1859, a Texan, urging the extension of slavery into Mexico, said:

> Thousands of rifles are sleeping in Texas and the Southern States, ready to awake at the call of a leader, and become an "Army of Occupation" in that broad territory between Monterey and the Rio Grande. They will be ready to establish a protectorate over that portion of Northern Mexico, or annex it to the Union, under a democratic form of government . . .[25]

Despite the fact that further extension might have been uneconomical, some planters were not convinced. They acted on the assumption that the extension of the plantation system into new lands in the 1850's would have a salutary effect, hoping that the result would be similar to that which such an extension had brought about twenty or thirty years earlier.[26] Southerners would hardly have been willing to fight for land in the 1850's had there been no hope for economic gain. At the same time, the increased intersectional tension and the feeling on the part of the slaveholding states that they were at a serious political disadvantage in dealing with the North provided an important additional stimulus for seeking territorial outlets.

While spokesmen were trying to salvage the South's self-respect and dignity in the great Congressional debate of 1850, others, less articulate but more daring perhaps, were attempting to gain territory. For years there had been whispers about Cuba and its possibilities. In 1820, agreeing with Andrew Jackson, John C. Calhoun stressed Cuba's importance as "not only the first commercial and military position in the world, but is the keystone to our Union. No American statesman ought ever to draw his eye from it." [27] By 1850, there were bold suggestions, even in responsible quarters, that Cuba should be saved from Spanish oppression and introduced to the glorious traditions of American democracy.

Any lack of leadership among Cuba's advocates was soon remedied through the appearance in the South of that Venezuelan soldier and adventurer, Narciso Lopez, who dedicated himself to the liberation of Cuba. General Lopez had made one attempt to free Cuba in the summer of 1849, but got no farther than New York harbor, where President Taylor's proclamation and United States marshals caught up with him.[28] He then attempted to secure Northern support, but, finding the people in that section "timid and dilatory," resolved to "rest his hopes on the men of the bold West and chivalric South." [29]

Lopez proceeded across the mountains and down the Mississippi Valley, traveling incognito, conferring with those who were interested in his scheme. The first step would be the establishment of a secret Southern committee for the annexation of Cuba. At Jackson, Mississippi, he visited Governor John A. Quitman and offered that veteran of the

Texas Revolution and Mexican War the office of "general-in-chief of the organization, movement, and operations of all the military and naval force which shall or may be employed in behalf of the contemplated revolution . . ." Lopez and his supporters hoped that Quitman's leadership would "tie into one single action Southern interest and Cuban annexation." Lopez told Quitman, "Were the extreme Southern men, possessing influence like yourself, to stretch forth a friendly hand to all Southern Unionists on the guaranteed condition of striking together one great and bold blow for Cuban annexation, positive force and probable advantages would result to the South . . ." This was a tempting offer to the militant expansionist. To lead such a movement "in aid of an oppressed people and for the introduction of American civilization and Southern institutions," his biographer said, had been the dream of his life. Only his strong sense of duty as governor of his state during the growing intersectional struggle restrained him. Quitman assured Lopez that if he were free to act he would at once embark upon the patriotic enterprise. He did not close the door, however, for he indicated that there was a possibility that his obligations to his state would soon be discharged.[30] For the present this was a great loss for Lopez and the Cuban cause. Moreover, even in 1850, Quitman was to find that association and communication with conspirators could be a dangerous business.[31]

A warm and friendly reception awaited Lopez in New Orleans. Numerous citizens helped to organize and equip the proposed expedition to Cuba. He also found "many gallant and gifted young men, ready to become soldiers of fortune — willing to respond to the simultaneous calls of the oppressed for sympathy and assistance; of ambition to 'glory or the grave' and the allurements of golden ease in the 'Garden of the World.' " The prospect of a fight quickened and warmed many hearts, and his recruiting efforts bore fruit as men from Kentucky, Tennessee, and Mississippi began to arrive in New Orleans. Not only the "very flower of the Mississippi Volunteers" that had served in Mexico were standing by, awaiting the orders of their leader, but also "many of the worthless characters and blackguard rowdies" of New Orleans.[32]

The outfit that set sail for Cuba late in April 1850, may be called the Lower Mississippi Valley Liberation Army, as the vast majority were fiery expansionists and adventurers from that part of the country. The guns and ammunition that were placed on the ship at the mouth of the Mississippi were supplied from the stores belonging to Mississippi and Louisiana.[33]

The victory that Lopez won upon landing at Cardenas on May 19 was short-lived. Not one Cuban volunteer answered his plea for reinforcements, and when large numbers of Spaniards reached the place, the American liberators were forced to withdraw. They put in at Key West where they were given a hearty welcome by the citizens who aided some of the filibusters in reaching their homes.[34] In Savannah Lopez was arrested and charged with violating the neutrality laws of the United States, but was released for lack of evidence.[35] He then went to New Orleans to prepare for another expedition. There, however, under pressure from the federal government, a grand jury indicted Lopez and fifteen other leaders, including John A. Quitman who at first had threatened to use the militia of the state of Mississippi to defend its impugned sovereignty. He finally resigned, however, and allowed himself to be arrested.[36] Sympathy for the indicted men revealed the great enthusiasm in the Crescent City for filibustering. Upon leaving the courthouse, Lopez was cheered by a large crowd, and that evening he was serenaded by several hundred young men. The New Orleans *Delta* praised him, as did the *Courier* and the *Crescent*. When the suits were finally dismissed, there was a wild celebration in the city. In Lafayette Square thirty-one salvos were fired for the Union and one for Cuba.[37] If the warriors could not have Cuba, at least they could have a military celebration.

This was not the end, however. The Mobile *Tribune* said of Lopez, "Unless we are greatly mistaken in the impression we have formed of him, he will again be heard of in some new attempt to revolutionize Cuba." [38] De Bow was brutally frank when he predicted that this second attempt was but the beginning of the end "which looks to be the acquisition of that island by the United States . . . Call it lust of dominion — the restlessness of democracy — the passion for land and gold, or the desire to render our interior impregnable by commanding the keys to the gulf — the possession of Cuba is still an American sentiment . . ." [39]

It would take more than failure and a federal indictment to force Lopez to abandon his schemes. Having found a congenial community, he resumed planning for the liberation of Cuba almost immediately. During the fall and winter of 1850–1851, preparations proceeded in New Orleans, in several Florida communities, and in Savannah.[40] In October 1850, Lopez was secretly drilling about eighty men in his New Orleans "School for the Soldier." A visiting New York physician reported that the Lopez group had "several thousand rifles, a large quantity of ammunition, and military stores" placed at convenient points to be removed at the appointed time. He added that "several leading and influential men at the South were engaged with them and had advanced large sums of money on their bonds, some of them having sold as high as forty cents on the dollar." [41] In the spring of 1851 several volunteer organizations were formed and military parades were held in the interest of Cuba. The proclamation against filibustering issued by President Fillmore on April 25 seemed not to deter them. That same spring the Louisiana legislature appropriated $5,000 for its military corps, and many believed that this was an indirect means of strengthening the forces of Lopez, as the man most responsible for the passage of the appropriation was L. J. Sigur, Lopez's New Orleans host and intimate friend.[42]

Late in July 1851, when news reached New Orleans that the Cubans had revolted, the people were delirious with joy. "In their jubilance some young men obtained a cannon and fired numerous salutes while waving the flag of free Cuba." The *Delta* got out an extra, while meetings on behalf of Cuba were held in Lafayette Square and elsewhere. Proclamations of Cuban liberty were read, Cuban bonds were sold, $50,000 were raised within a short time, and there was a scramble of men seeking a place in the liberation army. With a portion of the money Sigur purchased a ship, the "Pampero," to transport the Lopez expedition. Meanwhile, the United States government was strangely silent. On August 3, 1851, the "Pampero" sailed from the foot of Lafayette Street in New Orleans as hundreds of spectators cheered the four hundred liberators on their way.[43]

This last Lopez expedition was no more successful than the previous ones. Indeed, it was less successful, if such was possible. The Cuban insurrection had been quelled, and the Spanish army was prepared to give the liberating invaders a "warm" reception. In encounters with the Spaniards, the Americans suffered costly losses; their dwindling force was not only impotent but demoralized. Finally, Lopez himself was captured and executed before a firing squad. The news of his execution infuriated many Americans, but the wildest reactions were in the South where the majority of the members of the ill-fated expeditions lived. Rioting broke out in New Orleans and disorderly demonstrations were held before the Spanish consulate.[44] The *Courier* shouted, "American blood has been shed. It cries aloud for vengeance . . . blood for blood! Our brethren must be avenged! Cuba must be seized." Hundreds of filibusters poured into the city and joined the press in loudly demanding an expedition of revenge against Spain. At "The Oaks," where so much personal warfare had taken place, the Washington Artillery honored the dead in a solemn ceremony.[45] At Baltimore a procession of mourners moved through the streets, burning in effigy the American consul at Havana. In Mobile an angry mob was barely restrained from assaulting the crew of a Spanish ship that called at the port shortly after the news arrived.[46] Tempers were high, and the mourning was extensive. For the moment, however, Cuba seemed to be beyond the grasp of the Southern filibusters.

John Quitman, who had resigned as governor of Mississippi when he was under indictment for alleged assistance to the Lopez expedition of 1850, was a worthy successor to the Venezuelan. In 1853, he visited his native Rhinebeck, New York, his chief motive being to secure support for a move against Spanish control of Cuba. He visited New York, Philadelphia, Baltimore, Washington, and other cities, earnestly soliciting support for an expedition of liberation. He discussed his designs with various "distinguished persons at the seat of government, and he left there with the distinct impression . . . not only that he had their sympathies, but that there could be no pretext for an intervention of the federal authorities." [47] Quitman's success was limited largely to moral support. Rumors got around, however; and the modest accumulation of men and money was magnified into a gigantic filibustering project by those who gave free rein to their imaginations. An Ohioan was so alarmed that he wrote the British Prime Minister, Lord Palmerston, in September 1854, that there was an expedition of immense magnitude on foot in the United States for subjugating Cuba. He named General Quitman as its leader and indicated that it flourished chiefly in the slave states. "General Quitman proposes to raise 200,000 men, of which I have been informed 150,000 are enrolled already. The place of rendezvous is New Orleans, where they also purpose to embark for their descent on the island." Palmerston's informant said that the expedition was to embark the following February and it appeared that the United States was not going to interfere. "I have no motive . . . in giving this information, but to prevent, if possible, the consummation of as dark a piece of villainy as can disgrace the nineteenth century, to be carried out under the hypocritical pretext of enlarging the area of freedom." [48]

But the federal government had already acted, albeit feebly, to prevent further filibustering in Cuba. At the spring term of the United States Circuit Court for Eastern Louisiana, Quitman, A. L. Saunders, and J. S. Thrasher [49] were asked to show cause why they should not be required "to enter into recognizance to observe, for the term of nine months, the laws of the United States in general," and especially the Neutrality Act of 1818. At first Quitman refused to pay the $3,000 bond. Finally his friends prevailed upon him to do so. Shortly, he and the others were discharged. Quitman strongly resented the treatment accorded him by the court, and in the public press he severely reproached the presiding judge. But he was effectively restrained from further activities in connection with Cuba.

That sympathy for Cuba still prevailed in many quarters, however, is attested by the attitude of the marshal who had arrested Quitman. At a public dinner honoring Quitman after his release, the marshal offered the following toast:

> Cuba —
> We'll buy or fight, but to our shore we'll lash her;
> If Spain won't sell, we'll turn in and thrash her.[50]

Although Southern filibustering in Cuba seemed effectively checked with the bridling of Quitman, the cause of militant expansionism in the South still found support in high quarters. Out of a conference of the American ministers to England, France, and Spain, held at Ostend, Belgium in

October 1854, came a document that was, perhaps, more militant than any troops that Quitman might have raised. Two Southerners, Pierre Soulé and John Y. Mason, and a Southern sympathizer from Pennsylvania, James Buchanan, issued what properly has been called the *Magnum Opus* of the school of "Manifest Destiny and Southern Imperialism." [51] The United States could "never enjoy repose" or "possess reliable security," the ministers solemnly announced, "as long as Cuba is not embraced within its boundaries." And if Spain should refuse to sell, "then by every law, human and divine, we shall be justified in wresting it from Spain if we possess the power." [52]

This saber rattling by the authors of the Ostend Manifesto was not Union policy; it was Southern policy, and as irregular as any filibustering expedition. It expressed Southern will in language, as Channing has said, that "no one could fail to understand." [53] In the South only was there widespread support of the Manifesto. Not even the President and his Secretary of State, who had approved the holding of the conference, could give full support to the views expressed in the strange document. The Philadelphia *Pennsylvanian,* the only Northern journal to support the plan wholeheartedly, called the Manifesto "a dignified and powerful paper"; but the *Public Ledger* of the same city called it a "barefaced filibuster document." [54] In New Orleans, journalistic sentiment ranged from the critical attitude of the *Commercial Bulletin* to the unqualified enthusiasm of the *Delta.*[55]

The South's desire to absorb Mexico was stimulated both by enthusiasm for the war with Mexico and by the Wilmot Proviso which looked to the exclusion of slavery in territories acquired from Mexico. It is not necessary to assume that slavery was the ruling motive in the South's desire for Mexico; nevertheless, during the war there was a marked increase in this sentiment.[56] In December 1846, Wilson Lumpkin wrote Calhoun, "We cannot now get out of the war with any degree of credit except by large accessions of Territory." [57] The Mobile *Herald* felt that evils arising from the concentration of slaves in the lower South could be overcome "by taking new territory adapted to slave labor; or indeed by taking any kind of territory in the direction of Mexico." [58] The Governor of Virginia expressed a similar view, saying, in his annual message in 1847, that territory acquired from Mexico would be a natural outlet for slaves from Virginia and other Southern states. "The South can never consent to be confined to prescribed limits. She wants and must have space, if consistent with honor and propriety." [59]

There was sentiment opposing the absorption of Mexico, but it seemed to be felt largely by those who feared that slavery would be excluded from the newly acquired areas or that bitter antislavery opposition would render the effort unsuccessful. Most Southerners opposed the acquisition of territory that fell under the control of Free Soilism; otherwise, any and all was desirable.[60] Others, like Calhoun who was unfriendly to the Polk administration, opposed absorption for various reasons, including, perhaps, a desire to discredit the administration.[61] The Calhoun Democrats, as well as the Whigs, insisted that Polk had precipitated a needless war and that the fight over the status of slavery in the new territories would disrupt the Union.

That tireless militant expansionist, John A. Quitman, conceived a most ambitious plan for the occupation of Mexico. Toward the close of the Mexican War, the hero of Monterey went to Washington and urged the President and the Secretary of War to adopt his scheme for the permanent military occupation of Mexico. He had a plan to keep occupation expenses at a minimum and to avoid incurring the hostility of the Mexicans. This recommended the holding of a selected number of key positions "in the vital parts of the country" by a relatively small force of 28,000 men, and, later,

Quitman insisted that only Nicholas Trist's bungling of the treaty and generous concessions to Mexico prevented its acceptance. However, his biographer ascribes the defeat of the plan to the hostility of the non-slaveholding states to any expansion that might strengthen slavery. Quitman continued to believe that it was to the advantage of the United States, and especially the South, to hold all of Mexico. He could not see any evils that would arise from adding to the United States "one of the most beautiful and productive countries on the face of the earth, abounding in agricultural and mineral wealth, and possessing withal the power of taxing the commerce of the world by the junction of the two oceans." [62]

Many supported the idea of incorporating Mexico into the United States, and seemed to increase in numbers, as well as in fervor in the final decade before the Civil War. Perhaps the South's appetite for Mexico increased "in direct proportion to the increase of political power in the hands of the Black Republicans" who were pledged to no further extension of slavery.[63] In 1857, Robert Toombs, aggravated by the abolitionist attacks on slavery, expressed the hope that the country would soon get much of Mexico, along with Cuba.[64] William Burwell of Virginia insisted that the South should advocate the immediate acquisition of Mexico which he regarded as essential to the South's future growth. "Your only chance to secure the good will and forbearance of the world," he wrote his friend, Robert M. T. Hunter, "is to seize upon all the territory which produces these great staples of social necessity which the world cannot go without. Do so and you are safe. Fail to do so; you will be slowly and certainly enveloped in the coils of an avaricious and ambitious power, and your subjugation will be perpetual." [65]

The classic statement was made by George Fitzhugh in 1858. He argued, first, that Mexico could not stand alone; if the United States did not acquire it, some European power would. The United States should not permit abolitionism to paralyze her and prevent her from heeding the voice of humanity. Nor should the United States be dissuaded, his second argument ran, from annexing Mexico for fear that such a move would be associated in some minds with filibustering. What was wrong with filibustering, anyway?

> The filibustering that commenced with Vasco de Gama and Columbus, and in a short period gave to Christendom America, New Holland, the East Indies, and Polynesian Isles, is the most glorious epoch in the history of man. . . They who condemn modern filibuster, to be consistent, must also condemn the discoverers and settlers of America, of the East Indies of Holland, and of the Indian and Pacific Oceans.

Finally, Fitzhugh contended that the annexation of Mexico was desirable in order to extend slavery southward, denying that there was much Northern opposition to this. With the reopening of the slave trade, which he anticipated, Northerners would be appeased by the large profits which they could derive from such commerce. "We have but to will it, and Mexico is ours," he concluded. "She knows, from the past, how utterly incapable she is to resist us." [66]

The final effort to seize Mexico was reserved for the most successful of all Southern expansionists, Sam Houston, leader in the Revolution of 1836 which freed Texas. He had been influential in annexing Texas to the Union, which led to the Mexican War and the acquisition of the Southwest.[67] If anyone could succeed, it was Houston. The bill that he introduced in the United States Senate in 1858 to establish a protectorate over Mexico proved too bold even for the most militant expansionists, and failed. But in 1859, as Governor of Texas, Houston could strike out on his own. Complaining of Indian depredations on the frontier, he asked the federal government for military equipment for 5,000 rangers, forty times more than he was entitled to. He sent armed men to various points on the Mexican border and ordered the justice of the peace of each border county to organize small military groups that could be used in an emergency.

Houston had in mind the "boldest and most daring fili-bustering expedition that his fertile brain had ever con-ceived, namely, to lead ten thousand Texas Rangers, supported by Indians and Mexicans, into Mexico, establish a protectorate, with himself in the leading role . . ." He discussed the plan with friends and concluded that the time for action was at hand. He wrote the Secretary of War that conditions on the frontier were in a state of uncertainty, and that there was a possibility that he might be forced not only to repel invasion "but to adopt such measures as will prevent the recurrence of similiar inroads upon our frontier." He made it clear that he would not embarrass the government at Washington, and seemed to be willing, if necessary, to resign his governorship in order to lead the forces into Mexico.[68]

Houston proceeded with characteristic energy. In casting about for able assistance, he asked a friend to approach Colonel Robert E. Lee; but the wary Virginian would have nothing to do with the scheme. Houston was no more suc-cessful in his attempt to obtain money. The London finan-ciers from whom he sought backing held depreciated Mexican bonds, but seemed unimpressed by his argument that an investment in his enterprise would be a sure way to secure the full payment. They declined the offer.[69] Time had run out. The Civil War was upon Texas and Houston, and there was neither time nor money for filibustering.

The scheme to seize Nicaragua excited the admiration of a considerable portion of the Southern population, eliciting their enthusiastic support. Some believed that too much of the South's energies were going into the effort to win Kansas when it would be better to make Granada the "*point d'appui* of Southern strategy." [70] One editor said that the South had been shamefully negligent of Cuba and Central America, with the resulting danger of Black Republicanism in Nicaragua as well as in Ohio. Several months later a correspondent of the same paper expressed the hope that more leaders would, like Colonel H. T. Titus of Florida, yield their position in Kansas "in favor of a new galaxy of Southern States," of which Nicaragua would be the nucleus. Only in this way could the protective power be generated to prevent the South from falling under the permanent and humiliating subjugation of the non-slaveholding states.[71]

In 1860, William Walker, looking for greater support for his filibustering schemes, accused Southern leaders of giving too much attention to Kansas. He said that the Lecompton Constitution would not give another foot of soil to slavery, while the movement in Nicaragua might give it an empire. "Is it not time for the South to cease to contest for abstractions and to fight for realities?" "Of what avail is it to discuss the right to carry slaves into the territories of the Union if there are none to go thither?" If the South wanted to get her institutions into tropical America she would be well advised to do so before treaties were made that would embarrass her action and hamper her energies.[72]

None seemed more qualified to carry forward the expansionist cause in Central America than that restless, adventurous Tennessean, William Walker. Moving rapidly from medicine, to law, to journalism, he finally found excitement — a scheme to dismember Mexico and establish a government under his control. An unsuccessful attempt to seize Sonora in 1853–1854 merely whetted his appetite and gave him experience for more ambitious schemes. Between 1855 and 1860 Walker launched three expeditions to seize Nicaragua. The settlements on the Pacific coast and the increasing commerce in both the Atlantic and Pacific had already greatly enhanced the value of Central America to the United States and to certain European powers, notably England. Keenly aware of this, Walker planned to seize the initiative. Although he sought support in all parts of the country, there seemed little enthusiasm outside the slave states. His first expedition, composed of fifty-eight men, sailed from San Francisco in May 1855, and, within a few weeks, strong sentiment favoring the filibuster was expressed in several Southern communities. Soon advertisements for volunteers appeared in New York and New Orleans newspapers. Their language clearly indicates Walker's conviction that the South, in contrast with the North, appreciated filibustering. In December 1855, New York papers carried an advertisement that was a masterpiece in the omission of details.

Wanted — Ten to fifteen young men to go on a short distance out of the city. Single men preferred. Apply at 347 Broadway, Corner of Lombard Street . . . between the hours of ten and four. Passage paid.

The notice in the New Orleans papers left few questions unanswered.

Nicaragua — The Government of Nicaragua is desirous of having its lands settled and cultivated by an industrious class of people, and offers an inducement to emigrants, a donation of Two Hundred and Fifty acres of Land for single persons, and One Hundred acres additional to persons of family. Steamers leave New Orleans for San Juan on the 11th and 26th of each month. The fare is now reduced to less than half the former rates. The undersigned will be happy to give information to those who are desirous of emigrating. Thomas F. Fisher, 16 Royal Street.[73]

Not even in the New Orleans papers did Walker's agent intimate that fighting might be involved; but few Southerners failed to realize it.

As news arrived of the early successes of the Walker expedition, enthusiasm for the Nicaraguan cause increased markedly. In the spring of 1856 reinforcements began to reach Nicaragua from the Southern states. In April, more than two hundred filibusters embarked from New Orleans to the music of a so-called Nicaraguan band.[74] In June, Walker had himself elected President of the Republic of Nicaragua, but the United States did not extend recognition. In August, the Louisiana expansionist, Pierre Soulé, arrived in Granada. In addition to helping Walker secure a loan of $500,000 through the Bank of Louisiana he is said to have advised him to issue the proclamation of September 22, 1856 which paved the way for the reintroduction of slavery into Nicaragua. This decree called for the repeal of all acts and decrees, including the ban on slavery, that had been in force between 1824 and 1838; during that period Nicaragua had been a member of the liberal Federation of Central American States. While Walker was no ardent advocate of slavery, he appreciated the interest of the Southern planters in areas into which they could extend slavery. He admitted that the decree was "calculated to bind the Southern States to Nicaragua, as if she were one of themselves." His faith in the intelligence of Southern states "to perceive their true policy and in their resolution to carry it out" was one of the main causes for the decree. He said, further, that the true field for the extension of slavery was tropical America, which would be the natural seat of its empire "and thither it can spread if it will make the effort, regardless of conflicts with adverse interests. The way is open and it only requires courage and will to enter the path and reach the goal. Will the South be true to herself in this emergency?" [75]

Walker made it clear that he did not seek the annexation of Nicaragua to the United States. He was determined to establish and maintain a "powerful and compact Southern federation, based on military principles." With the reestablishment of slavery and the opening of the slave trade, his republic would have interests, identical, in many respects, with those of the slave states of the United States. The two regions would be drawn into a relationship resembling an *entente cordiale*. "In the event the Union were dissolved [a matter then freely discussed] the *entente cordiale* might be succeeded by a formal alliance with the seceding States." [76]

The South's reaction to Walker's appeals augured well for the Nicaraguan cause. The New Orleans *Daily Delta* lauded him, declaring that the South's "great directing minds are with the people, looking forward to such associations as may become inevitable." Another issue urged support of the "noble cause in which William Walker is engaged, knowing that it is our cause at bottom — help him onward, step after step, with money, with men, with voice and hand . . ." [77] Small wonder that Colonel H. T. Titus, despairing that the South might become a "Northern dependency," was seeking to establish a closer association with the "golden foliage of the NEW and partly Americanized Republic of Nicaragua." [78]

The willingness of men to fight to maintain the independence of the new republic was gratifying, and Walker was determined to make the most of it. He sent S. S. Lockridge to recruit in Texas and the Middle West; Walker's brother, Norvell, sought recruits in Nashville; while E. J. C. Kewen was to gather men in Alabama, Mississippi, and Georgia. Kewen raised more than eight hundred men, while Lockridge's efforts in the Southwest also were successful. [79] In October 1856, two companies of Louisiana men, the Jacques Guards, were ready to "do good service in Nicaragua . . . either as fighting men or as aiders in developing the agricultural or other resources of the country." [80]

On November 26, 1856, Lockridge left New Orleans with 287 men drawn largely from the Southwest. On December 24, 300 recruits sailed from New York, but were forced in at Norfolk by a violent storm. Another New York vessel, however, reached Nicaragua with 40 men. On December 28, the steamer "Texas" left New Orleans with 250 recruits. Laurence Oliphant, an English writer who went along for the ride, said that a large crowd at the pier cheered them as they departed. The crowd seemed to regard them "with mingled feelings of compassion (for those who have gone to Nicaragua hitherto have seldom returned), of admiration (for the desperate nature of the adventure commanded this), and of sympathy (for was not the object laudable?)." [81]

In February the "Texas" made another trip, carrying Colonel Titus and 180 recruits. March brought 130 fresh recruits from Texas and Louisiana.[82] By the spring of 1857 the Walker army in Nicaragua looked very much like a Southern army.

Throughout the period of filibustering in Nicaragua, New Orleans remained its stronghold of support. It was "the point of concentration for the more reckless spirits of the South, who find in the mixed and somewhat rowdy crowd which throng its streets and bars a congenial atmosphere." [83] The leading newspapers of the city looked with favor on the Walker expedition. The *Daily Delta* gave unqualified support, and even the more conservative *Picayune* spoke with pride of Walker and his men. Of the filibuster triumphs in the fall of 1856, the editor said, "The well proved and indomitable energy, determination and boldness of the man, combined with a singularly characteristic coolness and prudence, were never more conspicuous." The recruits also came in for considerable praise. "Never was there a better example of the adaptability of the wild American volunteer to the most fatiguing as well as dangerous military service; never was there a better example of what may be called, paradoxically speaking, his military characteristic — cool enthusiasm — deliberately hot headed valor." [84]

Walker's inability to "sell" his program to the other states in Central America and the growing hostility of certain American financial interests in the North led to disaffection both in Nicaragua and in the United States. Consequently, on May 1, 1857, he was forced to surrender to officers of the United States Navy. On his return to New Orleans, "a depu-

tation of the citizen-soldiery received the general as he left
the steamer, where the cannon boomed out a loud-mouthed
welcome." The fallen filibuster was lifted to the shoulders
of several men and borne to his carriage. The cheering
crowd followed him to the St. Charles, where he was compelled to make a speech from the balcony.[85] Two days later,
at a mass meeting, he delighted a large audience for two
hours with his account of the Nicaraguan experience. In
New Orleans, filibustering was not dead. In Washington
Walker filed a vigorous protest against the Navy's interference. At New York he received a hearty welcome, but it was
of short duration. However, in the Southern communities
he received a real hero's welcome. There were large demonstrations in Memphis and Louisville. Throughout South
Carolina, Georgia, and Tennessee, he was encouraged by
the lively interest in his fortunes, and in Mobile began to
make preparations for the next expedition. Recruiting was
already under way in Nashville. More than a hundred
Carolinians were ready to assemble in Charleston. A company
of Savannah fighters placed their services at his disposal.[86]
A visiting Canadian was greatly impressed by the enthusiasm
for Walker's cause. He learned that there were one thousand
Georgians and many Texans ready to take the field. "That
the organization has wide ramifications is undoubted," he
concluded.[87]

Although Walker was arrested by federal officials on November 10, 1857, for alleged violations of neutrality laws, he
secured bail and sailed for Nicaragua on November 14. The
federal government prevented recruits from sailing from
Charleston, Galveston, New Orleans, and Mobile, however,
and it was quite simple for a small United States naval force
to take Walker into custody shortly after his arrival in
Nicaragua. A group of New Orleans citizens described the
arrest as contrary to the law of nations and urged the administration to restore Walker to the position "from which

he had been violently and illegally removed." [88] Indignation meetings were held in other principal cities of the South, and the resolutions adopted were "remarkable for their fervid language." [89]

While Walker was repudiated by federal officials and his erstwhile Northern friends, support continued in the South. In Richmond, Montgomery, and Mobile, enthusiastic crowds indicated their confidence in Walker and his program. Senators such as Brown of Mississippi and Toombs of Georgia, and House members like Stephens of Georgia, Clingman of North Carolina, Warren of Arkansas, Taylor of Louisiana, and Quitman of Mississippi stanchly defended him. However, Southern Congressmen such as Winslow of North Carolina, Slidell of Louisiana, Lamar of Mississippi, and Hawkins of Florida upheld the government's right to arrest Walker.

In May 1858, Walker was brought to trial in New Orleans for violating the neutrality law of 1818. Pierre Soulé appeared for the defense, and Walker spoke in his own behalf. When the majority of the jury voted for acquittal, the district attorney entered a *nolle prosequi*. Walker remained in New Orleans to write an account of his experiences in Nicaragua and make preparations for his return.

As events encouraged the South to look for an area for future growth, the Nicaraguan cause seemed to win new support. In February 1858, the Alabama legislature chartered the Mobile and Nicaragua Steamship Company to ply between Southern ports and Central America. In March the Southern Emigration Society was organized to colonize Nicaragua, and soon it had branches in Alabama, Mississippi, South Carolina, and other states. During the spring and summer, Walker toured the lower South, winning new supporters. In June 1858, an editor said that his speech in Aberdeen, Mississippi, showed in words "as he has ever done in action, his devotion to the South and her institutions. He closed his speech by appealing to the mothers of Mississippi to bid their sons buckle on the armor of war, and battle for the institutions, for the honor of the Sunny South . . ." [90] Mobile was much excited by Walker's preparations for another expedition. "Thousands of hearts are throbbing with anxiety for his success," Steuckrath said, "as it is believed that the establishment of Anglo-Saxon rule in Nicaragua will add to the commercial prosperity of the South and the extension and safety of our peculiar institutions." [91]

Although preparations were freely discussed in the Southern press, it was difficult for the federal government to disprove Walker's contention that the prospective emigrants were merely peaceful settlers. However, when he made his final attempt to restore himself to power in Nicaragua by seeking to form an alliance with Honduran rebels, he was captured by British naval officers. Reinforcements arrived from New Orleans, but they could not have saved him from British seizure. Turned over to Honduran authorities, he was shot on September 12, 1860.

The most fantastic of all filibuster schemes evolved in the 1850's when the South keenly felt the pressure of Northern abolitionist policies. This was the Knights of the Golden Circle, the very name of which seemed worthy of a Southern cause. While there was no formal organization by that name until 1854, it had existed for many years, "like the earth in its primordial condition 'without form and void.' " [92] As early as 1834, there were various unaffiliated groups, commonly known as the Southern Rights Clubs, that advocated the reopening of the slave trade and the extension of slavery into new territories. [93] They had signs of recognition, met regularly, evolved a program for the development of the South, and even equipped and manned some slavers.

By the 1850's some men were thinking of an effective, formal organization for the protection and promotion of Southern rights. A group with such a view met on Independence Day 1854, at Lexington, Kentucky, and took the preliminary steps toward the organization of the Knights of the Golden Circle. The idea for the name came from the proposal that, with Havana as the center and with a radius of sixteen degrees, a huge circle could be drawn that would include the Southern portion of the United States, the Caribbean area, Mexico, Central America, and the Northern portion of South America. This area they would unite in a gigantic slave empire to rival in power and prestige the ancient Roman Empire. Within this dream-empire were the regions that produced nearly all the world's supply of tobacco, cotton, and sugar, and much of its finest rice and coffee. With a virtual world monopoly of these important commodities, it would have been in fact a rich region, stretching around the Gulf of Mexico like a great golden circle.[94]

The indefatigable physician-editor-promoter, George Washington Lafayette Bickley, was the founder and moving spirit of the Knights of the Golden Circle. Little is known of this native of southwest Virginia until 1850 when he appeared in Jefferson (now Tazewell), Virginia, as a practicing physician. If his earlier years had been uneventful, he more than made up for it in the following decade. He founded a historical society in Virginia, wrote a history of Tazewell, and published a "manifest destiny" novel, *Adalaska*, in 1853. Early in the decade he became a professor at the Eclectic Medical Institute in Cincinnati. Meanwhile he edited the *West American Review* and established the Wayne Circle of Brotherhood of the Union. In 1858 he gave up the practice of medicine and became a promoter of the American Patent Company of Cincinnati. In the following year he helped to establish in Baltimore a filibustering newspaper, the *American Cavalier*. During half these years he was the dominant figure in the Knights of the Golden Circle, calling himself "President General of the American Legion, K.G.C." [95]

It was not until 1858 that the K.G.C. was promoted with considerable vigor. The South's growing apprehension provided Bickley with an excellent opportunity to promote his fantastic cause with some success. In August 1859, the K.G.C. held an organizational meeting at White Sulphur Springs, Virginia. Rapid growth followed.[96] By 1860, the Knights were working throughout the South "with unabated energy for the increase of their numbers and 'the firing of the Southern heart.'"[97] Another meeting was held in Raleigh, North Carolina, in May 1860, at which the claims of some critics that Bickley was an imposter and a fraud were promptly disavowed. During much of this crucial year Bickley toured the South and Southwest working up support for his organization. At a meeting in Atlanta he succeeded in generating much enthusiasm. At Lynchburg he vowed that the flag of the K.G.C. would fly over Mexico City on January 1, 1861.[98] Since the K.G.C. was an organization whose members were pledged to secrecy, it is not possible to know the size of the organization or who its members were. In November 1860, Bickley claimed to have 115,000 members, including most of the important officials and leading citizens of the Southern states. Ollinger Crenshaw, a careful student of the movement, is convinced that these figures are exaggerated, that the members were not politically prominent.[99] A former member has insisted, however, that some of the most important men of the South were active members. In an obviously exaggerated *Narrative* of his experiences, Edmund Wright asserted that John Breckenridge, Robert Toombs, and John B. Floyd were devoted fellow members.[100] Another former member, generally more sober in his account than Wright, said, "There is no doubt that the original members . . . were men of little, if any, moral character. They were generally broken down hacks, gamblers, and drunkards. The accession to their ranks of such men as Yancey, about the time of the Charleston Convention, gave new life to a concern that was nearly defunct." [101]

While the specific personnel and numbers remain unknown, the qualifications for membership were widely broadcast. Bickley welcomed any Southerner of good character and "such worthy Northern men as live in the South and heartily concur with us in our determination to stand by the Constitutional rights of the South." [102]

The organizational structure of the K.G.C. was most elaborate and shot through with military trappings and an atmosphere of conquest. There were three divisions: the first, or military, degree, called the Knights of the Iron Hand; the second, or financial degree, called the True Faith; and the third, or political degree, called the Knights of the Columbian Star. The Knights of the Iron Hand, the most numerous, were to spearhead the invasion of new territories as well as provide adequate defenses at home against insurrections and abolitionist subversion. It has been claimed that upon initiation the Knights of the Iron Hand were addressed in the following manner by one of the officials:

Gentlemen, we must now tell you that the first field of our operations is 2 [Mexico]; but we hold it to be our duty to offer our services to any Southern State to repel a Northern army. We hope such a contingency may not occur. But whether the Union is reconstructed or not, the Southern states must foster any scheme having for its object the Americanization and Southernization of 2 [Mexico].

The new members were told of the plan to divide the Southern states into military districts, each to be presided over by a colonel who would be responsible for raising a certain portion of the four divisions of 4,000 men each, to be sent into Mexico.[103] It has also been claimed that each local organization, called "Castle," was required to have regular military drills, in order to prepare for the "impending crisis." [104]

The members of the second degree bore the responsibility for financing the program, while the Knights of the Columbian Star were the governing arm. Bickley proposed to acquire Mexico and cut it up into slave states, twenty-five perhaps, thereby permanently establishing the political balance in the Union in favor of the South. If for some reason this acquisition was delayed and secession became a reality, then the K.G.C. would be in the forefront in any scheme to acquire Mexico for the Southern Confederacy. Indeed, two threatening moves were made, in the spring and fall of 1860, toward the Mexican border. Lack of support and the growing unpopularity of filibustering due to the Walker debacle prevented the successful prosecution of the scheme.[105]

By 1860 it was impossible to rally any real support for filibustering in the South, for it seemed necessary to direct all militancy toward the North. While the South still felt it desirable to expand, the task of holding on to what it had was more urgent. Within a few months, the filibusters, like others, North and South, were swept into the vortex of civil war. It was fitting that most of those restless spirits who survived the strange operations in Cuba, Mexico, and Nicaragua should join the ranks of the Confederacy.[106] Several "Castles" of the K.G.C. joined the Confederacy *en masse;* even Bickley, in 1863, was willing to give up his title of "General" in the K.G.C. to become a mere surgeon in a North Carolina regiment of the C.S.A.[107]

# 7

# A Little Learning

If the men of the South showed a predilection for militancy and violence, their educational institutions and leaders did little to discourage this. Free public schools developed very slowly and failed utterly to exercise any considerable influence over manners and morals. After the War for Independence, a strong aristocratic tradition persisted in the South, giving encouragement to the small oligarchy that qualified for participation in government. Among people who regarded government as an instrument of the privileged few, education was viewed as an individual responsibility rather than a state function. Planters and others of the upper class could provide for their children's education in a manner convenient to them. The remainder of the community had little or no need for an education; so there was no problem.

The disinclination of Southern leaders to support free public education was a powerful, if not a decisive, factor in retarding the movement. Several other factors, however, militated against the improvement of schools. One was the almost universal aversion to taxation for education, resulting from a conviction that intellectual improvement was a personal responsibility. In 1832, the president of the University of North Carolina expressed the view that the people of his state were so opposed to taxation that any effort to maintain a tax-supported educational system was doomed to failure.[1] In most Southern states a literary fund, supported by uncertain and irregular revenue from fines, licenses, and franchises, was established as a substitute for taxation to support the public schools. The sparse population and the absence of satisfactory means of transportation made an effective program of public education all but impossible. In 1852, the most densely populated state below the Potomac was Virginia with 23 persons per square mile. Meanwhile, Massachusetts had 127 persons per square mile.[2] In the face of such overwhelming odds, there was little opportunity to develop and maintain free public education.

Nor did there seem to be any unquenchable thirst for knowledge on the part of the Southern people. Unaccustomed to using their meager training, few saw any relevance of education to the life they lived. Their aversion to book learning was almost as strong as their aversion to taxation. This attitude was doubtless a product of the practical-mindedness that came from frontier experience; and in many places in the South it displayed the same tenacity and permanence as other frontier characteristics. In 1853, the superintendent of schools in Rappahannock County, Virginia, reported that many indigent children were not sent to school. In Charlotte County, Virginia, children could not be induced to attend the schools in three or four districts.[3] In many quarters the pursuit of education was regarded as a reckless waste of time. Frequently teachers and pupils were held in simple contempt.

The conditions and attitudes regarding universal education in the South bore bitter and tragic consequences, not only in the general inability of the people to cope with rapidly changing conditions, but also in their intellectual debility. There was a frightening amount of illiteracy at the very time that the balance of power in politics was shifting from the privileged few to the masses. In 1831, in a contested election in North Carolina, 28 out of 111 voters could not sign their names.[4] In 1837, Governor Campbell of Virginia reported that almost one-fourth of the persons applying for marriage licenses in ninety-three Virginia counties could not sign their names.[5] There were more illiterates in Virginia in 1850 than in 1840. In 1850, the New England states had an illiteracy ratio among the native white population over twenty years of age of .42 per cent; the Middle Atlantic states, 3 per cent; and the Southern states 20.30 per cent.[6]

The increasing political strength of the individual American made the ignorance of those in power the more tragic.[7] Unscrupulous politicians encouraged the unlettered to regard their deficiencies as inconsequential or made a virtue out of ignorance and poverty. Taking advantage of the plight of the lower classes and their prejudices against the upper classes, the demagogues of the South rallied the most wretched elements and infused in them a determination to wield their new power against their enemies. But, since it was difficult, if not impossible, to keep venality out of the picture, there were times when this power was sold to the highest bidder. Not infrequently some member of the upper class was the highest bidder. As the contesting groups sought to lure the poor and ignorant into their respective camps, demagoguery and corruption became widespread.

The height of oratory was reached during the political canvass. The strongest appeals to the emotions were regarded as the most effective; and the real issues were subordinated to those matters that could arouse the greatest popular enthusiasm. Few veterans of political campaigns could resist the temptation to appeal to the basest emotions of their ignorant listeners. Even enlightened men like Calhoun encouraged a kind of intolerance that could easily lead to violence in connection with well-known, delicate questions involving the rights and honor of the South.[8] Under the spell of flamboyant, emotion-charged oratory, the citizenry was often moved to violent action. Its narrow intellectual horizons saw no other course. Violence, even rioting, became common-place in many communities in the period approaching and during elections.

Under such conditions politics was war. Regarding politics, a Tennessean observed in 1831 that "as in war, every cunning device is said to be fair when directed against the enemy. . . With a little judicious tempering of the steel I practice upon and admire your maxim of political warfare: 'War to the knife and the knife to the hilt.' " [9] The literal consequences of such a policy could be seen in the 1832 election riots in Charleston, where night after night a disorderly mob set upon and insulted its opponents who were obliged to arm themselves with bludgeons for self-protection.[10] Bishop Whipple's trenchant observations regarding the disorderli-ness of a Florida election in 1843 suggest that this was a wide-spread practice:

Today [November 6] is election day and I have had some sport in watching the speckled, coloured and streaked appearance of the voters who form the population of . . . St Augustine. Fight-ing, swearing, and drinking with the other usual accompaniments of a Southern election were served up in abundance and almost made one blush at such a specimen of republicanism.[11]

The bishop would have blushed even more if he had seen some of the bloody affrays that accompanied many New Orleans elections.[12] He had seen enough, however, to realize that disorderliness and violence were the logical results of the exercise of power by an uninformed, unlettered citizenry. While the more discerning doubtless saw this relationship, few were as blunt and direct as the editor of the *Alexandria Gazette* who suggested in 1835 that the best way to prevent mobs was to educate the people.[13] That was easier said than done, however, and the unlettered and uninformed, easily and regularly stricken by panics of fear, continued to be the main source of mob violence. It should be added, however, that the more articulate firebrands provided the inspiration.

Nor could the problem be solved merely by sending more young men to school. Southern schools did not always succeed in developing temperate, refined qualities in their students, and, in many instances, no attempt was made to do so. In fact, in many schools were found some of the most vigorous manifestations of the fighting spirit. From the Washington Academy in Virginia, John Campbell wrote his mother that the experience there, including sometimes a "little civil war" seemed well calculated to give him an idea of what the world was like. He added, however, "I endeavor to make it all improveing [sic] to me and shall never take an active part in belligerant [sic] power only when I see the liberty and rights of individuals trampled upon and truth and justice prostrated by prejudice and error." [14] If John Campbell was determined to control his belligerency, numerous other students apparently had made no such resolution. Discipline was a serious problem at many institutions in the North and in the South.[15] Almost from the beginning of his presidency, Dr. Thomas Cooper had difficulty with discipline at South Carolina College. Failing to understand or appreciate the Southern youth's idea of honor, he concluded that the only way to govern the institution was by a system of espionage, which was wholly unsuccessful.[16] Duels, though not often fatal, were almost common occurrences. In 1832, one student became involved in a fight with a man at a circus and killed him. He was tried, acquitted, and allowed to complete his course.[17] The maturity of the college and the development of a tradition of learning had little if any effect on the conduct of the students. In 1846, when one of the town marshals came on the campus, fifty students, armed with clubs, pushed him down the stairs and ran him off the campus.[18] In 1853, the "Biscuit Rebellion" at the South Carolina institution got so completely out of hand that the Columbia militia was called out to quell the uprising. When it was over, the wholesale expulsions and withdrawals left the college with only thirty students.[19]

Conditions were hardly less turbulent at other Southern schools and colleges. There were several serious riots at the University of Virginia; and in 1840, Professor A. G. Davis was killed in a fight with a student.[20] In 1837, six students at LaGrange College in Alabama were suspended for misconduct. In protest they threatened to burn the buildings and murder the faculty. One went so far as to draw a gun on the president, but then lost his nerve. After several days of anarchy the disturbance subsided.[21] A riot at the University of Alabama in 1848 led to the suspension of 102 students, leaving a total enrollment of three. Delaware College, the University of Georgia, William and Mary College, and other institutions experienced similar difficulties with their students.[22] Local regulations of the town or college against horseracing, cock-fighting, drinking, and the like did little to restrain them. Young men reared on plantations had not always learned the lesson of self-control. Removed from the restraint of comparative isolation, they seemed to have appreciated none of the proscriptions that were inevitable in most educational institutions.

Southern political fortunes had their effect on the thought and conduct of college students. Elections, Indian Wars, the Texas Revolution, the slavery controversy, and other problems frequently interfered with the normal routine of school life.[23] Augustus Longstreet encouraged secession sentiment among his students when he was president of the University of South Carolina in the late 1850's.[24] There were proslavery societies on many campuses, and enthusiastic young men frequently did not stop with a mere discussion of the problem, but on occasion were moved to violent action. After John Brown's raid the students of Roanoke College passed a resolution to burn William Seward, Joshua Giddings, and Wendell Phillips in effigy. They added that they would "ever be ready to enlist . . . to defend Virginia and her rights under all emergencies." [25]

Not unmindful of the inadequacies of their educational programs, some Southerners came forward with suggestions for improvement. The more enlightened saw a need for the extension of education to a larger number of people. Others saw a need for a program geared more directly to the peculiar conditions of the section. There was, moreover, the educational awakening in other parts of the country: as Horace Mann, Henry Barnard, and others undertook to strengthen and improve the schools of several Northern states, they influenced some Southern points of view.

Between 1840 and 1860, Southerners were becoming aroused over the whole matter of education. Men like Henry A. Wise of Virginia, Archibald D. Murphey and Calvin Wiley of North Carolina, and Robert J. Breckenridge of Kentucky spoke out in favor of free public schools.[26] By 1860 a few cities — including Charleston, New Orleans, Memphis, and Louisville — had creditable school systems; states like North Carolina, Maryland, Kentucky, and Louisiana had made significant steps toward establishing free public education on a state-wide basis.[27]

To many Southerners the question of the nature and content of the educational program was more important than that of broadening its base. Sensing the importance of having a system of instruction with a Southern orientation, they called for an intellectual independence of the South. This was vigorously suggested in the first issue of the *Southern Literary Messenger* when the editor decried the dependency of the South for "literary food upon our [Northern] brethren, whose superiority in all the great points of character — in valor, eloquence and patriotism — we are no wise disposed to recognize. . ." [28] In 1835 a speaker at the Institute on Education at Hampden-Sidney College expressed a similar view. Calling attention to the dangers threatening the Union, he suggested that it would be foolhardy not to recognize the need for a realistic educational program that considered the possibilities of a collapse of the Union. "Immense is the chasm to be filled," he said, "immeasurable the space to be traversed, between the present condition of mental culture in Virginia, and that which can be safely relied upon, to save us from the dangers that hem round a democracy, unsupported by popular knowledge and virtue." [29] Almost twenty years later these views crystallized into a specific program that looked to the education of Southern youth at home, the employment of Southern teachers, and the exclusive use of Southern textbooks and other materials. *De Bow's Review* argued that Southern "life, habits, thoughts, and aims, are so essentially different from those of the North, that here a different character of books, tuition, and training is absolutely required, to bring up the boy to manhood with his faculties fully developed." [30]

At the Southern commercial convention held in Memphis in 1853, a resolution was adopted embodying the program of Southern education.

Resolved, That this Convention earnestly recommends to the citizens of the States here represented, the education of their youth at home as far as practicable; the employment of native teachers in their schools and colleges; the encouragement of a home press; the publication of books adapted to the educational wants and the social condition of these states, and the encouragement and support of inventions and discoveries in the arts and sciences by their citizens. [31]

By 1856 the movement for a distinctly Southern educational program had gained considerable momentum. James De Bow stated the case when he said that it was impossible to overestimate the importance of training the youthful mind under home influences. He added that it was the imperative duty of those having the guardianship of their progress, "to cherish and *give preference to our own institutions of learning and native instructors.*" When such duty is neglected, "its effects are often perceived in the festering of unnatural prejudices, which are seldom uprooted, even after the youth has grown up to manhood." [32]

Something had to be done about a situation like that; and many of De Bow's associates were anxious to take the necessary steps. At the Savannah Convention later in the year a committee was appointed to prepare textbooks for Southern use. It could hardly have been a more distinguished group of scholars, composed as it was of Professors Albert T. Bledsoe and William H. McGuffey of the University of Virginia, Presidents David L. Swain of the University of North Carolina and Augustus B. Longstreet of the University of Mississippi, Stephen Elliot of Georgia, and Charles E. A. Gayarré, the Louisiana historian. The convention urged parents to send their children to Southern schools, because attendance at Northern institutions would be "fraught with peril to our sacred interests." [33]

One of the most exhaustive statements was made by William H. Stiles, in 1858. Speaking before the Alpha Phi Delta Society of the Cherokee Baptist College on "Southern Education for Southern Youth," Stiles argued that independence in education was not only more important than the financial and commercial independence of the section, but it was actually a prerequisite to it. He warned his listeners that the time was approaching, "nay, is already at hand" when the South would need the aid of all her sons. Educated and disciplined Southern minds would do much "to vindicate her peculiar institutions not only before our Federal councils, but in the judgment of the world." He reminded his audience that everything that exalts a nation and renders its institutions permanent depends on the character given by education to its youth. Northern institutions, he insisted, possessed no advantage over Southern institutions in "cultivating and producing the strength of a nation, *well-disciplined minds . . .*" [34]

Long before the South addressed itself seriously to the task of extending free public education or developing a special program for the education of Southern youth, there were those who were convinced that military education was the best way to cultivate the well-disciplined minds that Stiles called for. In the early decades of the century this conviction manifested itself in an enthusiastic support of the United States Military Academy and in various efforts to establish military schools in the South. In the generation immediately preceding the Civil War there was a substantial increase in the number of Southern military schools. The articulate element of the population advanced several cogent arguments in favor of military education, aside from the ever-present one based on military necessity.[35]

Since the problem of discipline was almost universal, the proponents of military education claimed support on the grounds that it would solve that aggravating problem. In urging upon the governor of Virginia a state program of military education, Claudius Crozet said:

At an age when passions are yet unmitigated by the lessons of experience, it is generally imprudent to trust to the self government of a young man. Habits of unrestrained indulgence have frequently laid the foundation of ruin of youths, who, if submitted to proper discipline and restraint at this trying season of life . . . would otherwise have become useful and distinguished members of society. The wise and prudent parent will choose for his son that education which will impart to him habits of order and regularity, and that seminary where a degree of parental authority may exercise a beneficial control over his activities.

Only in a military school could the young student have that kind of discipline and find "in each one of his associates the correct deportment of a gentleman and the honorable feelings of a soldier." [36]

Discipline was a major concern of Edwin Heriot in an address before a group in Charleston, South Carolina, in 1850. He said that "the necessity for a more rigid code of discipline than is supplied in any other plan of instruction . . . has been met by the establishment of an institution," in which "the martial spirit forms a prominent feature — viz: THE MILITARY SCHOOL." [37] Another advocate believed that, because of the discipline it imposed, the military school would produce better results than any other type of institution. "Every honourable principle is brought to bear upon the student; rewards attend success; while failure, when culpable, meets censure and disgrace. A sense of duty, ambition, patriotism, love of learning, are all inculcated, are all felt and appreciated." [38] Major D. H. Hill persuasively summed up the matter. He suggested that military schools were the places where the "imperious and self-willed" youths of the section could learn to submit to authority. "Who can estimate the influence upon society, of a body of young men, annually sent forth from our military schools, with stern notions of the supremacy of the law, and the necessity of carrying out its most stringent requirements?" Appealing to the teachers of North Carolina to support military education, Hill said that the state would be gratified to find that the military schools would give their students the "modest and manly bearing of the soldier instead of the impudent leer and blustering swagger of the rowdy." [39]

Military training, moreover, provided the type of experience that made for stronger, healthier men. Heriot pointed out that students in military schools would acquire "a robustness, a solidity of frame," which would enable them to bear hardships and labors, "under the pressure of which many annually sink into an early grave." [40] In urging a plan of military training at the University of Alabama, President L. C. Garland said that each year his school lost some of its best students from broken down constitutions. "We make good mathematicians," he said, "and incurable dyspeptics; good linguists and bronchial throats . . . The only schools, so far as we know, where anything like an effective system of physical education is carried out, is the United States Military Academy . . . and those schools which have been constructed upon it as a model." [41] George Fitzhugh suggested that the rigorous life of the gentlemen of the South made it possible for them to be better horsemen, have more physical strength . . . endure more fatigue than their slaves." [42] Presumably they would be even stronger when subjected to a program of military education. Major Hill called attention to the drill, parade, and guard duty in the military school, indicating that such activities gave "health to the body and vigor to the constitution." [43]

It was also argued that the military school was superior to other institutions in encouraging high scholarship and preparing the student for life. "I know of no institution," said S. W. Trotti, "better adapted to impart knowledge . . . for all the pursuits of civil life." [44] The whole program, said another, was "calculated to insure a far greater application to study, and a proportionately greater amount of knowledge and profit, than a residence of the same length of time under any college system whatever, now in vogue." [45] In an admirable way, said still another, the military school combined the advantages of strict discipline with a course of instruction better designed "than any other to fit the youthful aspirant for those public services, by which he may at once benefit society and acquire distinction." While there was still a place for the so-called classical institutions, the advocates of military education nevertheless insisted that the "exact sciences" and similar courses must yield the palm to the military schools.[46]

There was a good deal of fluctuation in the attitude of the people of the country toward the United States Military Academy.[47] At times they praised the work of the institution;

at other times they bitterly denounced it and demanded that it be abolished. While some Southerners joined in the periodic attacks on West Point, Northerners were both more numerous and more vigorous in their opposition. Seldom, moreover, did Southerners strike at the fundamental principle of military education, but some Northern opponents went so far as to declare that the military school was an improper medium through which to give training. In 1837, the legislature of Tennessee passed a resolution calling for the abolition of the Military Academy. It feared that the institution was a dangerous precedent that might lead to naval academies, national observatories, and other federally supported institutions. This view was labeled as "stupid" by an Alabama editor, who felt that the "scientific researches and military education carried on at West Point fully justified its existence." [48]

Much of the objection of Southern leaders to West Point stemmed from their conviction that it was largely for the sons of Congressmen and others of influence. In 1830, Tennessee's Davy Crockett told his colleagues in the House of Representatives that his constituents were under the impression that the Academy was a rich man's school, but admitted that the opposition to it "was possibly for want of knowledge." [49] Four years later David W. Dickinson of Tennessee objected to the Academy on grounds that it was too aristocratic; but he was unable to persuade the members of the House to hold up the appropriations for it. [50] When C. H. Williamson rose in the Tennessee House of Representatives to speak against the Academy in 1840, he did so because he believed that a system that did not encourage the further education of men from the ranks of the army was seriously defective. [51] If these spokesmen from the Volunteer State voiced the views of some of those who had been smitten by the leveling influence of Jacksonian democracy, they did not speak for Jackson himself. As early as 1823 he had referred to West Point as "the best school in the world," and during his Presidency he vigorously urged its support.[52]

By 1843, Tennessee's opposition to the Academy had spent itself, and from no other part of the South did any ardent enemies emerge. The Northern states, however, supplied a vigorous leadership against West Point. Perhaps the most articulate was Amasa Dona of New York who, in 1844, proposed to the House of Representatives that the school be abolished not only because it was aristocratic and expensive, but also because it fostered a spirit of pride and arrogance and was the parent of many "positive evils." [53] Questioning its constitutionality, Representative John Hale of New Hampshire said that the Academy trained more officers than the country needed; moreover, that they were inefficient as their conduct in the Florida war had demonstrated. A slight majority of the Representatives from the slaveholding states — 34 out of 40 — voted to table Hale's resolution to abolish the Academy.[54] In the same year, when U. S. Senator Sidney Breese of Illinois demanded a vote on his proposition to abolish the Academy, only three Southern Senators voted with him, while fourteen voted with the majority, 27 to 11.[55]

Meanwhile, Southerners came to the defense of the Military Academy with lavish praise. One enthusiast, signing his article "F. H. S.," [56] called West Point the "pride and ornament of our country" and decried the repeated efforts to abolish it. He saw no objection to giving West Point graduates the preference in army assignments. "Would any man hesitate to prefer the practiced skill of the physician to the inexperience of the quack . . . ?" "With all its defects," he concluded, "as American citizens we should be proud that we have such an institution as that at West Point, and low indeed must be the patriotism of that individual who, in view of all the good it has done, and all it is still destined to do, cannot give it his *hearty* GODSPEED." [57]

In the final decade before the Civil War there was more

praise for West Point, even some suggestion of the extension of national military education. One writer explained that the textbooks written by West Point graduates were excellent because the instruction at the Academy was complete and without sham. The public had become so impressed with the thoroughness of the teaching that "military schools, avowedly adopting West Point as their model, are rapidly growing up in several states . . ." [58] Even Tennessee Congressmen came around to an enthusiastic support of the Academy's program. In 1858, Representative Felix Zollicoffer of Tennessee proposed the establishment of a southern branch of West Point at the Hermitage, near Nashville.[59]

Many Southerners, moreover, testified to the value of the Military Academy. When he was Secretary of War, John Calhoun not only sought increased appropriations for the institution, but also recommended the establishment of another in the South or West. Calling the attention of Congress to the great importance of having scientific knowledge regarding the defense of the nation, he said that "the establishment of military academies is the cheapest and safest mode of perpetuating this knowledge." [60] In 1882, Cadet Benjamin Ewell's mother wrote him that she had been told that when a young man graduated from the United States Military Academy he was prepared to do almost anything. "Amidst all my pecuniary embarrassment, I feel cheered when I think your education is provided for," she concluded.[61] Another Southern mother, viewing the gathering war clouds in 1861, considered the possibility of her son's leaving West Point and enrolling in some military school in the South. "Still," she cautioned, "it is above all other things desirable to graduate at West Point if possible. No other school in the world gives its graduates such status. Other schools might even be better, but reputation is not won in a day and for success in this world, reputation is of vast importance." [62]

Southern opposition to West Point never seems to have deterred young men from seeking appointments to the institution; from the Academy's very beginning in 1802, the South had its share of prospective cadets. Between 1802 and 1829, 1,913 young Southerners sought admission, while the much more populous North and West could boast of only 2,160 young men who sought training at the Academy.[63] The South had more than its share of graduates. In 1820, for example, the sixteen Southern graduates constituted approximately 53 per cent of a graduating class of thirty, at a time when those states claimed barely 50 per cent of the country's total population. Thirty years later, when the Southern states could claim only 35 per cent of the population, the twenty-one Southern graduates represented approximately 47 per cent of the graduating class.[64]

Before they had their own military schools, young Southerners looked not only to West Point but to another Northern institution as well for a military education. In 1819, shortly after his resignation from the Army of the United States, Captain Alden Partridge of the class of 1806 at West Point founded the American Literary, Scientific, and Military Academy at Norwich, Vermont. By 1825 there were 480 students, the vast majority from the New England states, but a respectable minority, eighty, from the South. In the following year, when the school was located at Middletown, Connecticut, there were 102 students from the South, representing more than one-third of the student body.[65]

Despite his strenuous efforts, Partridge was unable to maintain a prosperous institution either in Middletown or in Norwich, to which he returned in 1827. Similar efforts of Partridge and his students to establish military schools were even less successful. In 1828 two graduates of Norwich — Truman Ransom and Elisha Dunbar — founded a school in Orange, New Jersey, which lasted hardly two years. In 1842, Partridge established the Pennsylvania Literary, Scientific, and Military Academy in Bristol. It was a failure there, and a transfer to Harrisburg brought no greater success. He set up a school in Reading, Pennsylvania, in 1850, but it did not last long. An attempt in Pembroke, New Hampshire, in 1850, had gone out of existence within three years.[66] His only Southern venture, at Portsmouth, Virginia, was a failure, for by 1839, when Captain Partridge appeared, they were concentrating on the newly founded Virginia Military Institute.[67]

Many Southerners would have denied that they lacked appreciation for education or that their institutions were inferior to those elsewhere. They would have admitted, however, that their educational needs were different. They needed schools and colleges to discipline young Southerners accustomed to disregarding law and order, to prepare them for living in a society having peculiar institutions and habits, and to educate them in the true values of Southern civilization. Few institutions in the South could qualify; those in the North, with the possible exception of West Point, were even less satisfactory. Increasingly, the most logical type of institution seemed to be the military school.

# 8

# West Points of the South

Even before the martial spirit clearly manifested itself in the South, a distinct interest in military education was apparent. Early efforts to establish military schools were not entirely successful, but were a portent of what was to come. In the first decade of the nineteenth century, North Carolina set up military institutes and incorporated the military feature into some of the academies already established. In 1809, an instructor at the Raleigh Academy organized a military company that paraded around the capitol square and received a stand of colors from the girls of the school.[1] In the following year Archibald Murphey began to conduct schools for the training of militia officers in Stokes County. The undertaking was so successful that he extended it to other counties and towns during the next several years.[2] In 1826, the *Raleigh Register* announced that Captain D. H. Bingham was opening the Scientific and Military Institute in Williamsborough. A full course of studies was to be offered, and the rules for the government of the school were to be on "the plan of the West Point Seminary and Capt. Partridge's Academy."[3] After moving his school to Littleton, then to Oxford, finally to Raleigh, Bingham closed the institution in 1833 and accepted a position as engineer for an Alabama railroad.[4]

Meanwhile, in 1830, Captain Ransom had opened a military school in Fayetteville; and in the inaugural year the cadets from his school and those from Bingham's institution paraded around the capitol and to the "Governor's House, where they passed in review before the Governor and partook of refreshments." The appearance of the young soldiers was "quite military," the *Register* reported, "and the regularity of their movements and precision with which they executed their various evolutions would not have dishonoured regular troops." [5] In 1833 Colonel Carter Jones opened a school in Raleigh in which he offered courses in "Infantry and Light Infantry Tactics, together with the Broad Sword Exercises and Cavalry movements . . ." He invited militia officers and all others who had an interest in the subject. Jones also organized schools at Rolesville and Wilmington, and divided his time among the three places.[6] By 1840, North Carolina could look back on a generation of military education which, although pursued in a desultory fashion, established important patterns and precedents for the future.

South Carolina lagged behind her neighbor before 1840, but showed some interest in military education as early as 1825. The coming of General Lafayette to Columbia in 1825 was the occasion for the organization of a cadet company at the College of South Carolina to participate in the gala event. The student group made such a favorable impression that it was permitted to remain permanently organized, and the state provided it with arms. It was deemed wise, however, to require that the arms be deposited in the public armory after each authorized use.[7] At Rice Creek Spring a young Dartmouth graduate, Rufus William Bailey, established a military, classical, and religious school in 1827. It was well attended and, for a time, its future seemed bright. Public sentiment during the nullification controversy, however, was opposed to a Northerner's operating a military school, and it was forced to close.[8]

It was difficult for the citizens of Mississippi to understand why Jefferson College had experienced such indifferent success since its founding in 1802. While there was nothing approaching an educational renaissance in the state, many wished for its success. Some thought that it should seek state support, but the authorities decided that such a plan might not be wise. In 1826, they did, however, place the governor and lieutenant-governor on the board of trustees and authorize the legislature to fill future vacancies on the board.[9] But even these steps did not solve the college's grave problems of finance and attendance. Finally, in 1829, it was decided to adopt a system of education similar to that of West Point. E. B. Williston was elected to the presidency, and Major John Holbrook, author of a book on tactics, was placed in charge of military training.[10] Almost overnight Jefferson College began to prosper. Within one year the enrollment increased from 98 to 150, with one cadet at the tender age of five years![11] It was said that under the military plan the college "was more flourishing in every respect than any other in the southwest." [12] When Major Holbrook died in 1832, the ubiquitous Alden Partridge was placed in charge of the military program. As he spent the larger portion of his time in the North and as his views on slavery were unpopular in the state, he failed to gain local support and soon resigned. The board decided to abandon the West Point system, and the enrollment declined almost immediately.[13] With the resumption of the military plan in 1850, Jefferson College again displayed the signs of growth that had been in evidence twenty years earlier.[14]

Alabama evinced some interest in military education before 1840. In May 1831, Colonel Jabez Leftwich proposed to conduct a military school in the vicinity of Huntsville for the training of officers. The announcement stated that the terms were "so reasonable, not amounting even to a consideration, and the opportunity so rare, that the commissioned and non-commissioned officers, and as many of the privates as may think proper, will benefit themselves and do the country a service by appearing . . . enrolling . . . and endeavouring by a strict attention to the talented master of the drill, to redeem the militia system from that disgrace under which it now labours." [15] In the same year, M. R. Dudley and Bradley S. A. Lowe announced plans for opening a scientific and military school at Huntsville, modeled after Partridge's Academy.[16] They proposed to add to "the ordinary branches of academical study the tactics of camps" and thus "to render instruction still more agreeable to the youth of our country." [17] On January 2, 1832, the school opened.[18] Presumably it did not flourish, for the local paper, which had been enthusiastic over the prospect, had nothing further to say about it. Alabamians had no need to worry, for in due time they were to lead the South as far as the number of military schools were concerned. The early experiments of the people of North Carolina, Alabama, and Mississippi could not be regarded as successful, and had neither support nor congenial surroundings.

If they were to be more than reformatories or physical education centers, military schools needed public support, not only because of the considerable expense involved, but also because of the very nature of their service. Nowhere did Southerners indicate an understanding of this problem until Virginians began to consider a military school. In 1834, the Franklin Literary Society of Lexington discussed the possibility of substituting a military school for the company of state guards. The idea appealed to a number of the leading citizens who explored the problem further. In August 1835, John T. L. Preston, a young lawyer, began publishing articles in the *Lexington Gazette* advocating a military school. Within a short time the Virginia legislature received a petition on the subject.[19] In March 1836, it passed a bill providing for the disbanding of the Lexington Arsenal, the establishment of a military school in its stead, and the appointment of a

Board of Visitors by the legislature. The board was to consist of four members, with the Adjutant-General ex-officio.

The Board of Visitors was set up under the presidency of Claudius Crozet, a distinguished engineer and graduate of the celebrated École Polytechnique. After formulating plans for opening the Institute and drawing up the regulations to govern it,[20] Francis Henny Smith was chosen superintendent, and the Board also appointed twenty regular cadets and thirteen paying cadets, "as fine young men as could have been desired, and of a character, indeed, exceeding our most sanguine expectations." [21] For three years the school was hardly more than a department of Washington College. On November 11, 1839, the flag of Virginia was raised over the Virginia Military Institute, by that time a completely separate school. It continued to serve the students of Washington College for the next six years, however, under an arrangement for the disposition of funds provided by the Society of Cincinnati.[22] Thus, for the first time in American history a state had become the sole sponsor of an institution for the military education of its youth.

In the spring of 1840, practical military instruction was begun, and the cadets, "in their trim coatees soon comprised a natty military company as excellent in drill as in discipline and personnel." [23] In June, when the Board of Visitors arrived to conduct the first annual examinations and to inspect the cadet corps, it was greatly pleased with what it found. The first year's work was so satisfactory in every respect that the school was promptly dubbed "The West Point of the South," and its fame rapidly spread abroad. At the same time the corps was more than doubled in size. Even so, the number of applicants far exceeded the number which in Institute could accommodate. Meanwhile, the legislature authorized the granting of commissions in the state militia to the professorial staff of the Institute.[24]

Within a few years Virginia Military Institute had not

only won its way into the hearts of the people but had also become an important factor in the educational and military program of the state. By 1850, a prideful Virginian expressed joy over the fact that one of the greatest charms of the institution was its "eminently State character. In all its features — in all its characteristics, it is Virginian — thoroughly and exclusively Virginian." He said that he was not an advocate of a narrow and confined type of state patriotism, but at a time when manners, institutions, and opinions were undergoing change, he was glad that there was one spot where something that was peculiar to Old Virginia could be preserved — "one hallowed altar where some portion, at least, of the vestal flame of Virginia spirit and Virginia pride may be sedulously watched over by a band of Virginia youths, and bequeathed in all its purity to succeeding generations." [25]

The example of Virginia's successful experiment was apparently all that South Carolina needed to launch a program of military education. When one recalls the serious tensions of the early thirties and the penchant for military things at that time, it is rather surprising to find that South Carolina was following instead of leading in the promotion of military education. By 1842 the Virginia experiment had so impressed South Carolinians that they were certain that such a program would be more than successful in their state. In his message to the South Carolina legislature, Governor John P. Richardson pointed to the success of the Virginia Military Institute. It proved to his satisfaction that a system of education could be fused with the duties of guarding the state. It would be a happy day, remarked the Governor, when the graduates of a military school in South Carolina would combine the "enterprise and decision of a military character with the acquirement of their scholastic opportunities." [26] The legislature agreed with him, and, on December 20, 1842, it passed an act to convert the Arsenal at Columbia and the Citadel and Magazine at Charleston into military schools.

If Virginia was doing well with one military school, perhaps South Carolina could do even better with two. At least Richardson and the legislators seemed to think so. They appropriated $8,000 for the Arsenal Academy at Columbia and $16,000 for the Citadel Academy at Charleston. The institutions were placed under a Board of Visitors, and provision was made for the education of fifty-four cadets at state expense. A similar number could be admitted upon their own payment of fees. Of each of these groups, thirty-six were to be educated at the Citadel, while eighteen were to be placed at the Arsenal. The apportionment was by judicial districts according to population. Most of the districts were entitled to one or two cadets. Charleston could send ten, while Beaufort could send three.[27]

Perhaps the person most responsible for developing the program of the academies in their early years was Major Richard W. Colcock, who became superintendent of the Citadel in 1844. Colcock brought with him the rich experience of a seasoned soldier and instructor in infantry tactics. He introduced a course of study and a body of regulations similar to the West Point system; and he persuaded a fellow West Pointer, Captain Abbott H. Brisbane, to join him.[28]

With the enthusiastic support of the members of the legislature and other public officials, the two schools prospered. When the Board of Visitors made its inspection in 1843, the members found it difficult to realize "that such a change had taken place in the appearance and conduct of boys, who, less than a twelve month ago, came into these institutions careless of their persons, awkward and untaught." The board was convinced that besides affording protection to the arms and public property at the two posts, the military training of the cadets greatly facilitated their instruction in other branches of study "by habits of good order and discipline." [29] Trotti was lavish in his praise of the work of the institution. Though "scarcely a day old," he said, the Citadel had "more than realized the most ardent hopes of its friends, and like Ringgold's brave little battery, vindicated its claim to the confidence of the country." [30]

The remainder of the decade witnessed no developments in other states even remotely approaching what was taking place in Virginia and South Carolina. There was, however, an inclination, in several places, to explore the problem and to give it a trial wherever practicable. In Tennessee, where there was some opposition to the United States Military Academy, a strong voice spoke out in favor of military education. In his baccalaureate address in 1826, President Philip Lindsley of the University of Nashville discussed the subject freely. He spoke of the need for cultivating the body as well as the mind and expressed the view that this could be done in an educational program with a military feature. He recalled that "even the ancients pursued various activities in the line of sports, games, and military tactics." [31] This early favorable disposition toward military education doubtless facilitated the introduction of such a program at that institution in 1855.[32] Before the University of Nashville embraced military education, however, the system was established at the East Tennessee University. In 1843, Albert Miller Lea became professor of mathematics and natural philosophy at the Knoxville school. Almost immediately he organized a company of cadets and put them in uniform. For a while the program prospered, but three years later it was abandoned.[33]

While Alabama was not yet ready to establish a state military school, it seemed willing to cooperate with private academies that incorporated the military feature. In Eufala, in 1843, the Alabama Military and Scientific Institute was incorporated by the state legislature. In the following year the legislature exempted the school from taxation and authorized the governor to provide the academy with "as many arms as shall be sufficient for its purposes." [34] In the following year a similar tax-exempt Scientific and Military Institute was established at Tuskegee. The legislature shortly gave it permission "to receive arms and accoutrements from the Governor of the State." [35] Both became important schools for the education of the youth of their communities. The one at Tuskegee was praised by the General Assembly in 1846. The lawmakers rejoiced that an academy in the state was preparing young men to assume direction of the militia in case of necessity. The condition of the school was described as "flourishing — the course of instruction the same as at West Point — its commanding officer well versed in Military Science, having served in the United States Army." It was a source of regret to the legislators, however, that the school did not have sufficient arms for the training of the cadets; consequently the commanding officer was authorized "to apply to the Secretary of War, for such description of arms as in his wisdom the Institute may require, in lieu of the muskets apportioned and furnished to the State of Alabama . . ." [36] This type of state support of private military academies remained the pattern in Alabama down to 1860.

Kentucky took its first steps toward a program of military education during the forties. Between 1847 and 1855 the Western Military Institute flourished in various Kentucky communities, including Georgetown, Blue Lick Springs, and Drennon Springs. It was founded by Colonel Thornton Johnston, "who wanted to combine the course of instruction at West Point with a thorough course of ancient languages and belles lettres." [37] Perhaps more responsible for the growth of the school was Bushrod R. Johnson, who came to the institution in 1848 as professor of natural philosophy and chemistry and became its superintendent in 1851. It was he who said that the military feature was not merely to diffuse military knowledge but to establish complete control and to secure to the student the personal advantages of a "uniform and economical distribution of time, habits, of punctuality, health, physical development and a consequent increase of mental vigor." [38] In its first year, the Western Military Institute boasted an enrollment of 136 students with two West Pointers and one graduate of the Virginia Military Institute on its eight-man faculty.[39] Despite the inroads of illness — a partial explanation for the moving of the school on several occasions — the enrollment continued to remain in the neighborhood of 150 cadets until the school was transferred, in 1855, to Nashville, to become the military department of the local university.[40]

In 1845 the Kentucky Military Institute, known also as the Kentucky Collegiate and Military Institute, was founded by Colonel Robert T. P. Allen, who hoped to subordinate the classical studies to the scientific and practical pursuits. This was a popular notion in Kentucky, and in 1847 the legislature granted the institution a very liberal charter. The governor of the state was designated as "Inspector," while the adjutant-general was named president of the board of visitors. The state also promised to furnish arms and other equipment with which to carry out a program of military education.[41]

James De Bow, who was visiting professor of political economy, commerce, and commercial law during a summer session, was most enthusiastic about the prospects for the school. Its location was "healthy and picturesque," the grounds well laid, and the buildings of the most substantial character. It had a faculty of six, and the number of students was "continually increasing from all sections of the West and Southwest." [42] Upon examining the catalog in 1857, the editor of a leading New Orleans paper was pleased to find the names of several Louisianians among its graduates and cadets.[43] Two years later the Institute was running regular advertisements in one Alabama newspaper.[44]

Colonel Allen was at the school only intermittently. In 1849 he was serving as a special agent for the United States Post Office Department in Oregon. In the following year he was publishing the *Pacific News* in San Francisco. In 1851, he returned to the school for a term of four years, and was then off to the Southwest.[45] The responsibility for the school's growth was in the hands of Colonel Francis W. Capers, "an eminent tactician and scholar," who "would raise the institution to the very highest point." [46] It was still flourishing in 1861 when it closed and most of its cadets and faculty went off to war.

The movement for military education in the South gathered marked momentum in the final decade before the Civil War. Of course, the growing interest, almost everywhere, in all types of education gave the supporters of military education a stronger hand. The success, moreover, of state-supported military academies like those in Virginia and South Carolina evoked the admiration of persons in public and private stations elsewhere. The prestige of the military life was immeasurably enhanced by the Mexican War, especially in the South from which warriors went in such preponderant numbers. As the conquering heroes returned, they inspired a people already inclined in that direction to put even greater emphasis on the type of training that would make good soldiers.

Some Southerners believed that there was an urgent need for highly trained citizen-soldiers to defend their homes in the emergency that seemed to be approaching.[47] One of the most eloquent statements regarding the role of military education in the impending crisis was made in 1854 by Richard Yeadon of Charleston. Urging the generous support of military schools, he said:

The nature of our institution of domestic slavery and its exposure of us to hostile machinations, both at home and abroad, render it doubly incumbent on us and our whole sisterhood of Southern States to cherish a military spirit and to diffuse military science among our people — Thus prepared and harnessed for conflict, should conflict come either from "higher law" traitors to the union and the Constitution at home or from foreign foes, the South may defy the world in arms.[48]

Apparently, many Southerners agreed with Yeadon and were willing to take action. In the final decade before the Civil War, they succeeded in establishing military education in more than twenty schools and colleges. Some were newly founded military schools; others were older institutions which modified their programs to include military education. By 1850, the trustees of Jefferson College in Mississippi were convinced that a military training program was the only thing that would insure the institution's growth. Consequently, they invited Captain James M. Wells to reestablish the military features that had been abandoned several years earlier. For the next ten years Jefferson College became, more and more, a military school. In most matters, including cadet uniforms, West Point served as the model. While it remained in the hands of a private board, the state, for a while, provided muskets for the cadets. Mississippi, thus, had its military academy without taxing itself to maintain it.[49]

In Tulip, Arkansas, Major George D. Alexander, who had conducted a coeducational school for several years, transferred the young men to a school that, in 1850, came to be known as the Arkansas Military Institute.[50] In the next ten years it gained a large following, and cadets were enrolled from all over the state. When the war came the faculty and students closed the school and went off to join the Confederate army.[51]

When, in 1849, West Pointer Arnoldus V. Brumby resigned as superintendent of the Alabama Military Institute, he had not completed his career as a military educator. Georgia seemed ready to take its first steps toward training its youth to become soldiers, and Brumby went to assist. In 1851, he organized a joint stock company which secured a charter for the Georgia Military Institute at Marietta. Although the school was under the control of a private board of trustees, the state manifested a deep interest in it.[52] That same year the legislature passed an act "to provide for the education of a certain number of State cadets in the Georgia Military Institute, to defray the expenses of the same, and for other purposes," thus, assuming responsibility for educating eight cadets from each Congressional district and two from the state at large. The governor was authorized to request the federal government to furnish the school with arms and accoutrements.[53] Only 7 cadets enrolled at the beginning of the first term, but there were 28 before the end of the year. Two years later the Institute boasted of 120 cadets, five professors, and one assistant professor. The curriculum and discipline were modeled after West Point, of course, and the pride of the state in the Marietta institution increased steadily. In 1857, the state purchased the entire establishment, and the Institute became a state college in every respect. Provisions were made for the erection of additional buildings and the purchase of apparatus for scientific instruction. The attendance increased, and in the years immediately preceding the Civil War the annual enrollment was approximately 200 cadets.[54]

By 1860, Governor Joseph Brown regarded the Institute as one of the state's most valuable assets. He hoped that the legislature would increase the appropriations which would make possible the diffusion of "a knowledge of military science among the people of every county in the State, which all must admit, in these perilous times is a *desideratum* second in importance to none other . . . Let us encourage the development of the rising military genius of our State; and guide, by the lights of military science, the energies of that patriotic valor, which nerves the stout heart and strong arm of many a young hero in our midst who is yet unknown to fame." [55]

When J. Berrien Lindsley became chancellor of the languishing University of Nashville in February 1855, one of his first recommendations was the reorganization of the literary department as a military college. The proposition met with immediate public favor. Since the previous year, when the cadets of the Western Military Institute visited Nashville to participate in a celebration at the University, many had favored the idea of a military school in Nashville.[56] Consequently, on March 17, 1855, the citizens of Nashville held a public meeting to discuss Lindsley's proposal to merge the Western Military Institute, then at Tyree Springs, Tennessee, with the University of Nashville. After inspiring speeches by Governor Johnson and others, the proposal was adopted, and plans were made to raise the requisite funds.[57] Colonel Bushrod Johnson promptly moved his cadets to Nashville, where new buildings were under construction. In 1860 the institution was thriving, with more than 600 cadets.[58]

As though its two flourishing state-supported military academies were insufficient to train the youth of South Carolina, two other academies sprang up to benefit from the growing martial spirit of the state. In January 1855, two graduates of the Citadel Academy established the Kings Mountain Military School, sometimes known as the Yorkville Military Academy, at Yorkville, South Carolina.[59] Within a year they laid the cornerstone of a new building. On that occasion a member of the Citadel's board of visitors was the principal speaker, and the young ladies from a neighboring college presented a stand of colors. The school continued to grow until 1861, when all the officers and some of the cadets entered the war on the side of the Confederacy.[60] Meanwhile, another Citadel alumnus went to Aiken and established a military school that was still in existence at the beginning of the war.[61]

No state approached Alabama's feverish interest in military education displayed just before the Civil War. The state

government was slow to assume full responsibility for training its citizen-soldiers, but it manifested an eager willingness
to facilitate the programs of private institutions. In 1852 the
legislature authorized the governor to secure arms and
accoutrements from the federal government for four schools
that were interested in introducing the military feature.
Under the arrangement 100 cadet muskets and the usual
accoutrements were to go to the Wilcox Male Institute, 64
to the Gibson F. Hill Academy, 75 to the Orville Institute,
and 64 to the Tuskegee Classical and Scientific Institute. In
addition the Tuskegee school was to receive "two six-pounder
brass pieces for instruction in artillery tactics." [62]

Succeeding years witnessed a continued interest of the
state government in the military programs of private schools.
In 1854, a school in northern Alabama received 80 cadet
muskets from the state arsenal.[63] In 1856 the Rehoboth Male
Academy got 50 muskets and accoutrements.[64] Two years
later the legislature authorized the Quartermaster General
of Alabama to furnish the Southern Polytechnic Institute
a stand of 110 muskets or rifles, together with "one hundred
copies of each and every work on Military tactics which may
be in the State Library." [65] In 1860, schools in Macon and
Barbour counties borrowed arms for the training of their
students.[66]

Moreover, schools that called themselves military academies received an increasing amount of support as the years
went by. Gibson F. Hill's academy in Chambers County was
actually a military school and was known as the Southern
Military Academy in 1852. In that year a Citadel alumnus
went there to serve as commandant of cadets, and it promptly
adopted more of the military features.[67] In 1854 the legislature authorized the school to conduct a three-year lottery
to raise funds to increase the staff of instructors, "enlarge the
apparatus, reduce the tuition, and to aid generally the said
military academy." [68] Two years later the legislature author-

ized the faculty to grant diplomas and to exercise certain other privileges. Governor John A. Winston vetoed the measure on the grounds that it granted no powers that were not already possessed by the Academy. The legislators, however, seemed anxious to proclaim their support of almost anything that might strengthen military education. They overrode the veto by a resounding vote of twenty to three in the Senate and fifty-four to fourteen in the House.[69] In 1860 the legislature authorized the establishment of another Southern Military Academy at Wetumpka. The governor was authorized to issue commissions of colonel to the superintendent and lieutenant colonel to the commandant of cadets and to provide the Academy with necessary and suitable arms and other equipment.[70]

The schools at La Grange and Glenville received the most generous support from the state of Alabama. Beginning as a small, private institution in 1830, La Grange College had constant financial difficulties in its early years.[71] In the hope of increasing its patronage, it introduced the military feature in 1858, becoming La Grange College and Military Academy. A former commandant of cadets at the Georgia Military Academy accepted the position as superintendent.[72] Almost immediately the school began to prosper. Within two years it was entirely committed to the military program, and the legislature changed its name to the La Grange Military Academy.[73] Meanwhile, citizens began to urge the state to grant more positive and tangible support to La Grange. "If you vote aid to this school," a citizen told his senator, "you will be applauded by your constituents as good and faithful servants who are willing to aid and protect an Educational and Military College that has no superior." [74]

Glenville Academy's early history had been even more dismal than that of La Grange. Beginning as an academy in the early forties, it was forced to close its male department in 1845 because of the lack of support. It continued to languish until, in February 1860, the legislature provided for the education, at public expense, of two young men from each county in the state. They could attend either La Grange or the Glenville Military Academy, but each was required to return to his respective county upon leaving the academy and "there teach school and drill the militia . . . for the same length of time during which he may have been a State Cadet." [75] The state also agreed to provide arms and other equipment for the two institutions.[76] The law was praised as a measure that would provide the state with "competent, practical school teachers, and scientific military officers." [77]

It was almost inevitable that in Alabama, where the interest in military education was so widespread, there should be an even more positive commitment to the program than in the arrangements with La Grange and Glenville. As early as 1852, the President of the University of Alabama suggested that his board of trustees might explore the question of instituting the military feature at the University.[78] In several succeeding years bills were introduced in the legislature providing for a military department, but they were defeated, largely because of the expense entailed. Increased tension between the North and South, however, convinced Alabamians that no measures should be overlooked in preparing for a possible conflict.[79] Shortly after John Brown's raid, a bill to set up a military department at the University was introduced and passed in February 1860. Meanwhile, President Landon C. Garland of the University had been commissioned to visit the principal military institutions of the United States and to "institute an inquiry into the nature and bearing of the system." [80]

Under the act the entire University was placed under military discipline. The officers of the military department were to hold commissions from the governor. The state was to furnish "such ordnance, arms, equipments, and munitions as may be required for the exercise and drill of the students of said University." [81] The Secretary of War, John B. Floyd, designated Captain Caleb Huse, a former West Point teacher, to introduce the new system, and the board of trustees appointed him commandant of cadets.[82] In the fall of 1860, the new system was inaugurated. The students were greatly pleased, and even the academic professors who had opposed it were, within one month, praising it. When the war came, many of the cadets, though hardly beyond the stage of orientation, were assigned as drillmasters for newly created regiments.

Louisiana had not been wholly indifferent to the growth of military education in other states. Early in the fifties there was talk of a state military and naval academy. In 1856, the legislature passed a resolution directing the standing committee on the militia to inquire into the expediency of adding a military academy to the proposed state seminary and of appointing one cadet from each parish. Nothing came of this, but General George Mason Graham, an ardent supporter of military education, was appointed chairman of the board of trustees of the new seminary. Graham busied himself in working up support for a military feature at the state school; indeed, he hoped to replace the seminary with a military school. Classical education had failed, he claimed, and only a military system would solve the problem of disciplining turbulent Louisiana youth. West Pointer Braxton Bragg and General Zachary Taylor's son, Richard, heartily endorsed Graham's stand.[83]

In 1858, a permanent organization law was passed. Among other things, it provided for the appointment of a board of supervisors, consisting of the Governor, the superintendent of education, and twelve other members. In May 1859, the board decided that the seminary should be "a literary and scientific institution under a military system of government, on a program and plan similar to that of the Virginia Military Institute." [84] James De Bow was among those who rejoiced in the decision to have a military school.[85] At once, Graham began to correspond with candidates for the faculty. William T. Sherman was elected superintendent. Of the six who made up the first faculty, only one was without military training.[86] On January 1, 1860, the Louisiana State Seminary of Learning and Military Academy opened its doors to sixty cadets.

Sherman did not seem to be strongly in favor of military education. He wrote a relative that the military colleges of the South might be a "part of some ulterior design," but he doubted that it was so in the case of the Louisiana institution.[87] With Graham at his side he established the military feature shortly after the opening of the term. The commandant of cadets was Francis W. Smith, whose uncle was superintendent of the Virginia Military Institute. In March 1860, the seminary was made the State Central Arsenal, but there was need for additional arms for training purposes. Consequently, in the summer of 1860 Sherman went to Washington with an authorization from the governor to secure arms from the War Department in the name of the state. Sherman was surprised to find that, although Louisiana had already drawn its full quota of arms, the Secretary of War, John Floyd, promised to fill the requisition and faithfully carried it out.[88] Meanwhile, Graham sent some ammunition to the Seminary and the police jury of Rapides appropriated $250 for powder, lead, and caps. There was much talk of Negro uprisings, and Sherman promised to move the cadets quickly to any point of threatened revolt.[89] When the war came, he felt it wise to leave the institution where he was extremely popular and where it was conceded that he had been an eminently successful administrator.[90]

In 1857 the people of Bastrop, Texas, decided that the local academy that had been languishing for several years could best be revived by its total reorganization as a military institute.[91] They were fortunate in securing the services of

Robert T. P. Allen, whose career at the Kentucky Military Institute was well known in the Southwest. The new superintendent, whom the cadets affectionately called "Rarin' Tarin' Pitchin' " Allen, brought with him his son, Major Bob Allen, who served as commandant of cadets. Soon the new institution became a popular center of learning, under a strict discipline, and boasted that its courses ranked with those taught in the best colleges.[92] The Bastrop cadets, locally referred to as "the military boys," drilled daily and attracted large crowds to observe their evolutions and exercises. General Samuel Houston was so favorably impressed that he placed his two sons there and visited the institution frequently.[93] When the war come, the superintendent served as a colonel in the 17th Texas Infantry, and many of the cadets served with him or in other outfits.[94]

North Carolina, whence had come the first interest in military education, remained actively involved. In 1858, Daniel Hill began to make plans for the establishment of the North Carolina Military Institute at Charlotte. Viewing events from his post as professor of mathematics at Davidson College, he was distressed by the growing tension and resolved to engage in a work that would have "wider usefulness." Hill greatly admired the service that the Virginia Military Institute had rendered in providing more than four hundred educated officers for the state and hoped that he could make a similar contribution to North Carolina, though he was not too sanguine over the prospects.[95] Charles C. Lee came to Charlotte to serve as commandant of cadets, and, with two other instructors, Hill opened his school in the autumn of 1859.[96]

Within one year the North Carolina Military Institute had more than one hundred cadets enrolled; when Fort Sumter fell there were one hundred fifty. In late April 1861, the ladies of Charlotte presented the corps of cadets with a secession flag, "made with their own fair hands." The superintendent was placed in charge of the First State Camp of Instruction at Raleigh, and Governor Ellis ordered the entire corps of cadets to Raleigh to serve as drillmasters. Later many of them joined the Bethel Regiment under their former superintendent.[97] Colonel Hill had not produced another Virginia Military Institute, but in less than two years he had made a significant beginning.

At the time that Hill was opening his school at Charlotte, Charles C. Tew was establishing the Hillsboro Military Academy in the central part of the state. Several men from the South Carolina military academies came to help him. Within a few months the corps of cadets, numbering more than one hundred, was uniformed, armed, and "superbly drilled after the precise close order tactics of the day." [98] When the war came, it was a novel sight to see the more seasoned cadets, "from thirteen years old and upwards, each tramping his squad of grown and sometimes grizzled men, over the parade ground." [99] Soon the work of the academy was suspended, and most of the cadets followed their superintendent into the Confederate Army.

Other military schools in North Carolina were, for the most part, mobile or temporary institutes such as those conducted by Murphey in 1809 and Bingham in 1826. Numbered among them were C. B. Denson's Franklin Military Institute in Duplin County, D. H. Christie's school at Henderson, and others at Raleigh, Oxford, and Statesville.[100] By 1860 and 1861, they were turning out thirty- and sixty-day officers for the coming conflict. There was little time; and North Carolina, a military pioneer, had lost much.

A strong factor in the growth of military schools was the zeal of their graduates. There were the West Pointers, who promoted military education with uncommon ardor.[101] Graduates of the Southern military schools joined the ranks, and the Virginia Military Institute served not only as a model for new schools but also as a supplier of teachers. Most zealous, apparently, were the graduates of the South Carolina schools.[102] Even the newer schools were sending out graduates to promote the cause of military education. By 1860, Southern military schools were well on the way to becoming self-perpetuating institutions.

These "West Points of the South" both reflected the martial spirit and contributed to its growth. Their slavish adherence to the customs of eminent military schools in the United States and abroad suggests the hold that the idea had on many Southerners. Southern military schools not only disclaimed any pretense to originality, but publicized the fact that they were modeled after West Point or V.M.I. They used, insofar as possible, the West Point curriculum, West Point texts, the West Point system of grading, and West Point discipline. Even in the 1850's there was only the rarest deviation, such as the Citadel's announcement of the substitution of Calhoun's writings for Story's *Commentary on the Constitution*.[103]

There seemed to be almost as much interest in the uniforms as in the courses of study. The design of the uniforms was usually one of the first matters to be settled when a school was founded. When the *Southern Advocate* announced the opening of a military school at Huntsville, Alabama, the prospective cadets were advised to call on a local tailor who would provide them with a uniform that they could wear, *before the formal opening*.[104] Even in this matter, there was little variation from the West Point model. At the Virginia Military Institute and at the South Carolina schools, the cadets' grey uniforms resembled those at West Point. They did, however, use buttons which bore the insignias of their respective states.[105]

There was more originality in Louisiana, where Sherman and Graham decided to use a dark blue coatee with trousers of a lighter blue.[106] At Bastrop, Colonel Allen adopted a uniform of dark blue, with red stripes down the sides of the trousers, while the La Grange cadets wore uniforms of grey and white.[107] In the attention given to sartorial details, one can see a desire to stimulate the ambition and vanity of the prospective soldier. In the South there was not enough finery, even among the upper classes, to render such ostentation unattractive. Even if the rather gaudy uniforms were not to be considered gay masquerade dress, they could be regarded as exciting substitutes in the relatively quiet and drab surroundings of the countryside.[108]

These military schools generally enjoyed excellent public relations. Indeed, they deliberately engaged in activities designed to excite the interest and admiration of the populace. Public examinations, then widely used in various parts of the country, became universal among them. These gave the more serious-minded citizens an opportunity to form opinions — usually favorable. For the general public there were the drills that were a part of the daily routine of each military academy. The cadet corps frequently visited other communities to exhibit their skills and their attractive uniforms and to receive the plaudits of the crowds. In 1842, cadets from V.M.I. visited Richmond, where they paraded on the capitol grounds and submitted to an examination before the legislature. The impression was profound and lasting. The lawmakers substantially increased the appropriations of the Institute. In subsequent years the cadets not only visited Richmond but also journeyed to Petersburg, Norfolk, and other communities.[109]

The South Carolina institutions early established the custom of visiting the larger towns and demonstrating their military skills. In 1854, the cadets of the two academies made "a peaceful but triumphal march through the State." They journeyed from Columbia to Chester, Yorkville, Spartanburg, Greenville, Laurensville, Newberry, and back to the capital. The expedition "no doubt tended to popularize the Institutions while contributing to the pleasure and instruction of the cadets." [110] In Alabama the La Grange cadets regularly attended large and festive gatherings. In 1859 they thrilled the crowds at the fairs in Decatur and Tuscumbia; [111] the following year they captivated those at the Athens fair.

Some of these institutions received greater public support in the last decade before the Civil War, because of the growing apprehension of many Southerners regarding the future. Advocates of preparedness looked upon the schools as important factors in the achievement of a measure of military and political independence. In 1854, a visitor told the cadets at the Virginia Military Institute that they constituted the nucleus for an effective citizen soldiery. In the days ahead they would be expected to "bring the freemen's arm to aid the freeman's cause." [112] Smith of the Virginia Military Institute rejoiced that, by 1856, graduates were scattered throughout the state; then added:

> God grant that our State may never need their services except against a foreign foe. But Virginia is loyal to the National Constitution, and should the terrible cry, "*To Arms!*" be ever heard from her, the graduates and cadets of her military school will be the main element of her defence, and they will rally around her standard as one man.[113]

In other states the preparedness value of military schools was recognized. In 1859, the governor of South Carolina declared that the wisdom of establishing the military schools at Charleston and Columbia was becoming more apparent each day. The fact that the young men who went out from the schools were competent to train the citizen soldiery was most gratifying. It meant that the state had at its command, "at all times, the means of an efficient organization to meet any emergency that may arise." [114] In 1860, Georgia's chief magistrate said that he fully appreciated the value of the Georgia Military Institute and called for its continued support. This should be done, he said, for "we know not how soon we may be driven to the necessity of defending our rights and our honor by military force." [115]

Thus, the relationship between military education and Southern policy was established. If they achieved nothing else, the West Points of the South succeeded in inculcating among a considerable portion of the population an appreciation for their role in serving and protecting the community. Out of these institutions, in increasing numbers, were coming leaders who could train and command human material to serve as the bulwark of the South's defense. By 1861, this had become very important. Indeed, in the crucial early months of that year cadets of the Southern military schools led the way for young Southerners, from peaceful pursuits to active military service. That spring every cadet at the Virginia Military Institute was mustered into service, and all left the institution with the exception of forty-eight quite young cadets, who were detailed to guard the institution for the duration of hostilities. [116]

Even before the war began, the Board of Visitors of the Citadel Academy had offered to the state of South Carolina the services of its officers and cadets. Shortly after the firing on Fort Sumter nearly all its cadets and graduates were in the service of the state or the Confederacy. [117] It was essentially the same at the North Carolina Military Institute, La Grange in Alabama, the new school in Louisiana, and the other Southern military institutions. [118] Southerners could be proud of the fact that in time of peace they had made formal preparation for war.

# 9

# The Citizen Soldiery

The founding fathers had a strong aversion to the idea of a large standing army. To avoid any necessity they decided to encourage the development of a citizen soldiery. That would be sufficient to protect the country in time of peril. In 1792, the Congress passed an act to provide for the national defense by establishing a uniform militia throughout the United States. Every able-bodied white male citizen between the ages of eighteen and forty-five was to be enrolled and was to provide himself with certain items of equipment, including a good musket or rifle, two spare flints, a bayonet, and a knapsack and was to appear, so armed, when called out to exercise or to enter the service.[1]

In 1803, when there was some prospect of difficulties with Spain, the Congress sought to strengthen the military establishment by authorizing the President to require the governors to hold in readiness a detachment of militia not exceeding 80,000, officers included. The law also authorized state officials to accept, as a part of the detachment, any corps of volunteers that would engage for a period not exceeding twelve months. Governors were to name the officers of volunteers, general officers being apportioned among the states at the judgment of the President. In 1808, the Congress began to appropriate funds with which to arm and equip the

militia. With periodic modifications these enactments remained the legal foundations for the citizen soldiery, composed of the militia and volunteers, down through the Civil
War.

In their constitutions and in their laws, the several states
undertook to complement the federal legislation on the military establishment. When Arkansas entered the Union in
1836, for example, its constitution contained an article on
the militia with provisions for its organization in conformity
with the federal regulations.[2] Most of the other state constitutions contained similar, if less elaborate provisions.

These statutes defined more carefully the organization and
role of the several state militias. The Tennessee law of 1798,
for example, required militia service of all free men and
indented servants between eighteen and forty-five. High state
officials, ministers, ferrymen, veterans with three years' service
in the Continental Army, mail handlers, and justices of the
peace were exempted. The militia, with the proper officers,
was broken down into brigades, regiments, battalions, and
companies. The law designated the days for regular musters
and listed the fines, according to rank, for men who failed to
appear or who were without proper uniforms and equipment.[3]

In giving the states an opportunity to build up a military
force composed of militia and volunteers, the federal government actually encouraged the growth of as many armies as
there were states. More than that, it made possible the
emergence of a strange, if not strong, citizen soldiery. The
most exacting federal legislation could hardly have brought
about a well-coordinated military organization, even within
a Southern or Western state. The widely scattered population
and the diversity of its interests and needs would have served
to render an effective state militia almost impossible. But the
encouragement given to volunteer military organizations by
the legislation of 1803 made possible the rise of as many

separate armies as there were communities — and, worse still, several small armies within one community.

In the South the volunteer military organization found a congenial atmosphere in which to flourish. The volunteer company made it possible for neighbors and friends to comply with the requirements of the federal and state militia laws and, at the same time, escape the irritating and aggravating restraints that would be imposed by an efficient military establishment. It was a welcome opportunity, moreover, for the volunteers and many others to brighten their lives by periodic gatherings, ostensibly for the purpose of learning the techniques of organized warfare, which, for many, constituted their major social activity.

It was a relatively simple matter for some interested person, not infrequently the prospective captain, to gather sufficient men for a volunteer company. Whether it was to be a light infantry, artillery, or cavalry was determined by the members. The decision was reached, not on the basis of the needs of the state militia, but on the basis of the interest of the members. Having done this, the company could then secure recognition from the state legislature as a part of the state militia and obtain authorization to proceed with activities consonant with its status as a military organization. Almost invariably the legislature permitted the volunteer company to elect its own officers and to make its own by-laws. It could also select its own name, design its own uniform, and determine the nature and extent of its activities. Under such favorable conditions the Southern militia grew — in numbers, if not in effectiveness — composed largely of local volunteer organizations.

Volunteer military groups were springing up even before the law of 1803. In Nashville, Tennessee, for example, in 1801, a group of citizens organized a company of light infantry, which became a part of the first regiment of the David-son County militia. An act of the legislature permitted the company to choose its uniform and to require each person to arm himself completely.[4] In 1821, some citizens of Murfreesborough, Tennessee, which was nothing more than a village, organized the Murfreesborough Independent Volunteer Company, which was empowered to hold an election of militia officers as soon as sixty-four persons had enrolled.[5] When there was an insufficient number in a community, those interested would organize a volunteer company of men from various parts of a county. In Alabama, in 1852, the legislature authorized the organization of several such groups, including the Pike County Rangers and the Montgomery County Rough and Ready Invincibles.[6]

If the town was of considerable size it would, in all likelihood, have more than one military organization. Friendly rivalry was stimulating, and new organizations were welcomed with enthusiasm. As a Memphis editor put it, "the glorious rivalry of the various corps will make all prosperous." [7] As Richmond grew in size and importance its citizen soldiery increased. In the early part of the century the uniformed guards at the state capitol were the only military men in evidence. By 1852, there were eight or more volunteer military groups, including the Light Infantry Blues, the Dragoons, and the Rifle Rangers.[8] Charleston's Light Dragoons had a glorious history in the late colonial period and were the sole military organization of the city down into the nineteenth century.[9] From the time of the nullification controversy in 1832 the citizen soldiery increased. By 1860, the Dragoons had rivals in the Moultrie Guards, the Palmetto Guards, the Irish Volunteers, the Independent Greens, and others.

Perhaps New Orleans had the largest number of military organizations. Before 1803 there was a mulatto corps in the city, but it was viewed with disfavor after the purchase of the territory by the United States, and ceased to be an official part of the militia.[10] While the Washington Artillery and the

Continental Guards were easily the best known, they found competition for public attention in the activities of the Louisiana Legion and the Orleans Grenadiers. By 1843, there were at least ten such groups in the vicinity of New Orleans.[11]

The citizen soldiery of Vicksburg was also increasing. In 1835, there were two companies, the Blues and the Greys, of about twenty men each. In 1857 there was at least one other company, the Volunteer Southrons, and all were increasing in size and popularity.[12] In Memphis there was the kind of enthusiasm for military organizations that was befitting this lively, bustling city where frontier conditions prevailed. The pride of the community was the City Guards, which had to share honors, in 1853, with the Washington Guards composed exclusively of German citizens. There was much praise for the new company: its men were called "worthy to represent their own warlike Fatherland."[13] As soon as it was clear that the Germans were organizing a volunteer corps, the editor called on the Irish to do likewise: "There are enough enterprising and hardy Hibernians for a first rate artillery corps. We would then have three companies — one of musketry, of rifles, and of artillery," he boasted.[14]

The names selected for the military organizations reveal a good deal regarding the tastes and self-esteem of the citizen soldiery. Some selected modest titles which described the type of activity in which they were engaged, such as the Clayton Guards, the Greensboro Artillery, and the Lowndesboro Cavalry. Others identified their uniforms in their names — the Brownsville Independent Blues, the Nashville Greys, the White Plume Riflemen. For others, a more positively martial designation was desirable. Some of these chose an outstanding military figure, among which were The Lafayette Guards, the Washington Artillery, and the Jackson Guards. When the units undertook to identify themselves with certain heroic qualities or activities, they frequently achieved some exciting results: the Alexandria Whigs, the

Rutherford Patriots, the Gallatin Spies, the Pickens DeKalb Minute Men, and the Trenton Invincibles – names bristling with courage and intrepidity.

The military companies were as enthusiastic about their uniforms as were the military school cadets. Of course, if the outfit was composed of men of less than modest means, who were merely complying with the requirements of being enrolled in the state militia, their uniforms — or lack of them — reflected this. On the other hand, if the volunteer company was composed of wealthier men who had much to gain, socially and otherwise, by membership, they might be extravagantly dressed. In Savannah in 1850, Emily Burke noticed that, among the ordinary militia men, "scarcely any two were dressed alike," while in the independent companies the men wore "elegant and expensive uniforms." [15]

The uniforms of the ordinary militia company were frequently the ragged, dirty, ill-fitting linsey-woolsey of the byways; they were easily overshadowed by the resplendent and gay uniforms of the independent companies.[16] Wherever it appeared, the well-dressed military company never failed to win admiration. When the Clarendon Horse Guards of Wilmington, North Carolina, paraded for the first time, the local editor said that the people expected them to be neatly dressed; but, he added, "we were by no means prepared for seeing one of the richest, and at the same time, one of the most tasteful costumes in which we have ever seen a Military Company equipped." Small wonder! The privates were dressed in blue uniforms, faced with scarlet, while the officers' uniforms of the same color were "gorgeously faced with gold lace." [17] Some of the uniforms were elaborate to the point of being gaudy. When Jane H. Thomas' father was a captain of a Tennessee company, his uniform was the delight of his daughter.

He wore white pants, white vest, blue cloth coat trimmed in red, and brass buttons. His hat was crescent shape with a cockade, with a silver eagle on one side and a large white feather tipped with red. He wore a sword and belt and a ruffled shirt and high boots.[18]

In Charlestown, Virginia, after the Harpers Ferry raid, an eyewitness saw men of various volunteer companies in uniforms "of all the colors of the rainbow." There were the modest gray uniforms of the Richmond Volunteers, "mingled with the cerulean blue of those from Alexandria, the glaring buff and yellow of the Valley Continentals, and the indescribably gorgeous crimson of the Southwestern men." [19]

Uniforms were a major consideration among the military companies of Mobile. "First private," the Mobile correspondent for the New Orleans *Daily Picayune,* rejoiced that the men of the Light Infantry had decided to return to their favorite red coats. They were to have new ones, using the pattern of the grenadier company of the Coldstream Guards. Even more exciting was the new uniform of the men of the Continental Corps. This outfit had chosen the uniform of the New Orleans Continentals as its patern, to which it added a little more red here and here. The salutary effect of these changes was clear, the correspondent claimed. "Since the resolution was made to adopt this change the applications for admission have been unprecedented, and they talk of an immediate order for a hundred uniforms." [20]

This dressed up citizen soldiery needed some place to go. The logical place to display their finery was the muster and review. The various state militia laws differed, but all called for periodic muster and review of the military organizations. In South Carolina the brigadier general was to hold a review and drill of each regiment of his brigade at least once every year; and it was the same for most states.[21] For obvious reasons, in a rural section, the brigade musters, usually statewide, were on the whole unsuccessful. It was the company muster that was feasible and important. The company captain was required in South Carolina to conduct such an event at least four times each year.[22] It was the same for Virginia.

In Tennessee the company muster was to be held three times each year.[23]

The muster was held under the general supervision of the state adjutant general, who required detailed reports regarding the strength of the organizations and the condition of the arms at the time. It was the single opportunity for some central authority to exercise control over the military of the state. But this fact had far less significance in the community than the fact that muster and review gave state and local military dignitaries an opportunity to perform before the local citizenry; such an occasion was one of the rare opportunities for social intercourse. The regularity and frequency of the muster, therefore, were determined more by feasibility and desirability than by the requirements of the law.

Although the citizen soldier generally knew the time of muster, local newspapers usually carried in several successive issues the announcement of the forthcoming event,[24] and would undertake to work up enthusiasm regarding the muster's significance. When the regularly scheduled quarterly review of the New Orleans volunteer companies were changed from the Place d'Armes to Annunciation Square, the editor of the *Picayune* was gratified. "It is not often," he said, "our up-town residents are gratified with a military display of this kind, and they will no doubt be pleased with this contribution to their amusements and pastimes in the holiday sports of war." [25]

Every company had its regular place of muster, such as the county court house square or some easily accessible parade ground. For muster and review the citizen soldiery were required to be present at the announced hour, in uniform and with proper arms. They were called to order by their sergeant. Then the captain, along with any visiting military dignitaries, inspected uniforms, arms, and equipment. Slowly the crowd would gather and settle down for the day, with baskets of food and a variety of confections and refreshments. When the inspection was over, absences recorded to be presented later to a court martial, and the reports made regarding the conditions of the arms, the show was ready to begin.

To the command of their leader the men would go through their various evolutions according to some standard manual of tactics such as Scott, Hardee, or Cooper. The drill was enlivened by the services of at least two musicians, not infrequently Negroes, who played the drum and fife. They provided what one enthusiastic spectator called "music most divine, bringing out the most thrilling patriotic demonstrations." [26] If the military group could boast of the kind of talent that the Natchez Fencibles had, it could march to the strains of its own song, two stanzas of which express its fighting spirit.

> Our Maiden banner courts the wind,
> Its stars are beaming o'er us;
> Each radiant fold, now unconfin'd
> Is floating free before us.
> It bears a motto proud and high,
> For those who dare defy us;
> And loud shall peal our slogan cry
> Whene'er they come to "try us."
>
> The hallow'd ray that freedom gave us,
> To cheer the gloom that bound us,
> And shone in beauty o'er the brave,
> Still brightly beams around us.
> The day our fathers bravely won
> Shall long be greeted by us;
> And loudly through our ranks shall run
> The gallant war-cry, "TRY US." [27]

After an hour's drilling the men were ordered to be at ease. After refreshments, the drill was resumed for another hour. Then, dismissed, they were free to move among the crowd, and to eat and drink. Frayed nerves, fatigue, and excessive drinking conspired to create misunderstanding and, ultimately, fighting. This was the time for the settlement of feuds and grievances and the entertainment of spectators. Combatants fought with their hands, feet, and teeth until one of them was "whipped." If the feeling ran deep, knives or pistols might be used.[28]

By its very nature, the muster and review, with its requirements of precision on the part of a group of untutored amateurs, easily lent itself to the broad farce. Writers who where unsympathetic or who had a penchant for the humorous could exploit the occasion; the more objective, even the sympathetic writer, could frequently find amusing or ridiculous incidents.

As long as there were a few old Revolutionary soldiers in the vicinity of Fisher's River, they kept the " 'militeer spirit' at blood heat in the rising generation." The May muster was one of the outstanding events of the year, and the men of Captain Moore's company were present in large numbers. After the sergeant ordered them to "fall in," the captain appeared in an old-fashioned uniform and began to drill them according to Duane's *Manual of Tactics*. The "gingy cakes" of Josh Easley, popular Negro vendor, and the "licker" that Hamp Hudson was serving proved to be too much competition for Captain Moore. He finally conceded the victory of food and drink over the military spirit of the men of his company.[29]

At times the borderline between fact and fiction in the descriptions of musters was rather indistinct. The account of "A Militia Training" that appeared in an Alabama newspaper in 1830 is clearly a caricature. At the appointed time the Captain marched with measured step to the muster ground, "having a clean buck tail stuck in his hat, and woollen sash tied round his body, whereby was suspended a large cut and thrust sword." When the "double lunged" commander shouted "shoulder arms" a general confusion ensued among the broomsticks and cornstalks. As the women of the community looked on, the men went through their drill. Then a pail of whiskey was passed around. Each of the citizen soldiers drank on the average of a half pint.

When the best part of the day's sport was over, the troops were again called to order, and what few rifles there were among them proved by their unsteadiness that their bearings had lost the best part of their understanding, though they had taken in an additional quantity of new spirits.

Toward the end of the day one of the ladies presented a new stand of colors to the company. Captain Barney Blim, chewing tobacco and expectorating profusely, accepted it with a semi-literate, but very vigorous speech.[30]

There is every reason to doubt the efficacy of the muster and review as an instrument of military training and organization. Few groups won such praise as the volunteer companies of New Orleans whose display of skill in intricate military movements was described in 1856 as "brilliant," [31] or the Mississippi muster, regarding which an observer remarked that the men "acquitted themselves with so much credit that our hearts swelled with pride." [32] At the same time there is little reason to doubt the importance of the muster and review as a social institution or to question its effectiveness in suffusing a kind of martial spirit, however ill-defined and misdirected, in the people who attended. In De Kalb County, Tennessee, the "surging crowds" admired the soldiers on muster day and looked forward to the occasion with eager interest.[33] The martial spirit was virtually kept alive in Clark County, Alabama, by means of the musters of the regular militia and independent companies. It was a great day for a boy when he was allowed for the first time to attend a muster.[34] At Hurricane Hill in West Tennessee everyone, young and old, Negro and white, gathered for each muster and found the experience "most enthusing."[35]

In the more isolated areas muster and review was a time

of refreshing in a secular vein, as the camp meetings were in a religious — and secular — vein. There were trading, gambling, and courting. There were games of sport, such as footraces, kicking the hat, throwing the rail, and gander pullings. There were salesmen from the cities to press on the rustics their "slow" merchandise. At the first opportunity, an ambitious politician would harangue the crowd on the issues of the day and shout reasons why he should be elected to office. It was the event of the season, or year! And no person, isolated and with few such opportunities, would miss it if possible.[36]

Where the martial spirit was sufficient and where it was feasible, as in the larger towns, military companies engaged in activities other than those prescribed by law. Parading and target practice were popular pastimes, and some communities were favored with them as frequently as once per week.[37] The Huntsville Fencibles were having weekly parades and "target shooting" in 1844.[38] In Memphis the City Guards marched and engaged in target practice frequently during the final decade before the Civil War. In 1853, when they passed the offices of the *Daily Appeal* they saluted the editor, in tribute to the enthusiastic support he had given the citizen soldiery in the columns of his paper.[39]

New Orleans had enough parades to satisfy the most enthusiastic militarist. The Washington Artillery paraded every week.[40] The Continental Guards engaged in frequent parades and then retired to Algiers or some other appropriate place for target practice.[41] Night parades were a favorite in the Crescent City. In June 1857, the Washington Artillery "turned out with full ranks in their handsome uniform . . . for a moonlight parade." They marched through several streets and then serenaded the mayor, who called for "three cheers for the Washington Artillery," in which the crowd of civilians joined lustily.[42] Later that year several companies of General Tracy's brigade turned out for a moonlight parade on the night the Continental State Artillery of Mobile was doing the same thing.[43] The Creole Volunteers of New Orleans paraded in the Place d'Armes immediately in front of the Cathedral on Sunday mornings. James Creecy observed that "while the organ in the venerable edifice is pealing anthems to *Him* on high . . . the words of command, clash or arms, rolling of drums, the fife's shrill whistle, and the crack of rifles, are heard above all!" [44]

These independent military companies whose members could afford it took delight in making excursions to other communities to display their martial accomplishments. Their hosts were the military organizations of the towns visited, but the entire population cooperated in entertaining them. The preparations involved in such visits resulted in the improvement in appearance and movements of all participants. For several days preceding the visit of the Natchez Fencibles in 1835, the military companies of Vicksburg sought to improve their precision by drilling and parading. The Natchez group, expected on November 11, arrived two days earlier under the command of its founder and captain, John A. Quitman. Caught by surprise, the Vicksburg citizen soldiery scurried down to the river where they exchanged salutes with the visitors. Then they escorted the Natchez soldiers to a hotel, where accommodations were provided at the expense of the hosts. Later that day both groups drilled and paraded, to the delight of the local citizens who had made a holiday of the affair. There were parties in the evening and more parading the next day. The final event was an elaborate "military dinner" in honor of the visitors. After the drinking of many toasts and the exchange of best wishes, the Fencibles were on their way back to Natchez, obviously quite refreshed.[45]

For many years there was a close relationship between the military organizations of Mobile and New Orleans; they exchanged visits and stimulated each other by friendly competition. In the 1840's, for example, the Washington Artillery and the Mobile Artillery engaged in several marksmanship contests.[46] A similar relationship developed between the City Guards of Memphis and the military companies of neighboring Mississippi towns. In 1853, the Guards went to Somerville to celebrate the opening of a branch railroad. There they were greeted by the La Mar Cavalry, the Fayette Guards and "multitudes of men, women and children." The entire contingent marched through the town to the parade and picnic grounds where speakers of both places praised the citizen soldiery and the new railroad. After a huge barbecue the Guards returned to Memphis.[47]

Although distance was an obstacle to the execution of their plans, the military companies were not averse to entertaining the notion of traveling long distances for visits. In 1843 the Cannoneers of Donaldsonville, Louisiana, suggested to the volunteer corps of the state that they send a detachment of men, fifteen in all, on a very special mission. These military men should go to the Hermitage and "testify to General Andrew Jackson that gratitude and esteem due him for the military services he has rendered our beloved country and Louisiana in particular." [48] There is no evidence that the other companies acted on the suggestion of the Cannoneers. In 1859, the Chatham Artillery of Savannah was planning a June visit to Nashville. If the group went, little notice was taken of it.[49]

Much of the social life of the community centered around the military organizations, and these were quite willing to assume this civic role. Aside from the great balls in connection with patriotic celebrations, they sponsored other colorful and important social events.[50] Captain and Mrs. Basil Hall went to a very fancy military ball in Charleston in 1828, given by the officers of the various military corps. Captain Hall was the only man not in uniform. Mrs. Hall did not think that the change of dress improved the appearance of Charleston's military men. She conceded that they might be effective in the field, "but they are certainly not drawing room soldiers." [51] In Nashville, the Blues and the Rock City Guards set the city's social pace. Whenever money was needed by some charitable institution, they sponsored a military ball. The social affairs of the Guards, composed primarily of young society leaders, were usually the highlights of the season.[52]

That the citizen soldiery was public spirited and influential is clear. The activities of the Oak City Guards of Raleigh, North Carolina, show how wide and diverse the range of interests of a military organization could be. It held its regular muster and review; and there were times when it drilled and paraded even more frequently. It participated in various public functions such as the inaugurations of governors. It sponsored military balls and other social affairs. It maintained a reading room kept open day and night for the accommodation of strangers as well as subscribers. In 1857, it sponsored a series of public lectures and presented, among others, William Gilmore Simms.[53] Finally, it sought to fulfill the role of protector and defender of the lives and rights of the people of the community.

While it appeared that the citizen soldiers were, at times, preoccupied with matters that may be regarded as extraneous, they did not lose sight of the reason for their organization. Whenever they tended to overlook their function of protection and defense, either some incident or the articulate element of the civilian population reminded them of it. They busied themselves repelling Indians, putting down slave insurrections, and participating in the nation's wars with England and Mexico. If they were not altogether prepared for the emergencies, the apprehensions invariably led to efforts to strengthen the military establishment through enlistments and the commissioning of additional officers. At the time of the Turner insurrection at Southampton, the governor of Virginia issued several new commissions. One new colonel commanded his men to keep their horses saddled and bridled every night for three weeks, ready for any alarm or emergency.[54] At the same time a group of legally exempt men in Raleigh, North Carolina, organized a new military group to assist in the protection of the city.[55] In Nashville a group organized a new company of infantry and named it the Greys.[56]

The citizen soldiery were no less anxious to assist in the enforcement of local law. In Memphis, when the wharf master found it impossible to collect the customary charges, the mayor appointed a new wharf master and called on two volunteer military companies to assist him. Shortly thereafter wharfage receipts became the chief source of municipal revenue.[57]

While the public attitude toward the citizen soldiery depended to some extent on conditions that might produce fears and apprehensions, there was a reservoir of respect for the military that insured a measure of popular support at all times. Achille Murat saw this in 1833 when he spoke of the enthusiasm of most Southerners for their infantry as well as their mounted riflemen.[58] Buckingham saw it in Mississippi, where he found the people willing to arm and equip the militia at their own expense.[59] Even the critics were not so much opposed to the idea of a citizen soldiery as they were to the way in which it was organized and administered. The *Daily Picayune* admitted in 1843 that the whole militia system needed improvement and that the passage of bills for that purpose in the Congress was a "consummation most devoutly to be wished for." [60] The austere educator, Philip Lindsley, who was less than lukewarm toward the military, confined his criticism to the extravagance of many members who could hardly afford the expensive uniforms and military balls.[61] It would have been difficult, in 1855, when Lindsley spoke, to find many persons with that much temerity. Fears and apprehension in these final years before the Civil War had caused the people of the South to put an increasing amount of reliance on the citizen soldiery. They closed ranks on this, as on most questions, and pleaded with militiamen to improve their organizations and urged greater support of the entire military establishment. As early as 1845, when several members of the Huntsville Fencibles failed to show up for review, "A Citizen" was alarmed over the consequences of such dereliction. "Shake off the lethargy that binds you . . ." he exclaimed. "Procrastinate no longer — but buckle on your armour and once more gather up under the ample folds of that stardecked standard, presented by the Ladies of the town and resolve that henceforth you will be 'True to the line.'" [62]

There was concern in other quarters. After reading George White's *Statistics in Georgia*, James De Bow, disturbed over the apparent indifference of some people to the dangers he saw, pleaded with the Southern states to strengthen their defense. He was gratified to discover a determination on the part of many to reorganize the militia and to encourage militia companies. But there was room for still greater improvement. "Shall we not organize for armed opposition to any encroachment upon our rights?" he asked. "Shall we not be prepared against the time when abolition shall let slip the dogs of war to bathe their fangs in our vitals? . . . The next legislature we have no doubt will adopt some policy in regard to our military system which will put this state [Louisiana] in a position to defend herself in these perilous times." [63]

De Bow's fellow townsmen agreed with him. Five years later, in arguing for a comprehensive program of preparedness in Louisiana, the New Orleans *Daily Delta* recommended that the legislature encourage the organization of volunteer companies throughout the state and set up a fund for the purchase of uniforms and equipment.[64] In 1857 the *Picayune* came out for regular pay for the militia; and before 1860 some independent companies were receiving special appropriations, as the Washington Artillery had been receiving since 1850.[65]

Governor John Winston of Alabama was so greatly impressed with the activities of the volunteer companies that in 1855 he recommended that they altogether replace the militia. If the state could increase the number of volunteer regiments like that in Mobile, which was "equal to any citizen soldiery in the United States," it would be prepared for any eventuality.[66] Georgia's Governor Brown was similarly anxious about that militia system. In 1858 he recommended the encouragement of volunteer companies to be commanded by the graduates of the state military school. In case of war, the well-trained volunteers would constitute the nucleus of a powerful fighting force. Then, the untrained militia, "if called into the field, with such a force and such officers at their head, would at once become infused with the military spirit and soon with much of the military skill of the volunteers, and would constitute with them an invincible army."[67]

In the mid-fifties the anxieties of some citizens of the upper South regarding their militia bordered on hysteria. A Richmond paper said that the Virginia legislature would be faithless to its gravest duties if it failed to strengthen the militia. Indeed, it should provide for the drafting of 20,000 men. The graduates of the Virginia Military Institute could then train 200 regiments that would become proficient in offensive or defensive warfare.[68] With such agitation the state plunged into a program of preparedness that, by 1861, left little to be desired.

Throughout the South, militia systems were being strengthened, and volunteer companies were springing up. In the spring of 1858, the Alabama legislature incorporated seven new companies, and there were other groups that did not go to the trouble of seeking papers of incorporation.[69] In Memphis, Tennessee, the Washington Rifle Company and four other volunteer military groups were organized between

1855 and 1860. Older companies, moreover, were growing in strength, as their delinquent members returned to the fold, while, at the same time, the recruitment of new members was accelerated.[70]

The greatest stimulus to the growth of military organizations in the South was provided by the fears aroused by John Brown. The effect of this fantastic attempt in 1859 to put an end to slavery was electrifying. Volunteer companies and regular militia outfits bristled with action. Virginia was not alone in producing a veritable multitude of new and active groups of volunteers.[71] In many parts of North Carolina military companies were being formed.[72] The companies that had been recently organized in Atlanta – the Gate City Guards and the Atlanta Grays — now seemed to have a real *raison d'être;* and their increased activity showed that they realized it.[73] The newly organized Phoenix Riflemen of Savannah were drilling regularly.[74] By 1860, the South had come to rely more and more on its citizen soldiery for the military defense of the section. To be a man in arms in 1860 was claim to the respect and admiration of the entire community.[75]

Some men were, of course, more interested in the prestige value of military leadership than in defense. If military leadership was a key to success, then it should be exploited. This point of view doubtless had much to do with the proliferation of volunteer military companies. Every ambitious man's desire to command a company made it almost inevitable that some companies would be much under strength and that the ratio of officers to men would be relatively high. In 1852, for example, New York had twice as many men in the militia as Virginia, but the latter state had 84 per cent as many officers as New York. In the same year, Massachusetts had one militia officer for every 216 men, while Illinois had one officer for every 36 men. But North Carolina had one officer for every sixteen men in its militia![76] Small wonder that there were so many captains and colonels in the South.

The possession of high military titles by some Southerners was observed by many travelers and occasioned some ridicule. When Mrs. Frances Trollope made the trip from New Orleans to Memphis in 1828, she was surprised to find that most of the men on the boat were addressed by the title of general, colonel, or major. She related her findings to an English friend who said that he found the same thing when he made that journey on the Mississippi River. He told Mrs. Trollope that he had asked a fellow traveler why there was not a single captain among them, to which the man replied, "Oh, sir, the captains are all on deck." [77]

The architect Latrobe had the feeling that everyone he met in the South was either a captain, colonel, or general. Every house seemed to be presided over by an "officered head" of high rank, while backwoods taverns had "titled bonifaces of majority status." Latrobe, who was emotional on the subject of military titles, said that the multitudes of colonels and majors he saw in a tavern in Petersburg, Virginia, reminded him of the nobles of the Polish Republic. "The only difference is that instead of Count Borolabraski and Leschinski . . . we have here Colonel Tom and Colonel Dick and Major Billy . . ." [78] Another observer wagered that if a public carriage turned over with five males aboard, at least four colonels and generals would be injured. [79]

A visitor to Savannah in 1842 felt that the obvious delight of men of all classes in military titles reflected a strong military spirit. The principal banker and the principal bookseller were both colonels, while the hotel keeper was a major. "Captains abound in every class," he reported; "nor do they receive their titles on parade only, but in everyday address of business and conversation." In the Carolina hills he found a similar condition, where titles "once enjoyed by ever so short a service are continued through life." [80] Bishop Whipple got the impression that almost every third man in the South and Southwest was "blest with a military handle to his name." [81]

It was not necessary for one to have served in the militia or a volunteer company to be dubbed with a military title. To ascribe to a person the role of a high military officer was a gesture of respect which no gracious or ambitious gentleman would decline. When Felix Lebouve migrated to Mississippi in 1835, he was almost immediately addressed as "colonel." No one recalls how he won the distinction. His biographer speculates that it was given *"causa honoris* by the lavish spirit of republicanism, which scorns to confine her honors to doughty deeds with the sword, but has all worthy sons in every walk of life to kneel before her and dubs them 'captain,' 'colonel,' 'general,' 'Judge,' by right of freedom of speech and freedom of the press, thus vindicating the sovereignty of the people." [82] In Mississippi, in 1835, the people preferred military titles above all others. The preference was the same in Virginia, where the rage for military titles was such that the people were willing to confer the distinction gratuitously on anyone who did not possess a title. Most of the men of the better class were at least colonels, while every tavern keeper was a major. Occasionally there were a few "Kaptins . . . amongst the stage drivers, but such an animal as a Lewtenant only exists on the muster-roll of the militia, for I never heard of any one having seen a live one in Republican America." Featherstonhaugh related a conversation which took place between a resident of Winchester, Virginia, and a ferryman.

"Major, I wish you would lead your horse a little forward," which he did, observing to the man, "I am not a major, and you need not call me one." To this the ferryman replied, "well, Kurnel, I ax your pardon, and I'll not call you so no more." Being arrived at the landing place he led his horse out of the boat, and said, "my good friend, I am a very plain man, I am neither a Colonel nor a Major. I have no title at all, and I don't like them. How much have I to pay you?" The ferryman looked at him, and said, "You are the first white man I ever crossed this ferry that warnt jist nobody at all, and I swear I'll not charge you nothing." [83]

People at home and abroad could find humor in the military titles that so many proudly wore. If their social significance outweighed their military importance this can be regarded as a reflection of the extensive influence that the martial spirit had come to wield over so many phases of Southern life. When Southerners met in Memphis in convention in 1845 to deliberate some of their grave problems, they elected fifteen vice-presidents among whom were four generals, two colonels, one major, and one captain.[84] Whether for social, political, or military reasons, it seemed comforting — reassuring — to Southerners to have leaders of the citizen soldiery close at hand.

# Literary and Social Echoes

A visitor to Charleston in 1833 complained that the city was like an armed camp, and that he longed for a land of peace.[1] Twenty years later the same town appeared to be "in a state of siege or revolution."[2] To Buckingham, New Orleans resembled a vast "Champ de Mars."[3] Other Southern communities made similar impressions on visitors from less martial areas. While some of these observations were based on superficial experiences, there was, nevertheless, enough evidence of a martial tone in many of the everyday activities of Southerners to give them some validity. The activities of the citizen soldiery were a major manifestation of the martial spirit and an important factor in its diffusion. The Southern men in arms, however, had the assistance of other forces and factors in giving to their section the martial atmosphere that came to be associated with it.

While even the white population suffered from serious educational deficiencies, it had some literary interests that reflected and, perhaps, influenced the South's affinity for military things. Among the writers with a considerable following in the South, Sir Walter Scott is regarded by many as a leader. How extensively this master of medieval chivalry was read and what influence he wielded are difficult questions to answer. Some contend that the Scott novels were the Bible's only competitors for the attention of literate Southerners, that their martial and chivalric themes became the rule of life. Mark Twain and H. J. Eckenrode have gone farthest in ascribing the South's martial life to Scott's influence.[4] On one occasion, Twain said:

But for the Sir Walter disease, the character of the Southerner — or Southron, according to Sir Walter's starchier way of phrasing it — would be wholly modern, in place of modern and medieval mixed . . . It was Sir Walter Scott that made every gentleman in the South a major or a colonel, or, a general or a judge, before the war; and it was he also, that made these gentlemen value these bogus decorations . . . Sir Walter had so large a hand in making Southern character, as it existed before the war, that he is in great measure responsible for the war.[5]

In 1917, Eckenrode was hardly less critical. The South saw in Scott, he argued, the answer to the need for a reactionary social ideal to withstand any influence that might be exerted by revolutionary idealism both in Europe and America. The planters, who, a few decades earlier, had sanctioned the doctrine of equality, became aggressive aristocrats. The South, he said, returned to the medievalism which it has been the special mission of America to combat and the planters turned their backs squarely on modern tendencies. "Beyond doubt Scott gave the South its social ideal, and the South of 1860 might not be inaptly nicknamed Sir Walter Scottland. He did not create the state of feeling which held sway in the South so long, but he gave it expression . . . The term Southern Chivalry, unknown in the colonial period, came into use through his influence." [6]

There was, indeed, a conscious and widespread interest in Scott. Grace Landrum points out that the libraries in the better Southern country and city homes had the "inevitable rows of Waverly Novels." [7] Perhaps they were shipped into the South by the carloads, as has been claimed.[8] Many newspapers printed reviews of Scott's works and followed his activities with a lively interest. His works were not only read, but acted. The drawing room of a stately Southern mansion was, on occasion, the scene of the presentation of portions of his works by ardent admirers. On the professional stage, Scott was also popular. Between 1820 and 1832, seven of his novels and two poems were performed in New Orelans.[9] Not surprisingly, when he died in 1832, a Richmond newspaper edged its columns with black.[10]

It may be conceded that Scott and other romantic writers had some influence on Southern life and character. As ideas became stereotyped regarding the structure of society, the relationships of groups, and the role of the military, the works of Scott took on real significance. Dodd has correctly pointed out that *Waverly, Fair Maid of Perth*, and other such works reflected the old ideals of "fine lords and fair ladies which Southerners now set themselves to imitate and reflect." [11] Scott doubtless bolstered the social philosophy that gradually came to dominate the section. He also excited the imagination of those who, either in splendid or wretched isolation, pursued a vicarious existence through the colorful pages of *Ivanhoe*.

The South's literary activities did not possess the kind or the degree of the martial spirit that was in evidence in the more ordinary pursuits. Conditions placed limitations not only on the extent of the influence of Scott and others, but also on the literary expression of a martial feeling on the part of Southerners themselves. Just as the persistently rural character of Southern life tended to retard the growth of social institutions and the development of agencies for the advancement of culture, it also served to restrain the full expression, in a literary way, of some of the interests and points of view of the people. Even if the South was not wanting in talent, its more industrious and articulate element, as in all societies, found it necessary to devote its energies to strengthening its economic system, preserving its social order, and promoting its political views.

Some gave at least a portion of their talents to the delineation of Southern life, although the critical Southerner was
inclined to remark that even his educated neighbors were
provincial and not highly cultivated.[12] The discerning and
talented observer could easily see in the racy, swashbuckling
life of the back country a great source of material. And, he
could not overlook the martial air that was a significant phase
of life. It provided some of the best known humorous and
serious literary productions to come out of the South.

It is difficult to find a writer who used local materials to
better advantage than Augustus Baldwin Longstreet. His
*Georgia Scenes* contain several sketches illustrating the
genius of some Southerners for exploiting the materials connected with the martial life of the region. "The Militia
Company Drill," is unsurpassed in Southern literature as a
humorous account of this important activity.[13] "The Fight"
which brought together the two champions of their respective
battalions, illustrates how personal warfare was fostered and
stimulated.[14] "The Shooting Match," the subject matter of
which Longstreet describes as "coeval with the colonization
of Georgia," emphasizes the Southerner's attachment to fighting weapons for pleasure and for "business."

William Tappan Thompson, a sometime associate of Longstreet on the Augusta *Sentinel,* caught his friend's enthusiasm
for drawing from indigenous materials. In the 1840's he
brought out several works in a "Major Jones" series, including *Major Jones' Courtship, Major Jones' Travels,* and *Major
Jones' Georgia Scenes.* In the latter work, "The Duel" ridi-
cules with raucous humor all the etiquette and customs connected with the practice that still held sway in many quarters.
The names of Thompson's characters — Major Bangs, Gun
Brestin, Major Joe, and Major Bumblusterbus — suggest the
author's interest in emphasizing the military aspects of Southern life.

Johnson J. Hooper, the successful Southern journalist,

found that the martial life provided fruitful material. *Some Adventures of Captain Simon Suggs, Late of the the Tallapoosa Volunteers* is a classic caricature. The pressing Indian danger, the emergence of Suggs, the complete rascal, as captain of the "forty brave men," and their great fright at the fancied enemy — are fascinating and hilarious tales of frontier life in Alabama.

In his power of portrayal and delineation, Joseph G. Baldwin compares favorably with Longstreet. He saw the great possibilities in Hooper's *Captain Suggs*, and one of his best sketches in *The Flush Times of Alabama and Mississippi* is entitled "Simon Suggs, Jr., Esq., A Legal Biography." The subject — a son of the Captain of the Tallapoosa Volunteers — was himself a colonel and practiced law and soldiering in "Rackinsack, Arkansaw." Baldwin pointed up the prevalence and absurdity of dueling in "An Affair of Honor." The bully, who provided the weapons for the occasion, made the mistake of giving his adversary the *one* pistol that was loaded! Bowie knives, fence rails, muskets, and other deadly instruments are scattered through the pages of Baldwin's work.

Despite the levity in some of the literature relating to the South's militant ways, the vast majority of creative minds were engaged in polemical discussions involving Southern rights. In such works, rather extravagant claims were made regarding the fighting prowess of Southerners.[15] Even when there was no conscious discourse on strength, the writers, by the very temper of their arguments, displayed a bellicosity that could hardly be matched anywhere else in the country. Longstreet's *A Voice from the South* reveals a writer who could drop every pretense at humor and call on his people to prepare themselves to stand against the North. In 1836, Nathaniel Beverly Tucker's novel, *The Partisan Leader,* rattled the saber and predicted a glorious war of liberation if the North sought to prevent the secession of the slave states. Running through the speeches of Fitzhugh, Calhoun, Hammond, and numerous lesser figures is a stern, bitter argumentation that is itself barely a degree short of warfare.[16]

Few equaled the Southern poets in their grim depiction of the martial South. Occasional lighthearted poems about a volunteer company and its stand of colors appeared; but the medium of poetry seemed to have been reserved for tearfully earnest statements on the South's willingness to fight. In this spirit, in 1833, Mirabeau B. Lamar wrote "Arm for the Southern Land," which was reprinted in 1835 on the eve of the Texas Revolution, and again in April 1861. A portion of one stanza reads:

> Arm for the Southern land
> All fear of death disdaining;
> Low lay the tyrant hand
> Our sacred rights profaning!
> Each hero draws
> In Freedom's cause,
> And meets the foe with bravery.[17]

James Buckingham noted the vigor of the South's martial poetry in the anonymous eight-stanza poem, "Georgia," which he reproduced in his work on the slave states. Its spirit is eloquently expressed in the fifth stanza:

> Ay, there are hearts within thy land,
> As warm, and brave, and pure and free,
> As throbb'd among the Spartan band
> Of Old Thermopylae;
> And like that band, should foes invade,
> To seek thy rights from thee to tear,
> Thy sons will lift the sheathless blade,
> And bid them come who dare! [18]

The pride in home and a fiery determination to defend it ran through many Southern poems. It was, perhaps, what Judge Alexander B. Meek of Mobile called a happy combination of the beautiful and the patriotic which naturally arose from an appreciation for the South's climate, its institutions,

habits of life, and social conditions.[19] Meek himself was inspired to write "The Homes of Alabama" in which he said:

> The homes of Alabama
> Homes of the brave and the free, —
> Stout hearts beneath their Cabin roofs
> Pulsate with liberty!
> They scorn the despot's iron rule,
> The Zealots galling chain, —
> And the homes of Alabama
> Shall ever free remain!
>
> The homes of Alabama,
> Let the tyrant keep his own,
> The bigot nurse his narrow creed,
> But not pollute her zone!
> Should war and frenzy ever strive
> To crush her strength, they'll feel
> That the homes of Alabama
> Are filled by hearts of steel! [20]

Buckingham was deeply impressed with the strong attachment of Southerners to their section, which was greater than
anything he had seen in the North. He made a note of one
of Judge Meek's poems which eloquently expressed the pre-
vailing Southern sentiment:

> Land of the South! Imperial land!
> Then here's health to thee: —
> Long as thy mountain barriers stand,
> May thou be blessed and free!
> May stark dissension's banner ne'er
> Wave o'er thy fertile loam;
> But should it come, there's one will die,
> To save his native home! [21]

The two outstanding qualities of Southern ante-bellum
literature became quite apparent, in its martial poetry. One
was the pride in the section, increasing with each passing
year; the other, a political aggressiveness that, at times, encouraged a militancy that could aid in preserving the section.

But, while more apparent in the poetry, these qualities were also present in other forms. Thus, Southern writers contributed substantially to as well as reflected the martial life.

The limited intellectual interests of the majority precluded extensive preoccupation with any kind of literature. Such people, however, were not averse to participating in other, more tangible, activities for which their environment and experience prepared them. Agricultural fairs gave opportunities — all too rare — for extensive social intercourse. One of the real delights was the parading of the volunteer corps, a militia company, or a corps of cadets, without which the fair was hardly successful.[22] When the cadets of La Grange appeared at the 1859 fair in Decatur, Alabama, an observer said that it was one of the most pleasing incidents of the enterprise. "Their fine appearance in uniforms, good drilling and orderly behavior, attracted general admiration, and was well calculated to impress favorably the spectators with the Institution and the practical utility of its system of discipline and instruction for Southern youth."[23]

An important and exciting event at many fairs was the ring tournament. This resembled the game of medieval chivalry described by Scott. Each contestant mounted his favorite charger and carried a long lance. At the signal he charged a course about one hundred yards in length, over which were placed a number of rings, usually three, about thirty yards apart. The rings, varying in diameter from two inches to one-half inch, were hung on a hook at the end of a wire fastened to a bar. At the end of the course the contestant carried the rings on his lance to the judges' stand. The one who performed the feat with the greatest skill in the shortest time was declared the winner and would have the honor of crowning the queen of the tournament.[24]

There is disagreement over whether the tournament was a military activity. Professor G. Harrison Orians has argued, with much force, that the tournament was not a military activity any more than any athletic contest is a preparation for a soldier's discipline.[25] G. P. R. James, a historian of chivalry, has asserted with equal vigor that the tournament is one of the war games in which all military nations have engaged from earliest antiquity.[26] It is of little importance whether the Southern tournament was inspired by Scott,[27] or whether it can properly be associated with the history of war games through the ages; what is important here is whether the tournament was an activity which was related to the martial life of the section in some significant way.

There can be little doubt that the names the contestants assumed reflected a mental association of the tournament with military activity. Most designated themselves as knights, and the military nature of such can hardly be denied. Among these were the Knight of the Black Prince, Knight Don Juan, the Knight of Malvern, Knight of the South, and Knight of the Old Dominion.[28] In other instances, military school cadets or officers of military companies entered tournaments, designating themselves by their military rank.[29] The orator of the day, moreover, usually selected a theme and emphasized those virtues that had a military flavor. Even Professor Orians admits the possibility that the "charge" of the tournament orator could lead one to believe that there was more fieriness to the Southern tournament than that imparted by keen competition.[30] At the tournament in Tallahassee, Florida, in 1859, the orator sought to inspire the knights by calling on them to emulate George Washington, the "noblest knight and purest hero of any country or age." [31] The orator frequently traced the history of chivalry from the earliest times to the present, emphasizing the virtues of bravery and unselfishness. That the oration could be carried to extremes was the conviction of the *Vicksburg True Southron*, which said that the grandiloquent speech of the "Knight of Mount Vernon" at the Alabama fair was "quite enough to make a dog laugh — if dogs do really laugh." [32]

Perhaps the principal reason for associating tournaments with the South's martial life is that their chief sponsors were almost invariably military organizations. If a company of dragoons or infantry regarded the tournament as an activity worthy of promotion, it is not surprising that others would regard it as a military activity. Indeed, in some communities it was second only to the muster and review in the opportunity that it afforded for appearance of the military. On November 6, 1856, the Henrico Light Dragoons staged a highly successful tournament at the Petersburg Fair Ground; the following year the same group joined with the Young Guard Battalion in putting on a parade and tournament to to mark the anniversary of the Battle of Yorktown. Various military companies in Charleston — the Light Dragoons, the Light Infantry, and the German Artillery — sponsored tournaments and other chivalric contests. On occasion they were joined by visiting groups, such as the Georgia Hussars of Savannah.[33]

Tournaments enjoyed widespread popularity in the Southern states, providing exciting opportunities for people to mingle under the most pleasant circumstances. They were most frequently held on holidays, thereby affording a greater number an opportunity to attend. Tournament day came to be regarded as a holiday, whether or not it coincided with some anniversary or commemoration. Frequently they were held for the benefit of some church or charitable organization; this attracted some who otherwise might not have attended. Usually, there were added attractions such as military parades, elaborate banquets, and military or fancy dress balls. Small wonder that such huge crowds witnessed the tournaments: there were five thousand at the Fredericksburg tournament in 1856; in 1859, four thousand turned out for the spectacle at Arlington, six thousand at Jackson, Mississippi.[34]

Patriotism was a part of the concept of loyalty that permeated the Southern character. Loyalty was connected with the concept of honor which required every man of the South to profess a kind of fidelity to his nation, his state, his family, and even to his slaves. Such loyalty was manifested through the patriotism which Southerners practiced with zeal bordering on the religious.

National and local anniversaries gave Southerners an opportunity to demonstrate their appreciation for contributions toward strengthening the community and nation. These were exhilarating experiences: periods of revelry and relaxation which lifted many out of their drab existence and permitted them to relate themselves to the noblest and most heroic people in their history. At times like these they could pledge themselves to guard with their lives the precious heritage handed down to them.

Independence Day was the principal day for a great military celebration. "T.P." of Alexandria, Virginia, published in 1834 a fictional account of such a celebration. He said that every firearm that could be found was put under requisition, and the entire forenoon was consumed in collecting and preparing them for use. One could hear the discharge of guns at regular intervals, an indication that the parade was about to begin. Shortly after noon the soldiery made their appearance. "Their arms were of divers descriptions; double barrelled guns, deer guns, ducking guns, and a blunderbus . . . and, for volunteers, in number exceeding arms, poles were substituted." [35]

Many actual Independence Day celebrations were just as picturesque. That in Richmond in 1812 was a gala affair. The governor "appeared on the *martial plain* more richly and elegantly uniformed than any man" John Campbell had ever seen. "He was in his glory . . . pranced here and there and everywhere — A hollow square was form'd and he addressed the military in a style of Superior eloquence." [36]

In Tennessee the "Glorious Fourth" was a great occasion, "a spread-eagle day in the land," and every one was present for the speeches and parades. Several volunteer companies were usually on parade "handsomely uniformed." [37] In Rome, Tennessee, at the mouth of Round Lick Creek, a huge Independence Day celebration was held in 1830. Despite the remoteness of the village, five or six hundred persons were present, "and two beautiful and finely equipped uniform companies graced the occasion. The military display and martial music not only had a fine effect on the crowd, but excited in the orator of the day the most patriotic emotions, and inspired him with courage in the performance of the duty which had on that day devolved upon him." [38]

In 1856, the people of Charleston began their Independence Day celebration early. At three o'clock in the morning the cannon at the city arsenal heralded the nation's birthday anniversary. Military companies began their activities at dawn, between four and five o'clock. A morning parade of all the citizen soldiery preceded the public meeting at eleven. During the ceremonies there was great praise of the heroes of the Revolution, and patriotic and martial tunes were interspersed throughout the program.[39]

The Independence Day celebrations in Alabama were worthy of the efforts of that martial state. Every town with military companies centered their observances around such groups. In 1845, the Huntsville Fencibles and the Huntsville Guards dominated the celebration in their town. "Their neat, trim appearance, gay uniforms, glittering arms, fine martial music, and the skill and precision with which the evolutions were performed, made quite an imposing and gratifying display." The military ball in the evening completed the day's festivities.[40] In the following decade, the Madison Rifles occupied the center of the stage at the Huntsville celebration. They fired salutes at sunrise and sunset, put on a colorful parade, and listened to a stirring address. After the "bountiful Barbecue," the Rifles staged their annual target firing in the grove south of the town.[41]

The Montgomery celebration frequently attracted military organizations from other towns. Joining the Montgomery Blues and the Montgomery Rifles in 1855 were the Greensboro Light Artillery Guards, the Cahaba Rifles, the Grove Hill Cadets, and the Columbus Light Rifles. During the parade, when the La Grange Cadets marched by, "parents looked with pride upon their intelligent sons, sisters smiled approvingly, and many girlish hearts beat quicker as among the ranks they espied the faces of their sweethearts." [42] The Mobile observance of 1857 brought out the entire Mobile Rifle Corps. These teenagers, calling themselves the Mobile Blues, showed by their performance that they would be an important addition to the "armed might" of Mobile.[43]

In 1844, the Natchez orator, in addressing his remarks to the Natchez Fencibles, linked the movement to annex Texas with the movements in Europe. The Fencibles could not have failed to understand the implications when William Mason Giles said:

The revolutionary spirit has gone forth and will go forth; it was felt in revolutionary France, and shook the thrones of Europe to the centre. Poland caught its spirit, and poured out her blood like water, in its support — South America echoed the strains in shouts of victory . . . and it lighted the "Lone Star" of Texas with an undying lustre.[44]

New Orleans always had an elaborate military observance of Independence Day; and on occasion a part of the citizen soldiery of the Crescent City chose this day to share their martial enthusiasm with neighboring towns. In 1857, the Continental Guard marched in Biloxi while the Washington Artillery went to Pass Christian, where they created "quite a sensation" with their demonstrations in maneuvers and firing of salutes with cannon. A resident of New Orleans, visiting in Pass Christian at the time, wrote that the city had every reason to be proud of the bearing of the men as soldiers and artillerymen.[45]

The birthday anniversary of George Washington was a proper time to pay tribute to the father of the country. Perhaps no occasion during the winter months called forth such elaborate military displays as February 22. In the capital of Washington's home state, the celebration was one of the major events of the year. In 1841, both President-elect Harrison and Vice-President-elect Tyler were present at the Richmond celebration. The military of the city, "in their best and most splendid array, added splendor to the spectacle." Swords were presented to Virginia's heroes who had seen action in the War of 1812 and on other occasions. The tributes paid to Washington and the other heroes would do much, one observer felt, "to revive the generous ardor of patriotism . . . and kindle in youthful hearts a chastened and pure ambition, and give a keener edge to the sentiment, which cherishes and regards the national honor as a part of our own." [46]

In other communities the celebrations centered around the military. Buckingham found an elaborate military display in Savannah on Washington's birthday. The companies were "well dressed, well disciplined, and had as perfectly martial an air as the National Guards of Paris, to which, both in uniform, stature, and general appearance, they bore a marked resemblance." [47] At Nashville the Guards, "a handsome uniform company," dominated the celebration. In 1822, in his address to the citizen soldiery and others, the mayor praised the heroes of Tennessee who did so much to strengthen Washington's hand during the War for Independence. "They have decked the name of Tennessee with wreaths of laurels," he said, "and placed its character for patriotism and valor in a position so conspicuous and elevated, that we deem it honorable to be termed a son of Tennessee . . ." As a final word of admonition he urged the men to remain prepared for any eventuality.[48]

The Washington Artillery of New Orleans had an especially elaborate celebration on February 22. In 1857 it lasted for several days, with other companies participating. Included were a parade, a special military burial of a retired naval officer, the presentation of a stand of colors to the company, and a military ball. In response to the presentation of the colors the company lieutenant, catching the spirit of the occasion, said:

> Should the tempest of war overshadow our land,
> Its bolts can ne'er rend Freedom's temple asunder,
> While still on our banner shall Washington stand,
> And repel with his glance the assaults of the thunder!
> This sword from the sleep
> Of its scabbard shall leap,
> And conduct, with its point every flash to the deep!

The atmosphere at the ball was no less martial than Lieutenant Todd's poem. The gallery of the hall was decorated with the military accoutrements of the citizen soldiery, while at one end of the ballroom there was placed a piece of brass ordnance, "glistening like gold, and a stand of arms, surrounded by piles of cannon balls and canister shot, which were arranged in a most elegant manner." [49]

The anniversary of the Battle of New Orleans received an appropriate military observance in many communities. In 1856 the Adams Light Guard of Natchez planned a parade and a military soiree to celebrate the "Glorious Eighth." [50] In Huntsville, Alabama, the Madison Rifles commemorated the anniversary in 1857 by a parade and the firing of salutes. [51] In New Orleans the eighth of January eclipsed every other fete day. [52] In 1836 more than a thousand men in arms participated. On the square before the cathedral the troops engaged in a mock battle for more than an hour, and the fire was incessant and heavy. [53] In 1857 the surviving heroes of the battle were the guests of honor for the various military observances. [54] In the following year, Negro and white veterans were honored together, an incident which the editor of the *Pica-*

*yune* thought the Garrisons, Stowes, and Greeleys should notice. When the aged men rode by in carriages provided by the military organizations, the bands united in playing "See, the Conquering Heroes Come." [55]

While the anniversary of the Battle of New Orleans was, perhaps, the most popular event of its kind, other battles were also commemorated with military fanfare. In 1810, the citizens of Washington, Virginia, made elaborate plans to commemorate the Battle of Kings Mountain. A regimental muster was to be held and the various military organizations were called upon to parade in observance of the day.[56] The Battle of Fort Moultrie was celebrated in 1856 by the military of Charleston. The Moultrie Guards led the parade around the city, escorted by cadets from the Citadel. At the evening celebrations, the Moultrie Guards, a total abstinence company, conducted an orderly affair; while at the Palmetto Guards' ball there was an abundance of alcoholic beverages.[57] Two years later the Battle of Fort Moultrie was observed as a holiday. The military, this time led by the Dragoons, held a parade that preceded the luncheon and a commemorative program.[58] Other battles celebrated with various kinds of military displays included those of Lexington and Yorktown.[59]

Of the numerous special occasions that brought out the military, none surpassed the visit of General Lafayette in 1825. His tour through the Southern states was a triumphant procession during which time he was never without the company of a variety of military organizations. When he arrived in Yorktown, for example, three companies of Richmond volunteers went to the peninsula to greet him.[60] Many thousands of citizen soldiers greeted the distinguished visitor during his sojourn in the South. He must have been impressed with the military resources of the country as far as manpower was concerned.[61]

Other distinguished personages visiting Southern cities

were similarly favored. When Major-General Edmund P. Gaines arrived in Nashville in 1822, the Guards paraded during the morning and escorted the general to a public meeting in his honor that afternoon.[62] The military of Natchez turned out for General Quitman's return in 1848; and his company presented him with a sword.[63] Former President James K. Polk evoked an enthusiastic military display during his visit to Savannah in 1859. As the steamer approached the city, the Chatham Light Artillery fired a salute of welcome, while six other companies of volunteers waited to escort him through the city.[64]

One of the significant celebrations of the period was the observance of the Fifth Semi-centennial of the Landing at Jamestown, held on May 13, 1857. It was primarily a military affair, a fact that Governor Wise recognized when he said at the end of a brief speech:

But the civil celebration of this day is ended; the military are waiting for me, and the drum-beat calls me to review. I cannot longer detain you, for you must not forget that I am commander-in-chief of your army, and we must now go to the battlefield!

Among the fourteen companies awaiting their commander-in-chief were the Fayette Artillery, the Webster Cadets, the Portsmouth Rifles, and the Dismal Swamp Rangers. In addition to the lengthy parade and review, there was a reception for the military. The toast to the First Regiment of Virginia Volunteers indicate the deep respect of the people for their citizen soldiery:

Their soldier-like bearing evinces a high degree of military skill and proves that they are fully able to maintain the glorious motto of the Old Dominion, "Sic Semper Tyrannis." [65]

Even in Southern religious experiences, there was sufficient combativeness to suggest the presence of the militant spirit. There seemed to be no feeling that the church was or should be beyond such influence. Indeed, churchgoers were praised for participating in military activities. In 1842 the anonymous author of an article entitled "Christianity and Patriotism" praised the pious men of '76 who were among the leading actors in the drama of the Revolution. "Christians stacked their arms at the door of the Church," he said, "and from the altar of devout supplication to the God of Nations, went to the field, where was reserved for them, either liberty or death." [66]

The issue of slavery drew the lines of division as sharply in the church as anywhere else; and the leaders and members were not above engaging in militant activities. In 1800, when the conference of South Carolina Methodists issued a very strong antislavery statement, a Charleston minister was intimidated to the point that he burned the statement. He continued to remain under the suspicion of his members and of others. On the following Sunday a mob visited him and warned him against any collusion with the antislavery element.[67] In 1845, both the Methodist and Baptist churches split into Northern and Southern factions; and in 1857 the Presbyterians divided. While there was little actual violence connected with the schisms themselves, the feeling of bitterness engendered by the divisions doubtless stimulated the growth of belligerency and even violence in the churches in succeeding years.[68]

In 1846, the minister of the Methodist church of Guilford, Virginia, was suspected of holding antislavery views. In the midst of a sermon, a mob entered the church, compelled him to stop by shooting, shouting, and throwing stones, and ran him out of the community. The grand jury refused to grant him any redress. That summer the proslavery element in the Methodist Church of Salem, Virginia, sought to force the entire membership to join the newly organized Southern wing of the denomination. A mob broke up the Sunday morning worship service and *"dragged the minister out by his coat and hair."* When he sought redress in court on the following day, the mob ordered him to leave within fifteen minutes, a reprieve which, presumably prompted by their Christian teachings, they finally extended to an hour.[69]

As sectional feeling grew more bitter, the Southern churches assumed or were assigned a specific role in the movement to win support for the Southern cause. City officials and state legislators set aside days of fasting, humiliation, and prayer at which time Southerners were asked to give thought to the disadvantaged position which their section occupied in the national picture. Huge religious services were held on such days, and the leading ministers were assigned the task of preaching sermons that related the plight of the South to the historic position of embattled Christians.

In 1850, on the day of humiliation, the members of the South Carolina General Assembly heard the Reverend Whitefoord Smith preach, using as his text "God is our Refuge," that the Southern cause was the cause of justice and truth. "We appeal to God, as did our fathers in the darkest days of their peril . . . and we believe that He will safely guide us through." There was no doubt in his mind on which side God was.

Cast your eyes around you, and ask if we were disposed to lean upon earthly aid, whence is that aid to come? Yet this need not intimidate us. For, what though we were deserted by men? What though the world were in arms against us? Has God never delivered his people under circumstances threatening and desperate as even these would be? [70]

Nor were Southern ministers averse to assuming an active military part. The Reverend Richard Stewart, a Methodist minister of Iberville, Louisiana, was captain of a company of ninety volunteers which he led into battle during the Mexican War. He did not allow his position to prevent the "discharge of that duty every citizen owes his country in the hour of peril," one admirer asserted. Upon his return he was loudly proclaimed as "the fighting clergyman." [71] Other

Southern ministers served as chaplains to militia and volunteer companies. In 1858, the Washington Light Infantry, South Carolina's oldest volunteer company, elected the Reverend Anthony Toomer Porter as its chaplain. During the dark days of December 1860, Porter went to Castle Pinckney where the men were assembled and preached a sermon from the text, "As a Good Soldier of Jesus Christ." For this stint, Porter claims the distinction of having preached the first sermon to troops in the Civil War.[72] With considerable strife within their organization and with a leadership that was willing to inspire men to fight, Southern churches were far from exercising a neutralizing effect.

Perhaps some phases of life in the South escaped the influence of the martial spirit. It would seem, however, that such were not only few, but were relatively unimportant. Internal conditions of life lent themselves to the indulgence in martial activities — some for recreation and others for strengthening defenses. As the relations between the North and the South became strained, martial activities tended to increase and to take on a more serious nature.

The martial tone achieved did not necessarily involve continuous beating of the drums of war. At times it found expression in some literary activity — either in the extensive reading of heroic fiction or in the articulation of the martial flavor. It could even be seen in the militancy that flared up in the religious organizations and activities in the section.

When related to the larger picture, these social, cultural, and religious phases of life take on a new significance. The larger picture is one in which, as we have seen, rural isolation continued and the feeling of personal self-sufficiency, bordering on sovereignty, created endless conflicts. It is one in which the Indian danger persisted and the fear of slaves imposed on the plantation the necessity of becoming a citadel. It is a picture in which the desire to expand gave way to a dynamic jingoism and in which education for war was an important phase of the South's intellectual interests. In this larger picture the citizen soldiery enjoyed a position of favor and respectability that made it possible for the men in arms to lend a martial tone to many phases of Southern life. In such a picture the martial tone of some of the literature, of the county fair, or of the fighting sermon merely brought this militancy into sharper focus.

This was the picture that some observers saw when they reported that the South had a bristling martial life. One reporter felt the leading characteristic of men and women was "reckless bravery." [73] This was what Olmsted saw in Charleston in the "frequent drumming which is heard, the State military school, the cannon in position on the parade ground, the citadel, the guard-house, with its martial ceremonies, the frequent parades of militia . . . and especially the numerous armed police, which is under military discipline . . ." [74] While the picture varied from one community to another, its salient aspects appeared almost everywhere. This life produced "The Southern Man," as described by W. H. Holcombe:

> Is it a fight on hand?
> For sacred cause or none —
> For a silly word or Fatherland?
> With a dozen foes or none?
> Clear the ring my boys!
> Battle it while you can;
> But, for gallant bearing and reckless daring,
> There's none like the Southern man! [75]

# Toward a Unified South

As the South developed an intense interest in military matters and as it engaged in activities reflecting that interest, it did not, in the beginning, place any special emphasis on its sectional needs. The opinion prevailed that, with the dangers rising from the proximity of Indians and the presence of Negro slaves, military precautions should be taken in the interest of self-preservation. But there was no indication, for many years, that the section needed military strength to repel a Northern foe. As a matter of fact, early in the century, Southern leaders focused their attention on the task of strengthening national defenses. Between the close of the War in 1812 and the beginning of the conflict in 1861, the War Department was under Southern leadership a vast majority of the time; and many of these Southern Secretaries of War argued strongly for a program of greater national defense. In 1818, as Secretary of War, John Calhoun made an eloquent plea for a larger military establishment, while Joel R. Poinsett, also of South Carolina, did much to strengthen the nation's defenses during the Van Buren administration.[1]

Down to the 1830's there was considerable public support in the South for a strong army. In 1821, the editor of the *Nashville Whig* was alarmed over the prospect of a reduction in federal army appropriations. He thought that, in view of the movements in Europe, it was especially shortsighted to "extinguish every spark of martial spirit" in the United States.[2] The *Louisville Public Advertiser* was opposed to any reduction of appropriations, arguing that such a step would be in keeping with neither the character of the nation nor with its great and growing interest.[3] Perhaps the most bitter opposition to the proposed reductions came from the editor of the Charleston *Courier,* who pointed out that to cut the army after the recent acquisition of Florida would reduce the country not only to the liability of insult but to something "more painful, the consciousness of imbecility." He then put a series of questions that reflected his deep appreciation for the whole complex of the military cult:

Is it nothing to impair, if not destroy that confidence in the government which induces high-minded men to leave the pursuits of civil life for the profession of arms? Is this no longer to be a profession in our republic, which men of genius may study with the desire of serving their country . . . Is military experience, valor, and fame so cheap that we may dispense with all we have, and expect to find it always in the market when we need it?[4]

In the years that followed, various Southerners spoke out for a stronger military force. If none of them quite reached the vehemence of the Charleston editor in 1821 they, nevertheless, showed a real desire to maintain the defense machinery at a high level of efficiency. As late as 1845, "A Subaltern" wrote articles for the *Southern Literary Messenger* calling for a thorough reorganization of the army with a view to strengthening it. He decried the subordination of the commanding general to a civilian, the Secretary of War, and argued that it was a waste of training and talent to use West Point graduates in the Quartermaster and Commissary Departments as "corn, coal, or pork merchants."[5]

Even in the final decade before the Civil War, there was some Southern support for a stronger federal army. In 1852, De Bow was distressed over what he termed the insufficiency of the army.[6] Four years later the correspondent of a New

Orleans newspaper said that the army on the western frontier was greatly neglected and all but abandoned. The most tragic aspect of the matter, from that reporter's view, was that the Northern bloc in the Congress was trading its support of the army bill for acquiescence "in its fanatical and treasonable designs against the Constitutional rights of the South and the continuance of our glorious and happy union." [7] Since army reductions were associated with abolitionist schemes, small wonder that the South supported a stronger United States army as the intersectional feeling mounted. The willingness of some Southerners to continue such support is explained by the fact that between 1844 and 1861 every Secretary of War was a Southerner,[8] one in whom the South could have faith.

Before 1850, however, the feeling had emerged that the South's principal interest in military affairs should be directed toward strengthening local defenses. An increasing sensitivity, born of its way of life and relationship to the rest of the country, fostered this redirection of the South's martial spirit toward self-preservation. Southern sensitivity to criticism increased substantially during the abolitionist crusade, and the reaction was most often resentment and pugnacity.[9] It was this hypersensitivity that caused a Southerner like Edmund Ruffin to denounce his critics as "self-seekers" and "schemers" without even an examination of the merits of their criticism.[10] It drove some to the use of the most abusive language and the adoption of the most desperate measures against all forms of criticism. When the editor of the *Illustrated London News* criticized Preston Brooks for attacking Charles Sumner in 1856, a Southern editor called the English writer a "coster-monger" and dared him to come into the Southern part of the United States.[11]

Not only did the South react spontaneously and emotionally to what it regarded as unfair criticism, but it also argued that as a section it was treated unjustly by the rest of the country. It will be recalled that the feeling persisted that the federal government provided inadequate defenses against Indians on the south and southwestern frontier.[12] It hardly seemed an accident, moreover, that "every establishment of the government, navyyards, armories, military schools, etc." had been erected "to the north of the Potomac or on its borders." In fact it appeared "as if the Southern States were considered unsuitable for any national establishment, and all must, of necessity, be located at the North." [13]

Southerners came to feel that they were being deliberately mistreated. There was a record of exactions, they argued, by a ruthless majority of the hard earnings of the people of one section to build up overgrown monopolies in another; wasteful expenditures of the public treasury to create the necessity for high duties and depressive tariffs; and reckless expenditures for lighthouses, canals, and fortifications in one section, while the other was scarcely lighted, improved, or fortified. Past injustices were insignificant, one ardent Southerner contended in 1850, when compared with the effort to exclude Southern institutions from the Mexican cession despite the fact that the South contributed two-thirds of the forces in the Mexican War.[14]

This sensitivity combined with a growing regional pride to produce a distemper that was capable of the most volatile reactions when the South was subjected to strains and stresses. The pride that was characteristic of the person became a trait of the section; and gone was any disposition to make concessions. Southern pride in its institutions and ways of life was transformed into a fierce intolerance of everything outside of and the most uncritical and slavish acceptance of everything within the sectional sanctuary. "I'll give you my notion of things" declared a sturdy, old up-country planter shortly before the war. "I go first for Greenville, then for Greenville District, then for the up-country, then for South Carolina, then for the South, then for the United States

. . ." [15] A more articulate Southerner put a similar thought more cleverly when he said, "Our place in the union is provincial, and as such our peculiarities will have to be defended, excused, ridiculed, pardoned. We can take no pride in our national character, because we must feel that from our peculiar position we do not contribute to its formation." [16]

It would follow that persons living in an atmosphere charged with sectional pride would be extremely critical of persons of other sections. There was unconcealed delight when any Northern undertaking could be regarded as less than successful. In 1857, the *Daily Picayune* seemed joyous over the fact that less than one-third of the expected 12,800 citizen soldiers turned out for a military parade in New York City.[17] When Thomas Nichols made the trip from New Orleans to Mobile by boat in 1857, he engaged a "fiery Southerner" in conversation. The latter was critical of every phase of Northern life and bitter in his denunciation of Northern policies. He was unwilling to trust any Northern leader and was convinced that if a Southern President was not elected in 1860 the Union would be gone forever.[18]

This proclivity to criticize the North led Southerners to make disparaging remarks regarding the capacities of Northerners in such crucial pursuits as military activities. While one critic was willing to concede that they were vigorous and inventive, he insisted that Northerners were destitute of the capacity for control. And "while they evince no capacity to control, they are uncontrollable." In contrast the people of the South were the inheritors of a great tradition of command and ever remained masters of any situation in which they found themselves.[19]

The way in which large numbers looked on the South with increasing devotion and fidelity did not augur well for the spirit of American nationalism in the land below the Potomac. Indeed, signs of a nascent Southern nationalism became more apparent in the 1840's and 1850's. Even a unionist like Henry W. Hilliard manifested this growing spirit. In the Alabama legislature in 1839, he decried the growing hostility between the sections. "Yet, sir," he hastened to add, "the South is my own, my native land — my home, and the birth-place of my children. Her people are my people; her hopes are my hopes; her interests are my interests." [20]

Alexander Stephens was even more explicit, saying, in a speech in the Congress favoring the annexation of Texas, that he was "free from the influence of unjust prejudices and jealousies towards any part or section." Yet, he added, "I must confess that my feelings of attachment are most ardent towards that with which all my interests and associations are identified . . . The South is my home — my fatherland. There sleep the ashes of my sire and grandsires; there are my hopes and prospects; with her my fortunes are cast; her fate is my fate, and her destiny my destiny." [21] The expression of such sentiments by responsible men like Hilliard and Stephens reflected the deep attachment to the South eclipsing any loyalty to the Union, which helped to crystallize the movement toward Southern nationalism.

The notion that the South was unique, that it had a case to present to the world, and that its future course would be decided in terms of its own peculiar interests became more widespread in the period between the outbreak of the Mexican War and the election of Abraham Lincoln. When the *Southern Quarterly Review* changed hands in 1847, the new editor promised faithfully that the magazine would seek to stimulate Southern intellect and Southern learning. In addition, it would vigorously defend the peculiar forms of social life in the South for which the section was "arraigned before the bar of Christendom for alleged wrong-doing, oppression, and injustice." [22]

This was in conformity with the growing sentiment for Southern intellectual independence.[23] C. K. Marshall warned that if dissolution, "that sad catastrophe," should come, the South would not be as prepared as it should be to educate its own children. The real hope of the South lay in the development of a program for the education of Southern youth with Southern materials, he concluded.[24] A New Orleans editor argued that the effect of intellectual independence on the political and mental health of the South could not fail to have a good effect:

> Let us have independent thought. Push on the work. Stir up the apathetic. Wake up the dreamers. Shake off the incubus of mere party organization. Acknowledge fealty to nothing in party but principle . . . The fool is a slave to the past; the wise man understands the now, and equipping himself from the armory of the present, goes fotrh to meet the future. Push on the work.[25]

In 1857 *De Bow's Review* felt that the South had achieved a measure of intellectual independence, an important step toward the realization of a Southern nation. "Twenty years ago," the editor said, "the South had no thought — no opinions of her own. Then she stood behind all christendom, admitted her social structure, her habits, her economy, and her industrial pursuits to be wrong, deplored them as a necessity, and begged pardon for their existence. Now she is about to lead the thought and direct the practices of christendom; for christendom sees and admits that she has acted a silly and suicidal art in abolishing African slavery — the South a wise and prudent one in retaining it." [26] By that time Southerners could point with pride to various evidences of a growing sectional consciousness bordering on nationalism: academies, colleges, and universities were multiplying; literature was increasing; educational and commercial conventions were solidifying thought.

The relative absence of restlessness and lack of emigration seemed convincing proof to Southerners of the general prosperity of the section and the loyalty of its people. With a complacent air they pointed out that Northerners were to be found in every part of the hemisphere. While some regarded this continuous movement as evidence of an enterprizing character, their critical rivals preferred to think that such movement was "prompted by need and stimulated by the want of comfort at home." [27]

Professional Southerners even objected to their fellows' visiting the North for short periods. In 1850, the reviewer of Charles Lanman's *Letters from the Alleghany Mountains* dubbed as "Soft-heads" those Southerners who saw nothing good in their home surroundings. He insisted that it was not necessary to visit the North during the summer, that such visitors were "born and wedded to a sort of provincial servility that finds nothing grateful but the foreign." Only a cholera epidemic in the North forced some Southerners to discover that they had delightful resorts in their own section, he concluded.[28] The campaign to discourage Southerners from visiting in the North had met with some success. In 1858, a Southerner reported, with ill-concealed pleasure, that the springs and popular watering places of the Northern states were not as crowded with Southern families as they had been in previous years. Amid the South's own sublime mountain scenery, he said, "by the health-giving waters gushing out of the hillsides . . . they are gathering freshness and vigor, enjoying rustic pleasures and relaxation . . ." [29]

If the South was to turn its back on the world, build its own nation, become intellectually self-sufficient, and satisfy itself in the exclusive enjoyment of its own resources, it was desirable to develop ways and manners peculiar to itself. That arch protagonist Fitzhugh summed it up when he insisted that Southerners should become national, "nay, provincial, and cease to be imitative cosmopolitans." [30] William L. Yancey hoped that Southerners would cherish their peculiar ways. His aims, he declared, were to cast before the people of the South their great mass of wrongs, injuries, and insults. "One thing will catch our eye here and determine our hearts;

another thing elsewhere; all united, may yet produce spirit enough to lead us forward, to call forth a Lexington, to fight a Bunker Hill, to drive the foe from the city of our rights." [31]

The articulation of Southern aspirations by men like Fitzhugh and the leadership of men like Yancey contributed to the cohesion that bound the people of the South together in the struggle to achieve a measure of independence. Gradually, the geographic differences became unimportant, and the differences between the views represented by the moderate Jefferson Davis and the extremist Robert Toombs tended to disappear.[32] The differences decreased in importance under the pressure of "outside interference," and the overriding conviction was that the dispute between the North and the South was infinitely greater than any internal conflicts that could be imagined. As one writer put it, "under the pressure of foreign insolence and outrage, the Southern states have been drawing closer the bonds of a common brotherhood, and developing in self-reliance, energy, courage, and all the resources of independent nationality. They are rapidly aspiring to the station which God designed that they should occupy and adorn." [33]

That the North and South were drifting apart was a common view. Observers seemed to hope that, by discussion, they would make the rift more pronounced. In 1854, Henry C. Carey pointed out that differences between Northern and Southern thought were increasing daily, and "*must* eventually lead to separation." [34] In May 1857, the leading article in *Russell's Magazine* was "Southern and Northern Civilization Contrasted," which said, "the philosophy of the North is a dead letter to us . . . We cannot live honestly in the Union, because we are perpetually aiming to square the maxims of an impracticable philosophy with the practice which nature and circumstances force upon us." [35] In June 1860, the *Southern Literary Messenger* featured, "The Difference of Race Between Northern People and Southern

People," which emphasized the differences in temperament, religion, mental capacities, and numerous other areas.[36] A. Roane handled the problem for *De Bow's Review* in "The South, In the Union or Out of It." For him, one of the principal differences was the overwhelming military superiority of the South, which would ensure the achievement of political independence after separation.[37]

It was important to give some attention to the military, for strength in arms is an important factor in any nationalist movement. This aspect could hardly be overlooked by a section whose people took such great pride in their military prowess. It is not without significance that the rise of military schools and the growing interest in the citizen soldiery coincided with the rise of Southern nationalism. If the interest in military affairs encouraged the movement for independence, the latter, in turn, stimulated the growth of the martial spirit.[38]

The role of the military in the growth of nationalism was important, not only because of the promise of protection and defense that it gave but also because it provided the political symbolism required by the state.[39] The psychological effect of this display of power and symbolism on the people was profound but difficult to measure. If the Southern confederacy was not to die a-borning, it had to understand this factor and to exploit it as it struggled to emerge.

The evidences of unity in the final decades before the Civil War are an impressive manifestation of the emergence of Southern nationalism. In 1848, during the controversy following the Mexican War, sixty-nine Southern members of Congress issued an address to their constituents urging "unity among ourselves." Within a few weeks, Florida served notice that she was ready to join other Southern states "for a defence of our rights, whether through a Southern convention or otherwise." [40] In 1850, Mississippi warned that "the time has arrived when, if they hope to preserve their exist-

ence as equal members of the confederacy . . . they must prepare to act — to act with resolution, firmness and unity of
purpose . . ." [41]

Various organizations sprang into existence to facilitate
the achievement of Southern unity and to assist in the defense of Southern rights. Among them were the numerous
Southern Rights Associations, which appealed especially to
the younger men. In 1851, a chapter was organized at the
University of South Carolina, and its members urged other
college students to do likewise.[42] In May 1851, the Southern
Right Associations of South Carolina met at Charleston and
talked freely of secession and of the state's right to establish
adequate defense against the encroachments on its powers.[43]
Upon observing their inclination toward drastic action, Benjamin F. Perry said that the most prominent agitators were
young men "panting for fame and military laurels." [44]

In other states special conventions of Southern Rights
Associations were held; their recommendations were similar
to those of the South Carolina group.[45] The commercial conventions, moreover, gave attention to the rights of the Southern states and, in doing so, contributed substantially to sectional unity. At the New Orleans Convention of 1855,
Captain Albert Pike of Arkansas offered a resolution condemning the North and calling for unified Southern action.
He accused the non-slaveholding states of exhibiting an
"utter want of fraternal spirit" and said that their conduct
"not only fully warrants a union of the Southern states *within the* Constitution . . . but makes such a union an inexorable necessity . . ." The resolution then called on the Southern states to encourage those pursuits that would guarantee
the self-sufficiency of the section when the break with the
North came.[46]

These disparate, independent efforts did not satisfy the
vigorous champions of Southern rights.[47] In 1848, William
Yancey wrote a friend that the remedy for the South's plight

was in "a diligent organization of her true men, for prompt resistance to the next aggression." No party, national or sectional, could save the South, he argued:

But if we could do as our fathers did, organize Committees all over the cotton states . . . we shall fire the Southern heart — instruct the Southern mind — give courage to each other, and at the proper moment, by one organized concerted action, we can precipitate the cotton states into a revolution.[48]

Ruffin had suggested the organization of a League of United Southerners to operate "by discussion, publication, and public speeches" on the public mind of the South.[49] Taking the suggestion seriously, in the summer of 1858, Yancey organized the Montgomery League of United Southerners whose object was "to create a sound public opinion in the South on the subject of enforcing the rights of the South in the Union." [50]

Within a year the League had many chapters. Its March 1859 statement called for *"firm, united, organized* defence . . . Organization is indispensable . . . it is only by associated and well-directed effort that great objects are accomplished. And we solemnly believe that it is only by a union of the true men of the South . . . that we can avert a fate, the most ignominious that ever befell a people." Southerners were urged to form associations, to put them into communication with each other, to hold conventions, and to do everything possible "to meet and repel the inroads of an insolent foe, who already vaunts his triumph, and claims your native South as a 'conquered province.' " [51]

In an atmosphere of frenzied agitation such as that produced by the proclamations of the Southern Rights Associations, the commercial conventions, and the League of United Southerners, the people of the South were in no mood to meet the challenge of the North passively. Southerners almost invariably reacted to Northern criticism by hurling angry threats and defiances, as though these very acts strengthened the hand of the South. During the dispute over the admission of California in 1850, one Southern editor feared that war would follow California's admission as a free state, a war the South could not decline "without dishonor and disaster." He pointed out that the six states that opposed Clay's bill had half a million brave men with their own horses and rifles. "The liberties of these states were won by the sword — and if necessary by the sword they will be maintained." [52]

**1 2**

# Ready to Fight

In the final decade before the war, Southerners talked freely of the possibilities of conflict, and the most extreme dared the North to stand up and fight. In advocating separation, the editor of the *Southern Quarterly Review* said that this object could be achieved peacefully, because Northerners would not risk defeat at the hands of the South:

> The Yankees are a calculating people, and would easily understand that it is to their interest to keep quiet. They well know that, if once aroused, we could never be "subdued," and that the first gun would bring a million rifles to the defence of the country.[1]

"Rutledge" struck the same note in urging South Carolina to declare its independence. "A brave and determined people may be whipped," he said, "but, if united, they can never be subdued . . . We certainly have the 'sinews of war,' and from the nature of our population and territory, we could keep in check at least 1,000,000 men that might be sent to invade us . . ." [2] William H. Trescott of Charleston doubted that the North would fight to keep the South in the Union. If he was wrong in this opinion, he warned that "there are more terrible disasters than war, and in the perpetual cry of peace, peace, there is as much selfishness as sense." [3]

Many Southern leaders were openly defiant and showed a

willingness to fight that must have horrified their peace-loving brethren. In his 1855 message to the Alabama Legislature, Governor Winston accused the North of making war on the South and urged his people to reply with the only kind of action that the North would respect.[4] Governor McWillie of Mississippi called on his people to show the Northern warriors "that we cannot be attacked with impunity; but, on the contrary, that we are fully ready, willing, and able to take care of ourselves — in the Union if we can, out of it if we must." [5] The time had come, William Yancey said, to stand firmly. "Is your courage up to the highest point? Have you prepared yourselves to enter upon the great field of self-denial as your fathers did, and undergo, if necessary, another seven years' war in order that you and your posterity may enjoy the blessings of liberty? If you are, I am with you; if you are not, I am not with you." [6]

Although the Southerners might have appreciated fully the implications of Yancey's challenge, they could truthfully answer that they had devoted much energy to the problem. Between 1845 and 1860, the South's preoccupation with preparedness clearly indicates that some notions of independence were held. At the Memphis Commercial Convention of 1845, Southerners called on Congress to establish a national armory at some point on the western waters and to complete the military road from the Mississippi River through the swamps to the highlands of Arkansas. It called on Southerners to build their defenses in every way possible.[7] In 1846, Lewis Troost of Mobile pointed out that the Congress had done very little to provide the South with military strength. It was, therefore, left to the South, whose "laws and habits tend to make almost every individual a disciplined and effective soldier," to build its own defenses.[8]

As the years passed, agitation for preparedness increased. In 1847, Longstreet was certain that there would soon be a showdown. "Now we should begin calmly and prudently," he counseled, "to prepare for this event. We should have a military school in every State . . . Tactics should be a part of the study and training of every college. Our militia laws should undergo a thorough remodeling." There was no danger in building up the military defenses of the section, he added. But if so, it was not nearly as dangerous as abolitionism, "or apathy, or tardiness to meet the inevitable issues." [9]

Finally, very specific proposals appeared, urging that the South's military might be developed. In South Carolina, Governor Whitemarsh Seabrook urged the establishment of a third military academy, to be located in the piedmont section. Perhaps he had in mind "the ideal of a trinity of military and scholastic forces to embrace all of South Carolina from mountain to sea." [10] In November 1850, a South Carolina critic called for the strengthening of the military academies through improvement of the engineering departments, artillery instruction, and by establishing a pyrotechnic laboratory for the preparation of ammunition. "Victory is not to the strong," he concluded, "but to the confident; and he who has made the best preparations, is furnished with the best munitions, and expends them with the most skill, is sure of victory." [11] This was also the view of Walter F. Colquitt of Georgia who told the Nashville Commercial Convention that the Southern states should be moulding bullets, casting cannon, and filling arsenals in order to defend their rights.[12]

A spirit of self-sacrifice and Spartan austerity was advocated by those who were anxious to put the South's defenses in order. The *Self Instructor* of Charleston reminded its readers that men who dared to be free "availed themselves of the military resources of the swamps, and with guns whose locks were oftimes tied by a string to the stocks, with swords beat out of mill-saws, and with spears made of plough-bolts ground sharp, held the field against the well officered and well supplied troops of the oppressors . . ." [13] The *Daily Delta* warned that only the most complete and selfless devotion to the cause of Southern rights would achieve a victory over forces led by men like Sumner and Seward. There was no reason to be dismayed, however. With men like Stephens, Toombs, "and a host of other gallant sons of the South, we need not fear the joust of arms — for the God of Israel will be on the side of His children." [14]

The election of 1856 brought about the defeat of Frémont, the antislavery candidate; but ardent Southerners could find little satisfaction in Buchanan's becoming President. They knew that the Republicans were already preparing for victory in 1860, and there was despair in many Southern quarters. "Black Republicans" were scheming to complete their subjugation. One editor screamed, "they are brightening their weapons every day. The tramp of their gathering hosts may be heard on every Northern plain. The tocsin of war sounds shrilly through every Northern valley."

What is the South doing for defence? What is she doing for preparation? Where is her encampment, where are her leaders, and who is her Fabius, or her Scipio Africanus? Alas! Where? Alas! Who? But never despair; when the hour comes the man will come, doubtless. We may wait awhile for the coming man, but we can wait no longer with safety to prepare for the inevitable hour . . .[15]

Meanwhile, Ruffin offered similar advice. He asserted that the expected submission of the South had been imputed to the dread of the Southern people of certain ruin in the event of separation and war. He rejected the view that Southerners were timid or that they would be ruined in a military operation, but was willing to admit, however, that the idea of Southern weakness, together with the absence of military preparation, might easily produce a war as the result of separation. He was convinced, therefore, that due preparation for war was the best way to ensure the maintenance of peace.[16]

An important aspect of such agitation was the gospel of

self-sufficiency preached by the South's politicians and businessmen in the last two decades before the war. The gospel was propagated in the legislatures and in the Congress; it was preached from the pulpit and platform; it was urged in pamphlets and newspapers; it was vigorously promulgated in the commercial conventions and Southern Rights Associations.[17] While the desire for local prosperity was a compelling argument in favor of agricultural diversity and industrialization, other persuasive elements were not overlooked. Economic independence was an indispensable part of a program to throw off the yoke of political domination.[18] As early as 1839 an advocate for the rebuilding of Southern commercial life combined these arguments effectively. Of the South's economic leaders he said:

> Let them lay well their plans and come to the contest with capital and energy; and like the gallant yeoman in Ivanhoe the South will find us ever ready to add our halloo to a good shot, or a gallant blow.[19]

An 1845 argument insisted that, as long as the South was dependent on the North and on foreign countries for food, clothing, and other necessaries of life, it would be in thraldom.[20] Self-reliance and preparation for defense were necessary to the South's salvation.[21]

The most effective argument that related the need for prosperity to the need for defense through self-sufficiency was advanced by the far-sighted factory master, William Gregg. In *Essays on Domestic Industry,* he said that those "who look for so direful a calamity as the dissolution of the Union should, above all others, be most anxious to diversify the industrial pursuits of South Carolina, as to render her independent of all other countries." He was certain that the state's defense would be in better order if the idle people were put to work in textile mills instead of spending their time following military parades through the streets.[22] Originally of the opinion that manufacturing could best thrive on peace and union, Gregg later became an ardent advocate of preparedness.[23] In February 1861, he completely rejected the notion that the South should depend on the outside world for anything; and he urged the expansion of Southern manufacturing before it was too late.[24]

James D. B. De Bow did much to advance the idea of industrialization and self-sufficiency. Article after article on the subject appeared in his *Review* and elsewhere. He was disturbed by the fact that the military spirit of the times tended to discourage the accumulation of capital goods such as factories because they were rendered hazardous in time of predatory wars. The South would never be strong or capable of defending itself unless its factories were encouraged to produce the things needed.[25] In 1856 he reprinted an article which doubtless expressed his own views on the need for factories. "Let the South but adopt a system of manufacturing and internal improvements to the extent which her interests require, her danger demands, and her ability is able to accomplish, and in a few years Northern fanaticism and abolitionism may rave, gnash their teeth, and howl in vain." [26]

De Bow seemed more alert than most to the possibilities of radically different industrial enterprises. When the Southern Oil Company was founded in 1859, he immediately saw the relationship between the new industry and the intersectional struggle.

We may . . . congratulate the entire South on the acquisition of another powerful weapon of defence against the aggression of the North. The Southern Oil Company is a fixed and permanent institution of the South; and it will not be many years before it will be as important as a revenue as our sugar or cotton.[27]

By 1860, the gospel of industrialization and self-sufficiency had been written into the Southern platform. Some believed a diversified and prosperous economic structure to be absolutely necessary to the political independence to which an increasing number was committed. Others, moving beyond that position, regarded the expanded economic program as an important military precaution.[28] Under the pressure of strained intersectional relations, more and more Southerners were shifting to this latter position.

In the atmosphere of conflict the manufacture of arms assumed an importance that increased as the tensions accelerated. This was the final step toward industrial self-sufficiency. Virginia's tradition of arms manufacturing dated back to 1797, when the legislature authorized the erection of an arms factory on the James River near Richmond. For several years after the beginning of production in 1802, the Virginia foundry engaged in the making of muskets, rifles, powder horns, cavalry swords, and the like. Although it was disbanded in 1815, the sentiment favoring the local manufacture of arms persisted for the next generation.[29] In the forties and fifties Virginians took pride in the work of private foundries, such as the Tredegar Iron Works, the Welford Foundry, and smaller establishments.[30] By 1860 the Tredegar factory was in a position to produce large quantities of arms and ammunition with great efficiency.[31]

There were a few other arms factories scattered over the South. A prosperous brass and iron foundry was in operation in Natchez in 1848; at that time the owner, Maurice Lisle, was employing as many as twenty-three operatives and was filling orders for arms from various parts of the South. There was also a gun factory in Natchez, operated by the firm of Fitzpatrick, Odell, and Newcomb and employing six artificers. The business was so lucrative that the firm announced that it would like to increase its number of employees if good workmen could be found.[32]

Agitation for the establishment of arms factories increased. Governors called for it in their messages to legislatures; conventions of businessmen advocated it.[33] In 1856, a commercial convention resolution declared that "the establishment of foundries and works for the casting of cannon and the manufacture of arms should be recommended to the attention of the several Southern States." [34] Early in 1860, De Bow said that if the South was deficient in arms, "self-preservation requires that they should be speedily provided." He was happy to learn that state legislatures and local foundries were giving increasing attention to this urgent matter.[35]

It would be a real victory, Southerners thought, if they could persuade the federal government to establish an ordnance foundry south of the Potomac, and several vigorous efforts were made when the intersectional controversy was at its height. In 1848, Mark Cooper, proprietor of an iron foundry near Rome, Georgia, urged his friend Howell Cobb to use his influence to obtain a national foundry for the South, preferably to be located in Georgia.[36] In 1850 the Alabama Railroad Convention, meeting in Mobile, forwarded a resolution to the Secretary of War, declaring it the duty of the federal government to establish additional foundries for the manufacture of ordnance and arms. This contended that natural resources and transportation facilities presented to the national government persuasive inducements to establish the foundry in Alabama.[37]

In 1858, the citizens of Richmond forwarded a set of resolutions to the Secretary of War urging the establishment of a foundry in their city. After listing the factors that should be considered in making a decision regarding the proposed site, it asserted that Richmond presented the best qualifications of any place in the country.[38] None of these propositions received favorable or, perhaps, even serious consideration, but they suggest the enterprise of Southerners that was doubtless stimulated by their propensity for military matters and their growing apprehension. It would be well to keep new ordnance foundries out of the North; it would be even better to have them in the South.

Efforts were also made to persuade the federal government to establish new armories and other military installations in the South. In 1843 the Mayor and the Board of Aldermen of Memphis issued a pamphlet giving reasons why there should be established in that city a Western Armory and Naval Depot and Dock Yard. It set forth the argument "in a bold light," but the federal government did not heed the plea.[39] Several years later Troost urged the establishment of an armory in the West, where, he said the government would enjoy facilities superior to those at Springfield or at Harpers Ferry. In his opinion, Harpeth Shoals on the Cumberland River in Tennessee offered the best advantages to be found anywhere in the country.[40]

As in other matters of defense, the people of the South found that they had to provide their own armories; and they did not wait for federal action. States and local military companies had been building armories since the early part of the century. In 1816, the General Assembly of Virginia provided for the erection of three arsenals, in each of which were to be stored 20,000 stands of arms.[41] In 1823 the legislature of Tennessee appropriated funds for the erection of an armory in Nashville.[42] In 1847 the people of Savannah, Georgia, constructed an armory, regarded as a great ornament to the city, to house the arms of the Chatham Artillery.[43] In 1857 Mobile was excited over the completion of its new armory for the Continental State Artillery.[44] The new armory on Girod Street in New Orleans, one of the finest in the country, was for the Washington Artillery.[45] In other parts of the South the people were providing housing for the arms and accoutrements of their citizen soldiery.

The one area in which the Southern states had some legitimate claim on military support from the federal government was in the matter of arms for the state militias. Under an act of Congress passed in 1808, arms and equipment were to be distributed annually to state militias according to the latest returns of the number of effective militia in each state. In view of the fact that many states did not make prompt and regular returns and that numerous inequities were possible under the arrangement, it was not satisfactory. Despite the pleas of the Chief of Ordnance, there was no change until 1855, when representation in the Congress was made the basis for the distribution of arms to the several states.

In the final decade before the outbreak of the war there was a remarkable increase in the pressure placed on the War Department by the Southern states for more arms than the quotas assigned them. Some of the pressure was, perhaps, the result of unfamiliarity with the law and with the channels through which requests for arms were to go; some stemmed from efforts to take advantage of the fact that, throughout the decade, all U. S. Secretaries of War were Southerners.[46] There can be no doubt, however, that much of this frantic effort to secure arms grew out of the increasing apprehension on the part of the South regarding future relations with the North.

Laws governing the distribution of arms made it clear that state governors and adjutant generals were to make the requests and receive the arms, but numerous individuals as well as local military organizations sought arms from Washington. In 1851 two Tennesseans unsuccessfully requested rifles for their volunteer corps, neglecting to clear the matter with the governor.[47] The Natchez Guards were likewise unsuccessful.[48] During the summer, the people of St. Martinsville Parish in Louisiana sought a piece of artillery, but the Chief of Ordnance pointed out that he lacked authority to comply with the request.[49]

The anxiety of Southern officials to secure their full arms quotas began in 1856, by which time the South's preparedness program was proceeding with full speed. The Savannah Commercial Convention adopted a resolution asking the Southern Congressional representatives to inquire whether

their states were getting their "full quota of arms distribut-
able under the Acts of Congress; and whether there is placed
within their limits, in the arsenals of the United States, their
full proportion of arms of every kind, and all the munitions
of war, camp, and other equipage of the United States." If
irregularities were discovered they were urged to take immediate action to place the Southern states upon a footing
of equality with the other states.[50]

In 1859, requests for arms increased considerably. When,
in February, three Georgians requested eighty sword bayonets, they were informed that their state had already drawn
its full quota for that year.[51] A week later a cavalry company
in Rome, Georgia, sought to secure arms from the ordnance
office.[52] The disturbance at Harpers Ferry in the fall of that
year gave Virginia and other Southern states an excellent
opportunity to press for more arms, and they made the most
of it. By the end of October, the state's adjutant general had
requested more than half of the state's quota for the following year, and the requests had been complied with.[53] In
December the governor of North Carolina requested two
thousand long range rifles with bayonets. This was a fantastic
request which, as the Chief of Ordnance pointed out, would
not only have absorbed the state's quota for the next six years,
but would have made difficult the fulfillment of requisitions
from any of the other governors during the period.[54]

For more than a year Virginia used John Brown's raid as
a pretext for additional requests. In November 1860, the
adjutant general made a request for an advance in arms
equivalent to the quota for 1861. He explained that "the
pressure of extra-ordinary circumstances" prompted the request and that if Congress required it, Virginia would pay
for the arms or make a return "in kind and of equal value
as soon as they can be fabricated at the armory of the state
now going into operation." [55] In reply the Chief of Ordnance
reminded the Virginia official that his state had already

drawn its full quota for 1861, and arms equivalent to 203 muskets on its quota for 1862![56]

The ordnance office had a policy of ordering sufficient training muskets to supply the needs of the Military Academy at West Point and the Naval Academy at Annapolis. In the final decade before the Civil War, it had to handle requests for such arms from Southern military schools. In February 1851, officials of the Arkansas Military Institute requested fifty cadet muskets. At that time the Chief of Ordnance laid down his policy.

> The object of the application may be obtained by a requisition from the Governor for fifty muskets, as a portion of the quota due the State of Arkansas, under the Law for arming the Militia. They will then be immediately supplied; and when in possession of the state, they may be placed by the Governor in use of the State Institute, until the other arms, given to it by the Act of the Legislature, can be regularly required and furnished.[57]

It was not possible to comply promptly with such requests, since there was no means of predicting the extent of the needs. The Chief of Ordnance had to explain this to the Governor of Mississippi who had requested 150 cadet muskets and accoutrements for Jefferson College.[58] By May 1852, the ordnance office had received the following requests for cadet muskets: Virginia, 300, supplied; Alabama, 125; Mississippi, 150; Georgia, 125; South Carolina, 200, and Virginia, 200, second requisition.[59] In 1853, Connecticut became the first and only Northern state to request cadet muskets.[60]

The problem soon reached the point where the ordnance office not only had difficulty in filling the requests but questioned the service provided for the nation's militia system by such a program of training. Regarding a new request of South Carolina for 326 cadet muskets, the Colonel of Ordnance told the Secretary of War that the request did not seem to be in accordance with the purpose for which the rule had been relaxed. The office had undertaken to provide arms *temporarily* for the state's military schools. The thing was now out of hand. He therefore suggested "that the extent to which issues of cadet arms may be made, be specified, which . . . may best be done by limiting it to a certain portion of each State's quota for one year, say two thirds." [61]

By 1860, the Southern preparedness frenzy had assumed such proportions that no possible avenue to secure arms was left unexplored. Those states that had drawn and, in some cases, exceeded their arms quotas from the federal government investigated the possibility of purchasing arms — from the government or elsewhere. The amount of cooperation that Southern representatives received from some federal officials in the year of secession is little short of amazing. In January 1860, the governor of Georgia asked the Secretary of War to tell him where he could secure arms "of the most approved and latest patterns, consisting of muskets, rifles, and pistols, with all the necessary and usual accoutrements, and also some artillery equipments." William Maynadier, the Captain of Ordnance, supplied the names and addresses of the firms from which the federal government purchased pistols, swords, sabers, and accoutrements for cavalry, infantry, and riflemen. He explained that muskets, rifles, and artillery equipment were manufactured in United States armories and arsenals. He then noted that federal armories could not manufacture for states without additional legislation, but "such legislation would secure additional advantage of giving employment to the national armories in greater proportion to their capacity for manufacturing than is furnished by the means usually appropriated for the purpose." [62]

In April a group of Arkansans sought to purchase arms from the federal government. The ordnance office informed them that more than 26,000 old-style muskets — altered to percussion — had been placed on sale in April 1859, and that some were still available. Rifles, in which the group was interested, had not been offered for public bids and consequently none could be sold "in conformity to the regulation, by private sale." [63] In September, when the quartermaster general of Alabama sought to purchase a quantity of "Mississippi Rifles," the ordnance office informed him that the only such rifles that had been offered for sale were unserviceable. There were, however, at the Baton Rouge Arsenal, 122 flint lock rifles and 1,385 altered to percussion that were serviceable and were to be offered for sale.[64]

After the election of Lincoln, with the talk of secession and war, the Southern states pressed even harder for arms and other military equipment. On November 19, Virginia was impatiently waiting for the six 12-pound howitzers that had been ordered earlier from the Washington Navy Yard.[65] The following day a group of Louisiana citizens offered to purchase seventy small percussion muskets, together with bayonet scabbards, and cartridge and cap boxes. The ordnance office said that the only arms the federal government could sell were those that had already been advertised and that did not include items of the description requested.[66] A similar reply was given to George Gordon of Savannah, Georgia, who wanted to purchase "75 to 100 'Minnie Cadet Muskets' for the Phoenix Riflemen of that place." [67]

Two of the most irresponsible compliances with requests of Southerners who were arming for war were made in 1860. On November 21, G. W. Randolph requested permission for the master armorer of Virginia to use and take drawings of the government patterns of arms. William Maynadier, Captain of Ordnance, recommended that the request be granted. On November 26, the same request was made, and Maynadier again recommended that it be granted.[68] On November 24, Governor Brown of Georgia asked for sample sets of certain military accoutrements as part of Georgia's arms quota for 1861. Georgia's quota for 1861 had already been filled, Maynadier informed the Governor on December 1, and such articles could not be sold. However, in a spirit of cooperation, he added:

> There will be no difficulty, however, in Governor Brown's obtaining them if he will write to 'Major William A. Thornton, United States Arsenal, New York' and request him to purchase for the State,
>
> Two sets of Infantry accoutrements complete; two sabre belts and plates, complete; two sabre knots; two holsters (pouches) for Colt's belt pistols; all of the latest U. S. Army patterns.
>
> I doubt not that Major Thornton will make the purchase for the Governor with pleasure.[69]

By this time the union was all but dissolved.

With John B. Floyd of Virginia as Secretary of War in Buchanan's cabinet, Southerners had some reason to believe that they could secure advantages. This explains, in part, the numerous requests for arms and other war materials during the years of Floyd's incumbency. The laws covering the distribution of arms frequently acted as a restraining force, even if officials were inclined to honor the South's requests. What the Secretary of War could or would do, on his own and yet within the law, was another matter. The nearest that Floyd came to extending assistance to the South's preparedness program was in his policy of 1859–1860 of removing some goods of war from Northern to Southern arsenals.

On December 30, 1859, Floyd ordered Craig, his Chief of Ordnance, to remove some 115,000 old model muskets and rifles from the Springfield Armory and the Watertown and Watervliet Arsenals to five federal arsenals in North Carolina, South Carolina, Georgia, Alabama, and Louisiana. By the spring of 1860 the orders had been carried out.[70] These arms had been classified as unserviceable, and some were presumably removed to make way for more modern equipment that was being produced at Springfield and elsewhere. When the war came, Floyd, having resigned his cabinet post and become a secessionist, was accused of conspiring to provide the South with arms with which to make war on the federal government. This accusation was never proved.[71]

A more serious and questionable transaction was Floyd's verbal order of December 20, 1860 to Captain Maynadier to remove some heavy artillery from Pittsburgh to fortify Ship Island and Galveston, Texas. At the time, the fortifications were not even ready for the artillery. The people of Pittsburgh were indignant. They protested vigorously in a wire to President Buchanan. Before the heavy pieces were actually shipped, Floyd had resigned; and his successor, Joseph Holt, rescinded the order.[72]

At a time when the country was in grave danger of disintegration, Floyd did little or nothing to prepare it. It is entirely possible that he had no ulterior motives in ordering such large quantities of arms to the South. In doing so, however, and at the worst possible time, he provided weapons the South lacked, which although out-of-date, were an attractive prize for a weapon-starved section in the winter of 1860–1861. Meanwhile, he did little to put his department or the national military establishment in a condition to meet the impending emergency of which he must have been fully apprized. In permitting members of the ordnance office to give military advice to Southern states, even after the secession movement was under way, he showed clearly that he had been unduly influenced by the South's atmosphere of conflict.

The war spirit had all but captivated the South. The incident at Harpers Ferry confirmed its worst fears. Even in quarters where there was a disinclination to prepare for war, there was an almost complete surrender to the atmosphere of conflict that prevailed. There was a veritable outburst of military enthusiasm in Virgina, where the legislature appropriated more than $500,000 to put the state on a war footing.[73] New military companies sprang up, the Central Southern Rights Association of Richmond was reactivated, and more than 250 Southern students, studying medicine in

Philadelphia, descended on Richmond.[74] The air was so tense with excitement and the military preparations so extensive that an English visitor asked her host if he was expecting a war with England or France. When he said that soldiers might be required nearer home than that, "Canada?" she asked. "No, madam; we may require our soldiers at our own homes, if things continue to go as they have done of late." [75]

It was the same in other parts of the South. In November 1859, some North Carolinians were demanding the construction of at least three arsenals in the state, while others wanted a special "preparedness" session of the state legislature. At a Wilson County mass meeting, a resolution was adopted declaring that efficient military organization was necessary in the South. Indeed, "the system of aggression, insult and spoliation embodied in the words 'irrepressible conflict' from being preached in theory, has of late been practically inaugurated." [76] In South Carolina — which needed no outside stimulus for its warlike conduct — Henry Ravenel observed that the John Brown raid had increased the spirit of disunion and preparedness in his state as well as elsewhere in the South.[77] Turner Ashby summed up the South's attitude:

The war spirit of the country is aroused and yonder group of horsemen are not discussing field sport or the contents of the late number of the *American Farmer,* but the mysteries of the well-worn work on Military Tactics or the latest news from Washington City. Men are growing desirous to know, not how to cultivate, but how to defend their soil.[78]

With every state in the South actively readying itself for war long before the election of Lincoln, there was little chance for peace. It was disturbing to anyone who hoped that the Union would be saved. William T. Sherman, from his excellent vantage point as the head of the Louisiana State Seminary of Learning and Military Academy, wrote his brother John that he did not like the looks of the times. "This political turmoil," he complained, "the sending of commissions from State to State, the organization of military schools and establishments and universal belief in the South that disunion is not only possible but certain — are bad signs . . . Disunion would be civil war, and you politicians would lose all charm. Military men would then step on the tapis, and you would have to retire." [79] Sherman could have added that in the South the military and the political arm were all but one and that the influence of the former was already just about decisive.

The movement for nationalism, the angry threats and defiances, and the program of preparedness had combined to produce a warlike atmosphere throughout the South. In 1844, after reporting on the condition of the state arsenals, Governor Hammond declared that South Carolina was prepared, at any moment, to arm one-half of its whole militia.[80] In 1847, Edwin Heriot declared that Charleston's military resources were remarkable for a city of its size.[81] In the 1850's, talk of war prompted the Louisiana legislature to appropriate special funds for the improvement of the Washington Artillery of New Orleans and other volunteer organizations.[82] Feverish preparation, which resulted in the great improvement of every aspect of Richmond's fighting arm caused one observer to conclude that it was "admirably qualified to resist foreign invasion, or to put down intestinal war." [83]

Southerners saw nothing invidious in the comparison of the military resources of the colonies in 1775 with those of the South of the 1850's. William Martin boasted that America's independence was won "with an average of 56,042 continental militia, rank and file, many of whom never entered the field." Now, the South alone had a militia of 700,000, and in an emergency, the number could be increased to one million.[84] Speaking before the Southern Convention at Knoxville, De Bow said that if war should come, the South would be protected against invasion by the able leadership of well-trained officers, the availability of adequate manpower to fight the battles, and "her semi-military system of society that has at all times raised her martial character to the highest rank." [85]

In the spring of 1861, De Bow reprinted from the *Memphis Appeal* what might be regarded as the final accounting of the military resources of the South before the war. In the arsenals of the South there were 290,000 stands of arms, including those transferred on Floyd's orders; 417,000 arms that had been purchased by the several states; and arms already possessed by the Southern states, which would increase the number to more than a million. "Besides this there are thought to be 2,000,000 of private arms which will answer all practical purposes in case of invasion by the enemy. In face of the above figures, let no one deny that the South is sufficiently well armed to drive the last minion of federal power from her soil in any possible emergency." [86]

In any accounting of the South's military resources, consideration must be given to what De Bow had earlier called the semi-military character of Southern society. In the final months before the Civil War this aspect of the South's resources was one of the most obvious if not the strongest. Men casually spoke of war as a pastime, and plumed cavaliers with their jangling spurs and rattling sabers sat around discussing with infantrymen the relative merits of the several techniques of fighting.

Southerners had, for several years, been inclined to regard war as a beneficent force for the improvement of mankind. They had given only slight support to the peace movement.[87] Persons who actively opposed war were almost as rare as abolitionists.[88] Judge Alexander Meek said that brave men preferred to die in battle. "Sooner or later death must come to us all," he told the veterans of the Mexican War in 1848; "the fresh green turf is a far sweeter couch than the feverish bed, — and there is no nobler boon than to 'look proudly to Heaven from the death bed of fame.'" [89] Senator Herschel

V. Johnson of Georgia said, "The results of war and the developments of science are but the voice of prophecy. The one opens the door for civilization, and the other sends its ministers by the power of steam, and speeds them upon the wing of 'seraphic lightening.' " [90]

One writer stated that the day of battle was the birthday of the greatness of nations and that beneficial effects to civilization and "the general weal of man and nations" have followed great wars and conquests.[91] On the beneficial effects of war, none was more eloquent and persuasive than the superintendent of the North Carolina Military Institute, Major D. H. Hill. Assuming the inevitability of war, he contended that it was the better part of wisdom to do everything possible to secure the greatest advantage over one's enemies. One should not be disturbed over the inevitability of war for "the first great stimulus to action which the mind of man ever received proceeded from the necessities of war." The mental resources of a nation are never so fully and rapidly developed as during a period of active hostilities. The Revolution brought forth Washington, Hamilton, and Jefferson; while the War of 1812 produced Calhoun, Clay, Webster, and others. Since 1812, the situation had been miserable. "The dwarfing effects of a fifty-years peace has put pygmies in our Halls of Legislation instead of these mighty men of old." Wars, Hill concluded, "are the best stimuli for the intellectual, scientific, and moral development of mankind." [92]

"Je Reviendra" of Norfolk, Virginia, said, in "The Soldier's Remonstrance" which appeared during the Mexican War:

> Why would you check my proud career?
> I love the Hero's glorious life;
> Give me the rush, the din the cheer,
> Of Squadrons mixed in deadly strife:
> Be mine the sword whose flashes bright
> Are foremost in the thick'ning fight!
> Hark! The War-shout! I know it well —

Thy topmost speed my gallant grey!
I cannot stay to bid farewell —
Dash bravely on — away! away!
Methinks the eagle's wing would tire
To match my charger's heels of fire!
Ha! They have met — see, see the flash,
That gleams within yon sulph'rous cloud!
Hark! To the valley's hurtling crash! —
The requiem o'er the warrior's shroud.
Oh! What of all life's fleeting bliss,
Can match one glorious hour like this! [93]

In the frenzied years of the late fifties, Southern bards saw
in war not only release from oppression but a glorious opportunity to pay tribute to the gallantry of the man who would
save their homes. Adrian Beaufain, after describing the impending crisis in his "Songs of the South" gave the following
picture of how men of the South would rise up:

And that young virgin land shall no longer
By the Tyrant's stern hoof be debased,
For the God in his own clime grows stronger
And his altars now rise undefaced.
From mountain, from river, from valley,
The calls of the true heart ascend;
And the brave to the battle-field rally,
And the boom and the danger impend.
The blood of the foe streams like water,
And the fields wear the garment of slaughter.[94]

In the spring of 1860, De Bow did his part to whip up
enthusiasm among the fainthearted by publishing "The Love
of Danger and of War." This article called war man's favorite
and most honorable pursuit. While the most dangerous of
pursuits, it prepared nations to enjoy and make good use of
peace. War drew social classes closer together, as they united
for common defense. "Frequent wars of invasion" he concluded, "are necessary to keep nations progressive. War alone
subjects all to those perils, trials, vicissitudes, dangers and
privations that are necessary agencies in developing, matur-

ing, and fortifying character, and in exciting intellectual energy, activity, and inventiveness." [95]

Little was left to say except for George Fitzhugh to condemn the Republicans during the campaign of 1850 on the grounds that they favored peace. While wars might seem unnecessary and unnatural, "God, who is wiser than we, has instituted them for salutary purposes, and prompted mankind to prepare for them." The attempt to dispense with war altogether was "only one of the thousand forms in which Republicanism wars against nature." [96]

Carl Von Clausewitz, the Prussian militarist, could not have found words to give greater praise of war than the Southern leaders just before the Civil War. Like them Clausewitz contended that war was a dangerous and glorious undertaking that required courage as the first quality of the warrior. Unlike the Southerners, who seemed to rely almost entirely on the courage born of their martial spirit, Clausewitz was keenly aware of the elements of uncertainty and chance involved in any military operation. He, therefore, conceded the possibility of failure of such a venture.[97] By 1860, the eyes of many Southerners were closed to the possibility of failure in the impending conflict that they regarded as inevitable.

If they could no longer weigh such matters carefully, it was, in part, because the conditions that had led to such widespread bellicosity had created a milieu where objective considerations were practically impossible. The martial spirit had reached beyond the formal military groups, extending itself into every phase of life, transforming most institutions into semi-military agencies, and establishing forms of control which flourished in such an atmosphere.[98] By the time that its economic order, the legal and political institutions, and the social and intellectual life felt the impact of militarization, the South had a way of life that greatly facilitated the drift to war in 1861.

These developments must have warmed the heart of sixty-seven-year-old Edmund Ruffin. For years he had argued that there could be no compromise with the North; and he had led in the agitation for preparedness. In the early months of 1861, the feverish preparation for war which he saw in his adopted South Carolina was deeply gratifying to the old Virginia expatriate. It was entirely fitting that he should take an active part. He joined the Palmetto Guards of Charleston and assumed the duties of a regular recruit. The company selected him to fire the first shot on Sumter, and he was delighted. When Ruffin pulled the lanyard on the sixty-four-pound columbiad at 4:30 on the morning of April 12, 1861, he did what thousands of Southerners were willing to do. They, like Ruffin, had nothing more to say. They were ready to fight, and this is what they would do.

# Bibliographical Essay

No attempt will be made here either to duplicate the bibliographical information that is provided, in some detail, in the notes or to furnish a definitive list of the sources that have been used in connection with the research and writing of this book. Such a task would require a disproportionate amount of space and would not have sufficient value to justify it. This discussion is merely an attempt to direct special attention to materials that have had particular significance for this work and that indicate the vast potentiality of studies in the social and intellectual history of the South.

A number of works outside the field of the history of the South have been valuable in suggesting the nature of a society that manifests a proclivity toward militancy and the relationship between the institutions of that society and the emergence of a martial spirit. Among them are Alfred Vagts, *A History of Militarism, Romance and Realities of a Profession* (New York, 1937), which contains a broad survey of the forces that have encouraged militarism in some parts of the Western world; and Alexander Gerschenkron, *Bread and Democracy in Germany* (Berkeley, 1943), which points up the relationship between the agricultural and the anti-democratic interests of the Junkers. Others are Joseph I. Greene, *The Living Thoughts of Clausewitz* (Philadelphia, 1943); G. P. James, *The History of Chivalry* (New York, 1857); Baron de Jomini, *The Art of War* (Philadelphia, 1862); and Karl Paul Liebknicht, *Militarism* (New York, 1917).

Several writers have suggested, directly or indirectly, an interpretation of Southern history that takes cognizance of the martial spirit. W. J. Cash, *The Mind of the South* (New York, 1941) is, perhaps, the most sensitive and discerning analysis, while Rollin G. Osterweis, *Romanticism and Nationalism in the Old South* (New Haven, 1949), and Clement Eaton, *Freedom of Thought in the Old South* (Durham, 1940), discuss many aspects of life that have relevancy here. Suggestive, also, are Jesse T. Carpenter, *The South as a Conscious Minority* (New York, 1930); B. B. Kendrick and A. M. Arnett, *The South Looks at its Past* (Chapel Hill, 1935); Edd Winfield Parks, *Segments of Southern Thought* (Athens, Georgia, 1938); and some of the chapters in W. T. Couch, *Culture in the South* (Chapel Hill, 1934). Among briefer works that have great value in understanding the nature of the civilization of the South are William E. Dodd, "The Social Philosophy of the Old South," *American Journal of Sociology*, XXIII (May 1918); Wilson Gee, "The Distinctiveness of Southern Culture," *South Atlantic Quarterly*, XXXVIII (April 1939); and Ulrich B. Phillips, "The Central Theme of Southern History," *American Historical Review*, XXXIV (October 1928). New possibilities in the interpretation of Southern history are discussed in Richard L. Shryock, "Cultural Factors in the History of the South," *Journal of Southern History*, V (August 1939) and Edgar T. Thompson, "Purpose and Tradition in Southern Rural Society: A Point of View for Research," *Social Forces*, XXV (March 1947).

### UNPUBLISHED SOURCES

Among the numerous collections of manuscript materials in the Library of Congress that bear on this subject, the papers of John Ambler, the Virginia militia leader, John Strode Barbour, a member of Congress from Virginia, and Duncan L. Clinch, planter, soldier, and Whig politician of Georgia, provide information regarding militia activities in many Southern communities. Indian problems and various military matters are discussed in the papers of Dr. Benjamin King and David B. Morgan. Some of the correspondence of South Carolina's distinguished planter-politician, James L. Petigru, remains unpublished; and an examination of those letters in the Library of Congress is rewarding. The diary of John Pickett, Indian fighter in 1836–1838, indicates how interested many Southerners were in maintaining military defenses against a real or fancied enemy. Another diary is that kept by the young lady from Massachusetts, Caroline Poole, who taught in Louisiana from 1835 to 1837 and recorded her impressions of Southern militancy.

A careful examination of the enormous quantity of materials in the National Archives provides fruitful yields. Of special value is the correspondence of the office of Secretary of War, in Record

Group 107. Inquiries came to the office from state officials rang-
ing from militia captains to governors. They wanted to know how
they should handle Indian problems and slave insurrections; and
they wanted to know what the federal government proposed to
do in the way of giving aid both in men and materiel. The instructions of the Secretary of War to the Colonel of Ordnance,
together with the latter's replies, reveal Southern militancy before 1860.

Among other official or semi-official unpublished materials are
the legislative papers and the correspondence of the governors
of the Southern states. For example, the legislative papers of
North Carolina at the State Department of Archives and History
contain petitions for the revision of laws relating to the military
control of slavery, requests for the authorization of new military
outfits, and sundry observations of citizens regarding military
matters. In the papers and letters of governors, such as those of
John A. Winston in the Alabama Department of Archives and
History, one may find discussions of the laws of dueling, opinions
regarding the establishment of military schools, and the records
of action taken in connection with Indian depredations or slave
uprisings.

Many of the manuscripts in the Southern Historical Collection
of the University of North Carolina provide information on the
subject. Perhaps the most important are the papers of Robert C.
Foster, Jr., whose activities as an officer in the Tennessee militia
are unusually suggestive regarding excessive preoccupation with
military matters; the papers of William Porcher Miles, who, as a
planter, educator, and Congressman living in several Southern
states, represents a significant aspect of culture in the section; and
the Pettigrew family papers, which contain much about militia
activities, unrest among slaves, and the intersectional tension
preceding the Civil War. At Duke University the Bennette Bagby
papers, with their discussion of education in several Southern
states, the David Campbell papers, touching on almost every con-
ceivable phase of life, the Benjamin Huger papers, with invaluable material on the manufacture of arms and ammunition, and
the Mary Schooler papers, containing information on educational
and military activities, are among the outstanding collections at
that institution. At Louisiana State University the St. John
Liddell, the Henry D. Mandeville, and the Henry Wilson Collections are significant sources of information for this study.

## PUBLIC DOCUMENTS

It is possible to trace the changes in the state constitutions regarding such matters as fugitive slaves, militia organizations, and dueling in Francis N. Thorpe, *The Federal and State Constitutions, Colonial Charters, and Other Organic Laws of the States,* seven volumes (Washington, 1909). Applications, rejections, and enrollment at West Point, as well as many other matters relating to the military interests of the country may be followed in *American State Papers, Class V, Military Affairs,* seven volumes (Washington, 1860). Another valuable collection of public documents is *State Documents on Federal Relations: The States and the United States,* edited by Herman Vandenburg Ames (Philadelphia, 1906).

The session laws as well as the legislative journals of the Southern states may be consulted with profit. Moreover, special compilations of laws should be examined, such as *The Militia and Patrol Laws of South Carolina to December, 1859* (Columbia, 1860), and *The Militia Law of Virginia* (Richmond, 1858). From time to time the federal and state legislatures made special reports that were of great value. Among them is the exhaustive study of the Graves-Cilley duel made by the House of Representatives of the United States Congress, *Report of the Committee on the Late Duel* (Washington, 1838). Another is the *Report of a Special Committee of the Senate of South Carolina on State Rights* (Columbia, 1827).

## CONTEMPORARY PERIODICALS

The magazine and newspaper press of the South is surpassed by almost nothing as a source of the South's social, cultural, and intellectual history. It is indispensable to the study of the militant South. The magazines and newspapers were frequently irregular and short-lived, but some persisted and even flourished. The three outstanding magazines contain enormous quantities of pertinent material. They are *De Bow's Review,* 1846–1861, thirty volumes; *Southern Literary Messenger,* 1834–1860, thirty volumes; and the *Southern Quarterly Review,* 1842–1857, thirty volumes. Others, of briefer duration, that should not be overlooked are *Russell's Magazine,* 1857–1860, six volumes; *Southern Review,* 1828–1832, eight volumes; and *Southwestern Monthly,* 1852, two volumes.

Because of the large number of newspapers, it is necessary, of course, to be somewhat arbitrary in selection. Brief attention was given to many, while others deserved more sustained examination. Among the latter are the *Richmond Enquirer,* 1844–1861; *Raleigh Register,* 1830–1860; *Charleston Mercury,* 1836–1861; *Southern Advocate* (Huntsville, Alabama), 1834–1860; *Daily Picayune* (New Orleans), 1840–1860; *New Orleans Daily Delta,* 1855–1860; *Memphis Daily Appeal,* 1849–1858; and the *Republican Banner* (Nashville), with several variations in the name, 1826–1855.

### CONTEMPORARY ACCOUNTS: TRAVELS, MEMOIRS, DIARIES

Although Southern writers were not always objective in describing conditions and narrating experiences, their personal accounts are valuable sources in understanding the South. Among the most important descriptions of life are Joseph G. Baldwin, *Flush Times in Alabama and Mississippi* (New York, 1853); Joseph B. Cobb, *Mississippi Scenes; or, Sketches of Southern and Western Life and Adventure* (Philadelphia, 1851); Augustus B. Longstreet, *Georgia Scenes* (Augusta, 1835); and H. E. Taliaferro, *Fisher's River (North Carolina) Scenes and Characters, by "Skitt" "Who Was Raised Thar"* (New York, 1859). William F. Gray's *From Virginia to Texas, 1835* (Houston, 1909) is unique in the detail and apparent accuracy of a variety of aspects of life, while Theodore Clapp's *Autobiographical Sketches and Recollections During A Thirty-five Years' Residence in New Orleans* (Boston, 1857) gives a vivid picture of life in the leading city of the South. The experiences of Southern soldiers are described in Philip St. George Cooke, *Scenes and Adventures in the Army* (Philadelphia, 1857), and George C. Furber, *The Twelve Months Volunteer* (Cincinnati, 1849).

Northern travelers in the South have left a wealth of material giving their impressions. John S. C. Abbott, *South and North* (New York, 1860) is not uniformly good, while David Brown, *The Planter: Or, Thirteen Years in the South, by A Northern Man* (Philadelphia, 1853) is extremely pro-Southern. Much more penetrating, though obviously overdrawn in places, is Daniel R. Hundley, *Social Relations in Our Southern States* (New York, 1860). Neither Joseph Holt Ingraham, *The Southwest, by A Yankee,* two volumes (New York, 1835), nor the anonymous work edited by Ingraham, *The Sunny South; or the Southerner at Home, Embracing Five Years Experience of a Northern Governess in the Land of the Sugar and the Cotton* (Philadelphia, 1860) should be overlooked. Accounts of brief, though significant visits are given in William Kingsford, *Impressions of the West and South During a Six Weeks' Holiday* (Toronto, 1858), and Benjamin H. Latrobe, *The Journal of Latrobe* (New York, 1905). In this as in many other cases, Frederick Olmsted, *A Journey in the Seaboard Slave States* (New York, 1856), and his *A Journey in the Back Country* (New York, 1860) are of exceptional value.

Even more articulate were the Europeans who almost always included the South in their American itinerary. Among the most valuable of several scores that may be read with profit are the following: Francis Baily, *Journal of a Tour in Unsettled Parts of North America in 1796 and 1797* (London, 1856); J. Benwell, *An Englishman's Travels in America,* two volumes (London, 1842); George W. Featherstonhaugh, *Excursion Through the Slave States,* two volumes (London, 1844); Thomas C. Grattan, *Civilized America,* two volumes (London, 1859); Basil Hall, *Travels in North America in the Years 1827–1828,* three volumes (Edinburgh, 1830); Charles Lyell, *A Second Visit to the United States,* two volumes (New York, 1850); Alexander Mackay, *The Western World; or, Travels in the United States in 1846–47,* two volumes (Philadelphia, 1849); William H. Russell, *Pictures of Southern Life, Social, Political, and Military* (New York, 1861); and James Stirling, *Letters from the Slave States* (London, 1857). Also of value are: William Chambers, *Things as They Are in America* (New York, 1854); Achille Murat, *A Moral and Political Sketch of the United States of North America* (London, 1833); Francis and Theresa Pulszky, *White, Red, Black; Sketches of Society in the United States,* three volumes (London, 1853); and Joseph Sturge, *A Visit to the United States in 1841* (Boston, 1842). While not precisely a travel account, there is much relevant material in Alexis de Tocqueville, *Democracy in America* (New York, 1898).

Some of the most incisive accounts of life in the South were written by women travelers. Fanny Kemble was not a traveler in the ordinary sense, but her *Journal of a Residence on a Georgia Plantation* (New York, 1864), is especially important in understanding the influence of slavery on the character of the planters. The Swedish traveler, Fredrika Bremer, covered many aspects of life in the South in *The Homes of the New World; Impressions of America,* two volumes (New York, 1853). Other important travel accounts by women are Margaret Hunter Hall, *The Aristocratic Journey, 1827–1828,* edited by Una Pope-Hennessy (New York, 1931); Harriet Martineau, *Society in America,* three volumes (London, 1837); and Frances M. Trollope, *Domestic Manners of the Americans,* new edition (New York, 1949).

There are many other contemporary accounts of a miscellaneous nature that provide information on various aspects of life in the ante-bellum South. J. W. Pomfrey, *A True Disclosure and Exposition of the Knights of the Golden Circle* (Cincinnati, 1861) is only one of a number of exposés of that organization. Some historical accounts were written to argue a case or promote a program. Prominent among them were Alexander Hewat, *An Historical Account of the Rise and Progress of the Colonies of South Carolina and Georgia,* two volumes (London, 1779); William Gilmore Simms, *South Carolina in the Revolutionary War* (Charleston, 1848); and William Walker, *The War in Nicaragua* (Mobile, 1860). Works like J. D. B. De Bow, *Industrial Resources Etc. of the Southern and Western States,* three volumes (New Orleans, 1852–53), and George White, *Historical Collections of Georgia* (New York, 1854) are invaluable for statistical data and the like.

### CONTEMPORARY DISCUSSION: TRACTS, ORATIONS, SERMONS

As controversy arose regarding Southern institutions, a large body of discussion literature emerged that is important for the purposes of this study. These titles are merely an indication of the types of material represented in this group. E. N. Elliott, *Cotton is King, and Pro-Slavery Arguments* (Augusta, 1860), and Thomas R. Dew, *Review of the Debate in the Virginia Legislature of 1831 and 1832* (Richmond, 1832), contain the major arguments of the proslavery interests. Some of the most original and militant thinking in the South is in George Fitzhugh, *Cannibals All! Or, Slaves Without Masters* (Richmond, 1857), and *Sociology for the South; or, The Failure of Free Society* (Richmond, 1854). The argument for the industrialization of the South was put forth effectively by William Gregg, *Essays on Domestic Industry* (Charleston, 1845), while Thomas P. Kettell, *Southern Wealth and Northern Profits* (New York, 1860), insisted that the

South should put an end to its current habit of working solely for the benefit of Northern businessmen. Dueling was discussed at great length and defended by John Lyde Wilson, *The Code of Honor; or, Rules for the Government of Principals and Seconds in Duelling* (Charleston, 1838).

Many Southerners wrote brief tracts or articles stating their own position or the position they thought their section should take in the intersectional strife that preceded the Civil War. These statements not infrequently called for militant action, and were almost always charged with a martial air. Numerous articles appeared in the aforementioned magazines and newspapers. Others were published as pamphlets and circulated as widely as possible. A call to arms in defense of slavery was made by Edward B. Bryan, *The Rightful Remedy, Addressed to the Slaveholders of the South* (Charleston, 1850), while James D. B. De Bow sought to extend the appeal in *The Interest in Slavery of the Southern Non-Slaveholder; The Right of Peaceful Secession* (Charleston, 1860). Uncompromising stands were also taken by: Edwin De-Leon, *The Position and Duties of Young America* (Columbia, 1845); Edwin C. Holland, *A Refutation of the Calumnies Circulated Against the Southern and Western States Respecting the Institution and Existence of Slavery Among Them* (Charleston, 1822); Augustus B. Longstreet, *A Voice from the South, Comprising Letters from Georgia to Massachusetts* (Baltimore, 1847); "Rutledge," *Separate State Secession, Practically Discussed* (Edgefield, 1851); and William H. Trescott, *The Position and Course of the South* (Charleston, 1850). Added to these should be the proceedings of the various state rights or Southern rights conventions and associations with their "addresses" to the Southern people and the addresses and messages of leaders like R. Barnwell Rhett and William L. Yancey to their constituents.

The forensic tastes and interests of Southerners found ample opportunity for expression before the collegiate and community organizations. The following are a few of the addresses that dealt with military education or urged a militant course of action on the part of the South: Charles J. Faulkner, *Address Delivered to the Graduating Class of the Virginia Military Institute, July 4, 1850* (Lexington, 1850); Edwin Heriot, *The Polytechnic School, the Best System of Practical Education* (Charleston, 1850); Major D. H. Hill, "Essay on Military Education," *North Carolina Journal of Education*, IV (April 1861); Francis H. Smith, *Introduc-*

*tory Address to the Corps of Cadets of the Virginia Military Institute* (Richmond, 1856); and S. W. Trotti, *Address Delivered before the Calliopean and Polytechnic Societies of the State Military Academy* (Charleston, 1847).

The orations delivered to commemorate an event in the history of the section were usually full of fire. Typical were the *Addresses Delivered at the Celebration of the Third Anniversary in Honor of the Martyrs for Cuban Freedom* (New Orleans, 1854) by Gaspar Betaucourt and J. S. Thrasher; William E. Martin, *The South: Its Dangers and Resources; An Address Delivered at the Celebration of the Battle of Fort Moultrie, June 28, 1850* (Charleston, 1850); W. D. Porter, *Oration Delivered before the Calhoun Monument Association . . . upon their First Celebration in Honor of the Birth-day of Calhoun* (Charleston, 1854); and William H. Trescott, *Oration Delivered before the Beaufort Volunteer Artillery, on July 4, 1850* (Charleston, 1850).

Some Southern ministers preached against the evils of excessive militancy. The sermons against dueling, for example, such as: William H. Barnwell, *The Impiety and Absurdity of Dueling — A Sermon* (Charleston, 1844); Frederic Beasley, *A Sermon on Dueling, Delivered in Christ Church, Baltimore, April 28, 1811* (Baltimore, 1811); and J. R. Kendrick, *Dueling; A Sermon Preached at the First Baptist Church, Charleston, S. C., on Sunday Morning, August 7, 1853* (Charleston, 1853). Other ministers urged their listeners to prepare to meet and defeat the enemy — the North. Two such sermons are: Whitefoord Smith, *God, the Refuge of His People; A Sermon Delivered before the General Assembly of South Carolina, Friday December 6, 1850 — Day of Fasting, Humiliation, and Prayer* (Columbia, 1850); and James H. Thornwell, *Judgments, A Call to Repentence; A Sermon Preached by Appointment of the Legislature in the Hall of the House of Representatives, Saturday, December 9, 1854* (Columbia, 1854).

### RELEVANT SECONDARY SOURCES

While few studies have addressed themselves specifically to the problem that is the subject of this work, many have contributed to an understanding of it. Several of the volumes in Julian A. C. Chandler, *The South in the Building of the Nation,* thirteen volumes (Richmond, 1909–1914) are valuable, as is E. Merton Coulter and Wendell H. Stephenson, *History of the South* (Baton

Rouge, 1948 — in progress). Other works of a general nature are R. S. Cotterill, *The Old South* (Glendale, 1936); Clement Eaton, *A History of the Old South* (New York, 1949); and Francis B. Simkins, *A History of the South* (New York, 1953). Frontier conditions in the South are discussed in Thomas D. Clark, *The Rampaging Frontier* (Indianapolis, 1939), and Everett Dick, *Dixie Frontier* (New York, 1948). Information regarding the social and economic conditions among certain groups may be found in Edward Ingle, *Southern Sidelights* (New York, 1896), and Frank L. Owsley, *Plain Folk of the Old South* (Baton Rouge, 1949), while the article by Charles S. Sydnor, "The Southerner and the Laws," *Journal of Southern History*, V (February 1940) is valuable.

State and local histories are by no means uniformly reliable or valuable, but some monographic studies provide pertinent material. Among them are the two works by Thomas P. Abernethy, *From Frontier to Plantation in Tennessee* (Chapel Hill, 1932), and *The Formative Period in Alabama, 1815–1828* (Montgomery, 1922). Guion G. Johnson, *Ante-Bellum North Carolina* (Chapel Hill, 1937) is excellent, while Rosser H. Taylor, *Ante-Bellum South Carolina* (Chapel Hill, 1942) is satisfactory. Minnie C. Boyd, *Alabama in the Fifties* (New York, 1931) is good for social history; and Roger W. Shugg, *Origins of Class Struggle in Louisiana* (Baton Rouge, 1939) breaks new ground in the field of social and economic history.

County histories are almost uniformly unsatisfactory, but a few, such as William T. Hale, *History of DeKalb County, Tennessee* (Nashville, 1915), provide useful information. Urban histories are somewhat better; some — like Gerald M. Capers, *The Biography of a River Town; Memphis: Its Heroic Age* (Chapel Hill, 1939), and F. Garvin Davenport, *Cultural Life in Nashville on the Eve of the Civil War* (Chapel Hill, 1941) — are far above the average. Adelaide Wilson, *Historic and Picturesque Savannah* (Boston, 1889), and William A. Christian, *Richmond, Her Past and Present* (Richmond, 1912) are older, but contain much valuable material.

Dueling and other forms of violence have received much attention. Significant interpretations are made by H. C. Brearley, "The Pattern of Violence," *Culture in the South*, edited by W. T. Couch (Chapel Hill, 1935), and Clement Eaton, "Mob Violence in the Old South," *Mississippi Valley Historical Review*, XXIX

(December 1941). Lorenzo Sabine, *Notes on Duels and Duelling* (Boston, 1855); Don Carlos Seitz, *Famous American Duels* (New York, 1929); William O. Stevens, *Pistols at Ten Paces: The Story of the Code of Honor in America* (Boston, 1940); and Benjamin C. Truman, *The Field of Honor* (New York, 1884) are the leading general works on dueling. Stuart O. Landry, *Duelling in Old New Orleans* (New Orleans, 1950); A. W. Patterson, *The Code Duello, with Special Reference to the State of Virginia* (Richmond, 1927); Myra L. Spaulding, "Duelling in the District of Columbia," *Records of the Columbia Historical Society*, XXIV, XXX (1928); and Thomas Gamble, *Savannah Duels and Duellists, 1733–1877* (Savannah, 1923) deal with the problem in specific areas.

The relationship between slavery and the growth of militancy in the South may be seen in many of the contemporary sources already discussed. Some secondary sources bear directly on the subject. Among these are studies of slavery in specific states, such as Charles S. Sydnor, *Slavery in Mississippi* (New York, 1933). The most exhaustive study of Negro opposition to slavery is Herbert Aptheker, *American Negro Slave Revolts* (New York, 1943); other aspects may be examined in Howell M. Henry, *The Police Control of the Slave in South Carolina* (Emory, Va., 1914), and Ulrich B. Phillips, *Race Problems, Adjustments and Disturbances in the Ante-Bellum South* (Richmond, 1909). The impact of the danger of uprisings on the Southern community is explored in Frederick T. Wilson, *Federal Aid in Domestic Disturbances, 1787–1903* (Washington, 1903), and John S. Kendall, "Shadow over the City," *Louisiana Historical Quarterly*, XXII (January 1939).

The literature of expansionism is voluminous, but there has been no synthesis of it as regards the Southern part of the United States. Helpful, however, is Albert K. Weinberg, *Manifest Destiny; A Study of Nationalistic Expansionism in American History* (Baltimore, 1935). The leading arguments that deny the aggressive nature of slavery are Chauncey S. Boucher, "In Re That Aggressive Slavocracy," *Mississippi Valley Historical Review*, VIII (June 1921), and Charles W. Ramsdell, "The Natural Limits of Slavery Expansion," *Mississippi Valley Historical Review*, XVI (September 1929). Harris Gaylord Warren has covered several phases of Southern filibustering in "Southern Filibusters in the War of 1812," *Louisiana Historical Quarterly*, XXV (April

1942); "Pensacola and the Filibusters, 1816–1817," *Louisiana Historical Quarterly*, XXI (July 1938); and *The Sword Was Their Passport; A History of American Filibustering in the Mexican Revolution* (Baton Rouge, 1943).

The view that the South was opposed to the acquisition of Mexico is advanced by John D. P. Fuller in "The Slavery Question and the Movement to Acquire Mexico, 1846–1934) and *The Movement for the Acquisition of All Mexico, 1846–1848* (Baltimore, 1936). On this problem, however, the critical student would examine carefully the contemporary sources, many of which were cited above. Southern interest in Cuba has been handled in Gavin B. Henderson, editor, "Southern Designs on Cuba, 1854–1857, and Some European Opinions," *Journal of Southern History*, V (August 1939); Louis M. Perez, editor, "Lopez's Expeditions to Cuba, 1849–1851," *Publications of the Southern History Association*, X (November 1906); Chester Stanley Urban, "New Orleans and the Cuban Question during the Lopez Expeditions of 1849–1851: A Local Study in 'Manifest Destiny,' " *Louisiana Historical Quarterly*, XXII (October 1939); and Robert G. Caldwell, *The Lopez Expeditions to Cuba, 1848–1851* (Princeton, 1915). In addition to the contemporary materials, the best work on the effort to acquire Nicaragua is William O. Scroggs, *Filibusters and Financiers* (New York, 1916). On Southern expansionism, C. A. Bridges, "The Knights of the Golden Circle, A Filibustering Fantasy," *Southwestern Historical Quarterly*, XLIV (January 1941), and Ollinger Crenshaw, "The Knights of the Golden Circle," *American Historical Review*, XLVII (October 1941).

The history of education in the South may be followed in the several volumes that make up the United States Bureau of Education's Contributions to American Educational History, as well as Edgar W. Knight, *Public Education in the South* (Boston, 1922), and Charles W. Dabney, *Universal Education in the South* (Chapel Hill, 1936). Works of value that deal with specific institutions or phases are William Couper, *One Hundred Years at V.M.I.*, two volumes (Richmond, 1939); E. Merton Coulter, *College Life in the Old South* (New York, 1928); Walter L. Fleming, *Louisiana State University, 1860–1896* (Baton Rouge, 1936); John Peyre Thomas, *The History of the South Carolina Military Academy* (Charleston, 1893); and Jennings Cropper Wise, *The Military History of Virginia Military Institute from*

*1839 to 1865* (Lynchburg, 1915). Two works on an Alabama institution should be consulted: Walter B. Posey, *La Grange – Alabama's Earliest College* (Birmingham, 1933), and John A. Wyeth, *History of La Grange Military Academy and the Cadet Corps* (New York, 1907). Articles that provide useful information on military education are Mabel Alstetter and Gladys Watson, "Western Military Institute, 1847–1861," *Filson Club Historical Quarterly,* X (April 1936), and David F. Boyd, "W. T. Sherman as a College President," *The American College,* II (April 1910).

Many of the works that deal with the cultural and intellectual interests of the South have already been mentioned. These should be supplemented by studies such as Hamilton J. Eckenrode, "Sir Walter Scott and the South," *North American Review,* CCVI (October 1917); George H. Orians, *The Influence of Walter Scott on America and American Culture before 1860* (Urbana, 1929); and two articles by Grace W. Landrum, "Notes on the Reading of the Old South," *American Literature,* III (March 1931) and "Sir Walter Scott and His Literary Rivals in the South," *American Literature,* II (November 1930).

Military interest and experience have been treated in several works that deal with wars as well as governmental administration. Among them are Justin H. Smith, *The War with Mexico,* two volumes (New York, 1919); Alfred Hoyt Bill, *Rehearsal for Conflict* (New York, 1947); and A. Howard Meneely, *The War Department, 1861; A Study in Mobilization and Administration* (New York, 1928). Also, Claud E. Fuller and Richard D. Steuart, *Firearms of the Confederacy* (Huntington, W. Va., 1944); John P. Thomas, *South Carolina in Arms, Arts, and Industries* (New York, 1875); and Walter P. Webb, *The Texas Rangers; A Century of Frontier Defense* (Boston, 1935). There are many sketches of separate military organizations. Among the more commendable ones are Charles M. Blackford, *Annals of the Lynchburg Home Guard* (Lynchburg, 1891), and Powell A. Casey, "Early History of the Washington Artillery of New Orleans," *Louisiana Historical Quarterly,* XXIII (April 1940).

The relationship between the promotion of industrialization in the South and the interest of the section in preparedness is established in a number of works. There are even suggestions of it in Victor S. Clark, *History of Manufactures in the United States, 1607–1860* (Washington, 1916). More relevant, however, are Kathleen Bruce, *Virginia Iron Manufacture in the Slave Era*

(New York, 1931); J. G. Van Deusen, *The Ante-Bellum Southern Commercial Conventions* (Durham, 1926); Herbert Wender, *Southern Commercial Conventions, 1837–1859* (Baltimore, 1930); and Broadus Mitchell, *William Gregg, Factory Master of the Old South* (Chapel Hill, 1928). One should not neglect two significant articles that bear directly on the problem: Herbert Collins, "The Southern Industrial Gospel before 1860," *Journal of Southern History*, XII (August 1946), and Philip G. Davidson, "Industrialism in the Ante-Bellum South," *South Atlantic Quarterly*, XXVII (October 1928).

Literature on the movement for Southern unity and its consequences is abundant, although little can be described as objective. Some biographies are valuable, among which are: Avery O. Craven, *Edmund Ruffin, Southerner* (New York, 1932), and John W. DuBose, *The Life and Times of William Lowndes Yancey*, two volumes (Birmingham, 1892). The South's reaction to the aggravated intersectional tension is discussed in Charles S. Sydnor, *The Development of Southern Sectionalism* (Baton Rouge, 1948), Avery O. Craven, *The Coming of the Civil War* (New York, 1942), and Avery O. Craven, *The Growth of Southern Nationalism* (Baton Rouge, 1953). Melvin J. White, *The Secession Movement in the United States, 1847–1852* (New Orleans, 1916), and Dwight L. Dumond, *The Secession Movement* (New York, 1931) contain some relevant materials. A significant approach is made in Ulrich B. Phillips, "The Literary Movement for Secession," *Studies in Southern History and Politics* (New York, 1914). Conditions in the Southern states in the years immediately preceding secession have been handled in a variety of ways. Prominent monographs are: Harold S. Schultz, *Sectionalism and Nationalism in South Carolina, 1852–1860* (Durham, 1950); Henry T. Shanks, *The Secession Movement in Virginia, 1847–1861* (Richmond, 1934); Richard H. Shryock, *Georgia and the Union in 1850* (Durham, 1926); and Joseph Carlyle Sitterson, *The Secession Movement in North Carolina* (Chapel Hill, 1939).

# Notes

## 1. Background of Violence

1. Edwin (Edmund) Ruffin, "Consequences of Abolition Agitation," *De Bow's Review*, XXIII (September 1857), 270. The article appeared in the *Enquirer* in December 1856.

2. *Southern Literary Messenger*, XIII (July 1847), 430.

3. Alexander Hewat, *An Historical Account of the Rise of Progress of the Colonies of South Carolina and Georgia* (London, 1779), II, 298.

4. Alexander Mackay, *The Western World: or Travels in the United States in 1846–47* (Philadelphia, 1849), I, 104.

5. James Stirling, *Letters from the Slave States* (London, 1857), p. 273.

6. William H. Russell, *Pictures of Southern Life, Social, Political, and Military* (New York, 1861), p. 8.

7. Joseph Holt Ingraham, *The Southwest, by a Yankee* (New York, 1835), I, 208. Fanny Kemble asserted that the Southern planters, "with their furious feuds and slaughterous combats, their stabbings and pistolings, their gross sensuality, brutal ignorance, and despotic cruelty, resemble the chivalry of France before the horrors of the Jacquerie admonished them that there was a limit even to the endurance of slaves," *Journal of a Residence on a Georgia Plantation* (New York, 1864), p. 303.

8. See also Harriet Martineau, *Society in America* (London, 1837), II, 329.

9. *Southern Quarterly Review*, II (July 1842), 168.

10. Edward B. Bryan, *The Rightful Remedy, Addressed to the Slaveholders of the South* (Charleston, 1850), p. 89.

11. *De Bow's Review*, XXXIX (October 1860), 459.

12. "The Difference of Race Between the Northern and Southern People," *Southern Literary Messenger*, XXX (June 1860), 406.

13. *Ibid.*, p. 407.

14. E. Merton Coulter, *A Short History of Georgia* (Chapel Hill, 1933), pp. 30–60, 108–122. See also Charles C. Jones, Jr., *The History of Georgia* (Boston, 1883), vol. I.

15. See Wallace Notestein, *The Scot in History* (New Haven, 1946), pp. 31, 93–98.

16. See the views expressed in John Adams, *The Works of John Adams* (Boston, 1851), IV, 39.

17. *The Writings of George Washington,* edited by John C. Fitzpatrick (Washington, 1931), IV, 124.

18. *Ibid.,* p. 451.

19. John Richard Alden, *General Gage in America* (Baton Rouge, 1948), p. 212.

20. A notable exception is David Ramsay of South Carolina, whose *History of the American Revolution* was published in Philadelphia in 1789.

21. Lorenzo Sabine, *The American Loyalists* (Boston, 1847), pp. 39–42.

22. William Gilmore Simms, *Southern Quarterly Review,* XIV (July 1848), 51.

23. J. D. B. De Bow, "The South and the Union," *De Bow's Review,* X (February 1851), 160.

24. William E. Martin, *The South: Its Dangers and Resources* (Charleston, 1850), pp. 6–7.

25. Lawrence Massillon Keitt, "Patriotic Services of the North and South," *De Bow's Review,* XXI (November 1856), 491.

26. *Congressional Globe,* 34th Congress, 1st Session, Appendix, p. 543.

27. At that time Sumner was gravely ill from the lashing at the hands of young Representative Preston Brooks of South Carolina, who took offense at his remarks about Butler, his uncle.

28. *Congressional Globe,* pp. 627–628; see also *De Bow's Review,* XXI (August 1856), 197–198.

29. *Southern Literary Messenger,* XI (March 1845), 139–140. The account is by an unknown English traveler.

30. See, for example, Julius Pratt, *The Expansionists of 1812* (New York, 1925), *passim.*

31. James M. Callahan, "The South in the Wars of the United States, 1789–1860," *The South in the Building of A Nation* (Richmond, 1909), IV, 264.

32. John Campbell to David Campbell, July 12, 1812, MS in the David Campbell Papers, Duke University Library.

33. Callahan, "The South in the Wars," p. 264.

34. John M. Campbell to David Campbell, June 12, 1812.

35. Justin Smith, *The War with Mexico* (New York, 1919), I, 126.

36. August 10, 1845.

37. August 17, 1845.

38. Ulrich B. Phillips, "The Correspondence of Toombs, Stephens, and Cobb," American Historical Association, *Annual Report for the Year 1911,* I (Washington, 1913), 76.

39. Adelaide Wilson, *Historic and Picturesque Savannah* (Boston, 1889), p. 170.

40. *Natchez Courier,* June 24, 1846, quoted in James Byrnes Ranck,

*Albert Gallatin Brown; Radical Southern Nationalist* (New York, 1937), p. 44.

41. Charles Lanman, *Letters from the Alleghany Mountains* (New York, 1849), p. 152.

42. Ranck, *Albert Gallatin Brown*, p. 43.

43. L. M. Roper to Major St. John R. Liddell, June 2, 1846, MS in Liddell Collection, Louisiana State University Archives.

44. Susan Dabney Smedes, *Memorials of a Southern Planter* (Baltimore, 1887), p. 128.

45. *De Bow's Review*, VI (October, November 1848), 369; and X (February 1851), 160. See also the account of the reactions of Southern college students to the victories in Giles J. Patterson, *Journal of a Southern Student, 1846–1848*, edited by Richard C. Beatty (Nashville, 1944), p. 51.

46. Thomas Low Nichols, *Forty Years of American Life, 1821–1861* (New York, 1937), p. 127.

47. William Cary Crane, "The History of Mississippi," *Southern Literary Messenger*, XXX (February 1860), 89.

48. *Southern Quarterly Review*, XV (July 1849), 414.

49. Major D. H. Hill, "Essay on Military Education," *North Carolina Journal of Education*, IV (April 1861), 115.

50. J. E. Walmsley, "The Presidential Campaign in Mississippi," *Publications of the Mississippi Historical Society*, IX, 195.

51. Ingraham, *The Southwest*, I, 208.

52. *Southern Literary Messenger*, XXI (January 1855), 2.

53. *Southern Advocate*, May 9, 1828.

54. Henry Benjamin Whipple, *Bishop Whipple's Southern Diary, 1843–1844*, edited by Lester Burrell Shippee (Minneapolis, 1937), pp. 24–25.

55. John Hope Franklin, *The Free Negro in North Carolina, 1790–1860* (Chapel Hill, 1943), p. 100.

56. Quoted in *Plantation and Frontier Documents, 1649–1863*, edited by Ulrich B. Phillips (Cleveland, 1909), II, 120.

57. Stirling, *Letters from the Slave States*, p. 271.

## 2. *Fighters' Fatherland*

1. Hamilton Basso, *Beauregard, the Great Creole* (New York, 1933), pp. 5ff.

2. Robert M. Hughes, *General Johnston* (New York, 1893), p. 14.

3. Philip St. George Cooke, *Scenes and Adventures in the Army* (Philadelphia, 1857), pp. 197–201.

4. James L. Petigru to his sister Jane, May 18, 1836. MS in James L. Petigru Correspondence, 1826–1863, Library of Congress.

5. Francis W. Pickens to Armstead Burt, June 15, 1848. MS in the Duke University Library.

6. *The Making of a Soldier; Letters of General R. S. Ewell,* edited by Percy Gatling Hamlin (Richmond, 1935), p. 27.

7. George Washington Cullum, *Biographical Register of the Officers and Graduates of the U. S. Military Academy,* Third Edition (Boston, 1891), I, 587.

8. *Ibid.,* I, 587.

9. Daniel Robinson Hundley, *Social Relations in Our Southern States* (New York, 1860), p. 50.

10. Joseph Holt Ingraham, *The Sunny South* (Philadelphia, 1860), pp. 272–273.

11. Augustus Baldwin Longstreet, *Georgia Scenes* (Augusta, 1835), p. 297.

12. Frederick Law Olmsted, *A Journey in the Seaboard Slave States* (New York, 1856), p. 645.

13. Edward Ingle, *Southern Sidelights* (New York, 1896), p. 151.

14. Douglas Southall Freeman, *Lee's Lieutenants, A Study in Command* (New York, 1942), II, 703–704.

15. Stephen F. Miller, *Bench and Bar of Georgia* (Philadelphia, 1858), I, 318–319.

16. Stirling, *Letters from the Slave States,* pp. 177–178.

17. James Silk Buckingham, *The Slave States of America* (London, 1842), I, 188, 251.

18. Francis and Theresa Pulszky, *White, Red, Black; Sketches of Society in the United States* (London, 1853), III, 8.

19. David W. Mitchell, *Ten Years in the United States* (London, 1862), p. 30.

20. Olmsted, *Seaboard Slave States,* pp. 65–66.

21. Edd Winfield Parks, *Segments of Southern Thought* (Athens, 1938), pp. 146ff.

22. Olmsted, *Seaboard Slave States,* p. 405.

23. Stirling, *Letters from the Slave States,* p. 250.

24. Olmsted, *Seaboard Slave States,* p. 136.

25. Buckingham, *Slave States,* I, 222, 247.

26. George William Featherstonhaugh, *Excursion Through the Slave States* (London, 1844), II, 55.

27. Ingraham, *The Southwest,* I, 90; and Roger W. Shugg, *Origins of Class Struggle in Louisiana* (Baton Rouge, 1939), pp. 58–59.

28. Avery O. Craven, "The 'Turner Theories' and the South," *Journal of Southern History,* V (August 1939), 306.

29. Buckingham, *Slave States,* I, 351.

30. Craven, "Turner Theories," p. 313. See also Frederick L. Olmsted, *A Journey in the Back Country* (London, 1860), pp. 413ff.

31. Thomas Perkins Abernethy, *From Frontier to Plantation in*

*Tennessee* (Chapel Hill, 1932), pp. 161ff; and Clement Eaton, "Mob Violence in the Old South," *Mississippi Valley Historical Review*, XXIX (December 1942), 352.

32. John Francis Hamtramck Claiborne, *Life and Times of General Sam Dale, The Mississippi Partisan* (New York, 1860), pp. 83, 85.

33. Scott, *Acts of Tennessee and North Carolina*, II, 103.

34. See Robert S. Cotterill, *The Old South* (Glendale, 1936), p. 171.

35. D. L. Clinch to the Adjutant General, October 9, 1835. MS in the Clinch Letter Book, 1834–1835, Library of Congress.

36. *Southern Advocate* (Huntsville, Alabama), February 23, 1836.

37. Duncan L. Clinch Order Book 1834–1836, Order No. 75, April 27, 1836, Library of Congress.

38. Thomas A. Anderson, Jefferson County, Tennessee to Joel R. Poinsett, Secretary of War, March 17, 1840. Letters Received, War Department, National Archives.

39. F. M. Henderson to Dr. Benjamin King, February 13, 1838, MS in Benjamin King Letters, Library of Congress.

40. Order No. 29, Headquarters, Fourth Infantry, Ft. Broke, Tampa, May 6, 1836. MS in W. Henry Wilson Collection, Louisiana State University.

41. Order No. 73 and Order No. 75, April 27, 1836, Clinch Order Book.

42. James E. Broome, *Message to the Senate and House of Representatives, November 24, 1846* (n.p., n.d.), pp. 10–17. See also *The Daily Picayune* (New Orleans), December 6, 1858.

43. See Kenneth W. Porter, *Relations Between Negroes and Indians Within the Present Limits of the United States* (Washington, n.d.), pp. 35ff. See also Joshua R. Giddings, *The Exiles of Florida* (Columbus, 1858), pp. 57ff.

44. R. Garland to John C. Spencer, Secretary of War, November 8, 1841. Letters Received, War Department. MS in the National Archives.

45. A. Church, "The State of Georgia — Its Duties and Its Destiny," *Southern Quarterly Review*, VIII (October 1845), 444.

46. Charles Mackay, *Life and Liberty in America* (London, 1859), I, 289–290.

47. Memorial of the Citizens of Memphis, August 30, 1842. Letters Received, War Department. MS in the National Archives.

48. David Yancey Thomas, *Arkansas and Its People: A History, 1541–1930* (New York, 1930), II, 605.

49. Governor A. Yell to John C. Spencer, Secretary of War, January 10, 1842. Letters Received, War Department. MS in the National Archives.

50. Memorial of Arkansas Citizens to President John Tyler, July 4, 1843. Letters Received, War Department. MS in the National Archives.

51. See the distress of Louisiana citizens over the withdrawal of troops from Arkansas and Texas, *Daily Picayune,* February 24, 1858.

52. A. G. Haley to C. M. Conrad, Secretary of War, January 28, 1852. Letters Received, War Department. MS in the National Archives.

## 3. Personal Warfare

1. W. J. Cash, *The Mind of the South* (New York, 1941), pp. 34–35.

2. See the discussion in Rollin J. Osterweis, *Romanticism and Nationalism in the Old South* (New Haven, 1949), pp. 82–102.

3. Alexander Mackay, *The Western World,* I, 254.

4. Thomas Cooper DeLeon, *Belles, Beaux and Brains of the 60's* (New York, 1909), pp. 11–12; and William O. Stevens, *Pistols at Ten Paces; The Story of the Code of Honor in America* (Boston, 1940), p. 108.

5. See Frank L. Owsley, *Plain Folk of the Old South* (Baton Rouge, 1949), pp. 117–118; and H. C. Brearley, "The Pattern of Violence" in William T. Couch, *Culture in the South* (Chapel Hill, 1934), pp. 685–688.

6. Martineau, *Society in America,* II, 329.

7. Everett Dick, *Dixie Frontier* (New York, 1948), p. 140.

8. Whipple, *Southern Diary,* pp. 26–27.

9. Longstreet, *Georgia Scenes,* pp. 65ff.

10. John Donald Wade, *Augustus Baldwin Longstreet* (New York, 1924), p. 173.

11. Thomas Perkins Abernethy, *From Frontier to Plantation in Tennessee* (Chapel Hill, 1932), p. 162.

12. "Sketches of Our Volunteer Officers," *Southern Literary Messenger,* XXI (January 1855), 2.

13. William H. Russell, *My Diary North and South* (Boston, 1863), p. 301. The recent (1954) edition of the Russell diary edited by Fletcher Pratt does not contain this statement because of the cuts the editor made in order to make the reissue of this work practicable.

14. Stevens, *Pistols at Ten Paces,* p. 111.

15. Shugg, *Class Struggle in Louisiana,* p. 61. See also Abernethy, *Frontier to Plantation,* pp. 131ff.

16. Hundley, *Social Relations,* pp. 223–224.

17. *Ibid.,* pp. 239–243.

18. James L. Petigru to Hugh S. Legare, October 29, 1832, in James Petigru Carson, *Life, Letters and Speeches of James Louis Petigru, the Union Man of the South* (Washington, 1920), pp. 103–104.

19. *Niles Register,* August 31, 1833.

20. H. S. Fulkerson, *Random Recollections of Early Days in Mississippi* (Vicksburg, 1885), pp. 96–97.

21. *Ibid.,* p. 98.

22. Charles Hillman Brough, "Historic Clinton," *Publications of the Mississippi Historical Society* (Oxford, 1903), p. 290.

23. In February 1845, for example, a Memphis resident fought a man from Vicksburg at Foy's Point on the River. They used pistols and bowie knives. Shields McIlwaine, *Memphis Down to Dixie* (New York, 1948), pp. 101–103.

24. *Memphis Daily Appeal*, January 17, 1854.

25. John S. Kendall, "The Municipal Elections of 1858," *Louisiana Historical Quarterly*, V (July 1922), 362ff.

26. New Orleans *Daily Picayune*, June 9, 1858; and François Xavier Martin, *The History of Louisiana* (New Orleans, 1882), p. 455.

27. Alfred Vagts, *A History of Militarism, Romance and Realities of a Profession* (New York, 1937), pp. 185–186.

28. Rosser H. Taylor, *Ante-Bellum South Carolina* (Chapel Hill, 1942), p. 47.

29. James Ford Rhodes, *History of the United States* (New York, 1928), I, 362; see also Osterweis, *Romanticism and Nationalism*, p. 97.

30. James H. Hammond, "Governor Hammond's Letters on Slavery — No. 2," *De Bow's Review*, VII (December 1849), 491.

31. See the announcement, for example, of the opening of the Huntsville Military, Scientific, and Classical School. *Southern Advocate* (Huntsville, Alabama), November 26, 1831.

32. John Augustin, "The Oaks, the Old Duelling Grounds of New Orleans," in Thomas M'Caleb, *The Louisiana Book* (New Orleans, 1894), p. 76; and R. L. Desdunes, *Nos Hommes et Notre Histoire* (Montreal, 1911), pp. 107–109. Desdunes says that Crokere was regarded as the best maitre d'armes in the city.

33. *Daily Picayune*, February 7, 1845.

34. John Lyde Wilson, *The Code of Honor; or, Rules for the Government of Principals and Seconds in Duelling* (Charleston, 1838). The work was issued again in 1858. John McDonald Taylor's "Twenty-Six Commandments of the Duelling Code" were well known in New Orleans. See Heloise H. Cruzat, "When Knighthood was in Flower," *Louisiana Historical Quarterly*, I (April 1918), 367–371.

35. *Ibid.*, pp. 3–4.

36. See page 58.

37. Don Carlos Seitz, *Famous American Duels* (New York, 1929), p. 310.

38. Elizabeth Merritt, *James H. Hammond, 1807–1864* (Baltimore, 1923), p. 17.

39. Seitz, *Famous American Duels*, p. 120.

40. Whipple, *Southern Diary*, pp. 32–33.

41. Arthur Palmer Hudson, *Humor of the Old Deep South* (New York, 1936), pp. 430–431. See also the *Southern Advocate*, November 30, 1827.

42. Augustin, "The Oaks," p. 73.

43. John S. Kendall, "According to the Code," *Louisiana Historical Quarterly*, XXIII (January 1940), 143.

44. Mrs. D. Giraud Wright, *A Southern Girl in '61* (New York, 1905), pp. 31–32. Wigfall had engaged in several duels, including one in 1841, with Preston Brooks in which Brooks was shot through the hip and Wigfall through both thighs.

45. James L. Armstrong, *Reminiscences; Or An Extract from the Catalogue of General Jackson's 'Juvenile Indiscretions' Between the Ages of 23 and 60* (n.p., n.d.), p. 8. Armstrong listed fourteen fights, duels, etc. and said, "The foregoing is only a short extract from information sent me by my friends . . . since the attack has been made on my character by the General's minions, although I had knowledge of most of them myself. The list in my possession has accumulated to nearly ONE HUNDRED FIGHTS or *violent and abusive quarrels."*

46. John Spencer Bassett, *The Life of Andrew Jackson* (New York, 1928), pp. 62ff; and Seitz, *Famous American Duels*, pp. 123ff.

47. Lillian Adele Kibler, *Benjamin F. Perry, South Carolina Unionist* (Durham, 1946), p. 145.

48. Stephen F. Miller, *Bench and Bar of Georgia* (Philadelphia, 1858), I, 218; and Seitz, *Famous American Duels*, p. 115.

49. Miller, *Bench and Bar*, I, 21, II, 180.

50. Myra L. Spaulding, "Duelling in the District of Columbia," *Records of the Columbia Historical Society* (Washington, 1928), XXIX–XXX, 126–130. See John M. M'Carty's, *A View of the Whole Ground* (District of Columbia, 1818), for his discussion of the controversy.

51. Marquis James, *The Raven, A Biography of Sam Houston* (Indianapolis, 1929), pp. 66–67.

52. M. B. Blake to Dr. Benjamin King, April 8, 1826. MS in the Benjamin King Letters, Library of Congress.

53. Hugh A. Garland, *The Life of John Randolph of Roanoke* (New York, 1854), II, 260.

54. U. S. Congress, House of Representatives, *Report of the Committee On the Late Duel* (n.p., 1838), pp. 1–8. See also Seitz, *Famous American Duels*, pp. 251ff.

55. The *Report* cited above was the work of the investigating committee that was appointed.

56. *Congressional Globe*, 25th Congress, 2nd Session, March 2, 1838, p. 207.

57. Benjamin C. Truman, *The Field of Honor* (New York, 1884), pp. 427–428. *Ibid.*, p. 332. Webb was sentenced to two years' imprisonment at Sing Sing for violating the New York law against dueling. He was pardoned by Governor Seward. Marshall went unpunished.

58. John Witherspoon Du Bose, *The Life and Times of William*

*Lowndes Yancey* (Birmingham, 1892), I, 140ff. See also Seitz, *Famous American Duels*, p. 310.

59. *New York Times*, January 30, 31, 1856, and Glyndon G. Van Deusen, *Horace Greeley, Nineteenth Century Crusader* (Philadelphia, 1953), pp. 201ff. During these years there were numerous altercations of a similar nature, both in and out of the Congress. For an engaging account of several of them see Benjamin Perley Poore, *Perley's Reminiscences of Sixty Years in the National Metropolis* (Philadelphia, n.d.), I, 466, 532ff.

60. Preston Brooks to J. H. Brooks, May 23, 1856, in Robert L. Meriwether, ed., "Preston Brooks on the Caning of Charles Sumner," *The South Carolina Historical and Genealogical Magazine*, LII (January 1951), 3.

61. *Daily Richmond Enquirer*, June 14, 1856. These students presented Brooks with a goblet.

62. *Ibid.*, May 29, 1856; June 3, 1856.

63. *Charleston Mercury*, May 28, 1856; May 29, 1856.

64. Columbia Citizens, *Reception and Speech* (n.p., n.d.), pp. 4–5; and James E. Campbell, "Sumner – Brooks – Burlingame," *Ohio Archaeological and Historical Quarterly*, XXXIV (October 1925), 453ff. In the controversy that followed the caning, Brooks challenged three Northern offenders, all of whom declined. For Congressional reaction to this altercation, see the *Congressional Globe*, 34th Congress, 1st Session, Appendix, *passim*.

65. For a comprehensive discussion of the duels of Southern editors, see Frederic Hudson, *Journalism in the United States from 1690 to 1872* (New York, 1873), pp. 761–768.

66. Truman, *Field of Honor*, p. 306. See also Truman's account of the duels of other Vicksburg editors, pp. 306ff.

67. *Historical Sketch of New Orleans*, pp. 184ff. As late as 1859, Emile Hireat, a reporter for the New Orleans *Daily Delta*, killed C. Loquet, a French broker, in a duel. *Southern Advocate*, March 24, 1859.

68. F. Hudson, *Journalism*, p. 403. See the *Charleston Mercury* for September 13, 20, 24, 29, 30, and October 1, 2, 8, 1856.

69. A. W. Patterson, *The Code Duello, With Special Reference to the State of Virginia* (Richmond, 1927), pp. 43–44 and Robert R. Howison, "Duelling in Virginia," *William and Mary College Quarterly*, IV (October 1924), 240–244. See also the *Richmond Enquirer*, March 2, 1846.

70. Patterson, *The Code Duello*, p. 41.

71. *The Revised Code of North Carolina* (Boston, 1855), pp. 203–211. See also *The Revised Code of the Laws of Mississippi* (Natchez, 1824), p. 311.

72. *The Statutes At Large of South Carolina* (Columbia, 1839), V, 671–672. See also *A Compilation of the Laws of the State of Georgia* (Augusta, 1812), p. 529.

73. *The Consolidation and Revision of the Statutes of the State* (New Orleans, 1852), p. 187. See also *Digest of the Laws of the State of Alabama* (Philadelphia, 1833), p. 134.

74. George W. Crabb and J. T. Bradford, *Alabama Military Code* (Tuscaloosa, 1837), p. 51. In 1837 Alabama also forbade the carrying or use of any knife or weapon "known as Bowie knives or Arkansaw Toothpicks, or any knife or weapon that shall in form, shape, or size, resemble a Bowie knife or Arkansaw Tooth-pick." *Acts passed at the Called Session of the General Assembly of the State of Alabama, June 12, 1837* (Tuscaloosa, 1837), p. 7.

75. *Southern Advocate,* May 2, 1828. The address was delivered on October 3, 1827.

76. William H. Barnwell, *The Impiety and Absurdity of Duelling — A Sermon* (Charleston, 1844), pp. 5ff. See also J. R. Kendrick, *Duelling. A Sermon Preached at the First Baptist Church, Charleston, S. C. on Sunday Morning, August 7, 1853* (Charleston, 1853).

77. Whipple, *Southern Diary,* p. 115.

78. For an account of the organization of the Charleston Anti-Duelling Association see the Charleston *Courier,* October 19, 1826.

79. Thomas Gamble, *Savannah Duels and Duellists, 1733–1877* (Savannah, 1923), pp. 183–187. In September, 1834 more than one hundred citizens of New Orleans organized an anti-dueling association. Despite the pledges to fight the evil, several members were themselves involved in duels within a few months. Stewart O. Landry, *Duelling in Old New Orleans* (New Orleans, 1950), pp. 20–22.

80. *Southern Advocate,* March 14, 1828.

81. *Southern Advocate,* July 18, 1828.

82. *Acts, 1840–1841,* pp. 107, 144, 145.

83. *Acts, 1847–1848,* pp. 394, 409–410. See also *Acts, 1845–1846,* p. 216, for the special act releasing William L. Yancey from the dueling oath. It was vetoed by the Governor, but the Assembly overrode the veto on January 31, 1846.

84. This comment is an endorsement on a letter from Rush to Jackson, August 12, 1837, in Bassett, *Andrew Jackson,* p. 729.

85. Wilson, *Code of Honor,* p. 5.

86. Stevens, *Pistols at Ten Paces,* p. 75.

## 4. *A Militant Gentry*

1. See George Macaulay Trevelyan, *England Under the Stuarts* (New York, 1933), pp. 4ff.

2. See Thomas J. Wertenbaker, *The Planters of Colonial Virginia* (Princeton, 1922), pp. 28ff, 59.

3. See Louis Booker Wright, *The First Gentlemen of Virginia* (San Marino, Calif., 1940), pp. 38ff.

4. *The Writings of Thomas Jefferson,* edited by Paul Leicester Ford (New York, 1894), III, 266–267.

5. Captain Basil Hall, *Travels in North America in the Years 1827–1828* (Edinburgh, 1830), III, 230.

6. Alexis de Tocqueville, *Democracy in America* (New York, 1898), I, 507–508.

7. Buckingham, *Slave States,* II, 28.

8. Kemble, *Residence on a Georgia Plantation,* pp. 57–58, 305.

9. Max Farrand, *Records of the Federal Convention* (New Haven, 1927), II, 370.

10. Ulrich B. Phillips, *Race Problems, Adjustments and Disturbances in the Ante-Bellum South* (Richmond, 1909), p. 200.

11. Richard Hildreth, *Despotism in America . . .* (Boston, 1840), p. 37.

12. Charles Sumner, "The Barbarism of Slavery," Speech Delivered in the U. S. Senate, June 4, 1860 (Washington, 1860), p. 13.

13. H. S. Fulkerson, *Random Recollections of Early Days in Mississippi* (Vicksburg, 1885), p. 143. See also the account of the planter who was seriously considering putting his slaves in uniform and providing drill music for them. MS fragment, November 8, 1853, in the Mary Eliza Fleming Papers, Duke University Library.

14. Fulkerson, *Random Recollections,* p. 129.

15. Olmsted, *Back Country,* p. 30.

16. Helen T. Catterall, *Judicial Cases Concerning American Slavery and the Negro* (Washington, 1929), II, 57.

17. Olmsted, *Back Country,* pp. 82–83.

18. Howell M. Henry, *The Police Control of the Slave in South Carolina* (Emory, Virginia, 1914), pp. 31ff.

19. Charles S. Davis, *The Cotton Kingdom in Alabama* (Montgomery, 1939), p. 97; and Charles S. Sydnor, *Slavery in Mississippi* (New York, 1933), p 78.

20. *The Code of Alabama* (Montgomery, 1852), p. 235.

21. *Ibid.,* p. 235 and John B. Miller, *A Collection of the Militia Laws of the United States and South Carolina* (Columbia, 1817), pp. 71ff.

22. Henry, *Police Control,* p. 40.

23. *Ibid.,* p. 32.

24. Sydnor, *Slavery in Mississippi,* p 78; and Davis, *Cotton Kingdom in Alabama,* p. 97.

25. See the modifications of the Alabama law to meet these defects in Davis, *Cotton Kingdom in Alabama,* pp. 99ff; and *Code of Alabama,* pp. 235ff.

26. Thomas Colley Grattan, *Civilized America* (London, 1859), II, 242–243.

27. Hall, *Travels in North America,* III, 74–75. See also his wife's account of the same experience in Margaret Hunter Hall, *The Aristo-*

*cratic Journey, 1827–1828*, edited by Una Pope Hennessy (New York, 1931), p. 197. There are comments on the Richmond patrol in the John Ambler papers in the Library of Congress.

28. William Chambers, *Things as They are in America* (New York, 1854), p. 272

29. Buckingham, *Slave States,* I, 568.

30. J. Benwell, *An Englishman's Travels in America* (London, 1857), pp. 178, 184–185.

31. William Kingsford, *Impressions of the West and South During a Six Weeks' Holiday* (Toronto, 1858), p. 77.

32. Adelaide Wilson, *Historic and Picturesque Savannah* (Boston, 1889), p. 81.

33. *Daily Picayune* (New Orleans), January 2, 1857.

34. Edwin Clifford Holland, *A Refutation of the Calumnies Circulated Against the Southern and Western States Respecting the Institution and Existence of Slavery Among Them* (Charleston, 1822), pp. 61, 82.

35. Olmsted, *Back Country,* p. 203.

36. William Asbury Christian, *Richmond, Her Past and Present* (Richmond, 1912), p. 53; Herbert Aptheker, *American Negro Slave Revolts* (New York, 1943), pp. 218ff; and George Morgan, *The Life of James Monroe* (Boston, 1921), p. 228.

37. Theodore D. Jervey, *Robert Y. Hayne and His Times* (New York, 1909), pp. 131–132; Aptheker, *Slave Revolts,* pp. 273ff; and Henry, *Police Control,* pp. 152–153.

38. *Nashville Republican,* September 10, 1831.

39. *Norfolk Herald,* August 21, 1831, reprinted in *Nashville Republican,* September 10, 1831.

40. Frederick T. Wilson, *Federal Aid in Domestic Disturbances, 1787–1903* (Washington, 1903), pp. 56, 261–263.

41. In *American Negro Slave Revolts,* Aptheker calls attention to many instances in which military forces were used in connection with slave uprisings.

42. Charles Gayarré, *History of Louisiana* (New Orleans, 1903), IV, 267–268.

43. Aptheker, *Slave Revolts,* p. 255.

44. Harvey T. Cook, *The Life and Legacy of David Rogerson Williams* (New York, 1916), p. 130.

45. Guion G. Johnson, *Ante-Bellum North Carolina* (Chapel Hill, 1937), pp. 514–515.

46. Aptheker, *Slave Revolts,* p. 335.

47. *Journal of the Legislature of South Carolina for the Year 1833,* p. 6.

48. *Daily Picayune,* December 24, 1856.

## 5. *Defending The Cornerstone*

1. John C. Calhoun, *The Works of John C. Calhoun* (New York, 1854), I, 483–484.

2. *Ibid.*, II, 632–633. These remarks were made in the U. S. Senate on February 6, 1837, in the debate on the reception of abolition petitions.

3. *Southern Quarterly Review*, I (January 1842), 51.

4. John W. H. Underwood to Howell Cobb, February 2, 1844, in Phillips, "Correspondence of Toombs, Stephen, and Cobb," II, 54–55.

5. See William S. Jenkins, *Pro-slavery Thought in the Old South* (Chapel Hill, 1935); and E. N. Elliott, *Cotton is King and Pro-slavery Arguments* (Charleston, 1852).

6. *Southern Literary Messenger*, XXIII (October 1856), 247.

7. Calhoun, *Works*, II, 58–59.

8. Jenkins, *Pro-slavery Thought*, p. 125.

9. Quoted in Edward Ingle, *Southern Sidelights* (New York, 1896), p. 31.

10. William Harper, *The Pro-slavery Argument* (Philadelphia, 1853), p. 11.

11. George Fitzhugh, *Cannibals All! or Slaves Without Masters* (Richmond, 1857), pp. 97–98.

12. George Fitzhugh, *Sociology for the South; or The Failure of Free Society* (Richmond, 1854), p. 222.

13. *Selections From the Letters and Speeches of the Hon. James H. Hammond of South Carolina* (New York, 1866), p. 34.

14. Thomas Cooper to Mahlon Dickerson, March 16, 1826, in "Letters of Dr. Thomas Cooper, 1825–1832," *American Historical Review*, VI (July, 1901), 729. The idea of Negro inferiority was believed by some Northerners, but it neither was as widespread in that section nor did it constitute a whole body of thought as it did in the South.

15. S. C. Cartwright, "Diseases and Peculiarities of the Negro," *The Industrial Resources, etc., of the Southern and Western States* (New Orleans, 1853), II, 316.

16. See Alfred Vagts, *A History of Militarism* (New York, 1937), pp. 165, 479.

17. Thomas R. Dew, *Review of the Debate in the Virginia Legislature of 1831 and 1832* (Richmond, 1832), pp. 112–113.

18. J. D. B. De Bow, *The Interest in Slavery of the Southern Non-Slaveholder* (Charleston, 1860), pp. 3, 5, 8–10.

19. For discussions of inter-class harmony in the South see Frank L. Owsley, *Plain Folk of the Old South* (Baton Rouge, 1949), pp. 133–134; and Paul H. Buck, "Poor Whites of the Ante-Bellum South," *American Historical Review*, XXXI (October 1925), 41, 51–52.

20. Harper, *Pro-slavery Argument*, p. 80.

21. "The Black Race in North America," *De Bow's Review*, XX (February 1856), 209. (Italics in original.)

22. Buckingham, *Slave States*, I, 183.

23. Martineau, *Society in America*, II, 349.

24. Alfred Huger to Amos Kendall, July 30, 1855, in Theodore D. Jervey, *Robert Y. Hayne*, pp. 379–380.

25. Eaton, "Mob Violence," p. 358.

26. Sydnor, *Slavery in Mississippi*, p. 246.

27. *Ibid.*, p. 246.

28. Eaton, "Mob Violence," p. 366.

29. *The New Reign of Terror in the Slaveholding States for 1859–60* (New York, 1860); and *A Fresh Catalogue of Southern Outrages upon Northern Citizens* (New York, 1860).

30. Garrison, *New Reign of Terror*, p. 64.

31. *Ibid.*, p. 69.

32. Clement Eaton, *Freedom of Thought in The Old South* (Durham, 1940), p. 245; and *Dictionary of American Biography*, XIX, 114.

33. *De Bow's Review*, XXI (September 1856), 276–277.

34. David W. Stone to Thomas Ruffin, May 3, 1842, in J. G. de Roulhac Hamilton, editor, *The Papers of Thomas Ruffin* (Raleigh, 1918), II, 206.

35. For a detailed account of the experiences of Crooks and McBride, see Eaton, *Freedom of Thought*, pp. 138–139.

36. John Stafford to Thomas Ruffin, January 24, 1860, in Hamilton, *Papers of Thomas Ruffin*, II, 65–67.

37. Benjamin S. Hedrick to Thomas Ruffin, January 16, 1860, in *Papers of Thomas Ruffin*, III, 64–65.

38. Olmsted, *Back Country*, p. 478.

39. *Annals of Congress*, 12th Congress, 1st Session, p. 451. See also Hugh A. Garland, *The Life of John Randolph of Roanoke* (New York, 1854), I, 294–295.

40. Hildreth, *Despotism in America*, pp. 108–110.

41. Olmsted, *Back Country*, p. 477.

42. Hammond, *Letters and Speeches*, pp. 477, 128.

43. *Southern Quarterly Review*, XII (July 1847), 122–123.

44. Bryan, *Rightful Remedy*, p. 47.

45. A. P. Upshur, "Domestic Slavery," *Southern Literary Messenger*, V (October 1839), 681.

46. Hammond, *Letters and Speeches*, p. 128.

47. Edmund Ruffin, "Consequences of Abolition Agitation," *De Bow's Review*, XXIII (December 1857), 597.

48. *Southern Quarterly Review*, XIV (July 1848), 61.

49. *Southern Quarterly Review*, XV (July 1849), 306–307.

50. Harper, *Pro-Slavery Argument*, p. 81.

51. *Southern Literary Messenger*, V (October 1839), 682.

52. Dew, *Review of the Debates*, p. 13.

## 6. *Militant Expansionism*

1. See Jenkins, *Pro-Slavery Thought*, pp. 7off.

2. Quoted in Jenkins, *Pro-Slavery Thought*, pp. 57–58n.

3. A. S. Roane, "Reply to Abolition Objections to Slavery," *De Bow's Review*, XX (June 1856), 666–667.

4. *Address of the Committee of the Mississippi Convention to the Southern States* (Jackson, 1850), p. 15.

5. Albert K. Weinberg, *Manifest Destiny; A Study of Nationalistic Expansionism in American History* (Baltimore, 1935), p. 115.

6. George Frederick Holmes, "Relations of the Old and the New Worlds," *De Bow's Review*, XX (May 1856), 529.

7. For a discussion of the relation between filibustering and the South's martial spirit see William O. Scroggs, *Filibusters and Financiers* (New York, 1916), pp. 6–7.

8. "The Late Cuba Expedition," *De Bow's Review*, IX (August 1850), 167.

9. Holland, *Refutation*, p. 9.

10. Calhoun, *Works*, IV, 382–396; and Charles M. Wiltse, *John C. Calhoun Sectionalist, 1840–1850* (Indianapolis, 1951), pp. 303ff.

11. *De Bow's Review*, IX (August 1850), 250–251.

12. Julius W. Pratt, *The Expansionists of 1812* (New York, 1949), p. 121.

13. Harris Gaylord Warren, "Southern Filibusters in the War of 1812," *Louisiana Historical Quarterly*, XXV (April 1942), 294–295.

14. Harris Gaylord Warren, *The Sword Was Their Passport; A History of American Filibustering in the Mexican Revolution* (Baton Rouge, 1943), pp. 35–36.

15. *Ibid.*, p. 89.

16. Warren, "Southern Filibusters," p. 299.

17. Henry Putney Beers, *The Western Military Frontier, 1815–1846* (Philadelphia, 1935), p. 55.

18. For a different view see George P. Garrison, "The First Stage of the Movement for the Annexation of Texas," *American Historical Review*, X (October 1904), 72–96. Garrison contends that the "friction with Mexico brought about by the antislavery legislation of the Mexican government served for one or two brief periods to retard the growth of the colonies, but it disappeared before 1830 and played no appreciable part in bringing on the revolution." He then adds, "Neither was the material help given Texas from the United States in the course of the revolution the result, in my opinion, of any systematic thought for the expansion of slavery." (p. 80.)

19. James Winston, "New Orleans and the Texas Revolution," *Louisiana Historical Quarterly*, X (July 1927), 334.

20. *Ibid.*, p. 337.

21. John F. H. Claiborne, *Life and Correspondence of John A. Quitman* (New York, 1860), I, 141–142.

22. *Southern Advocate*, December 29, 1835, January 12, 1836.

23. Rosalie Q. Duncan, "The Life of General John A. Quitman," *Publications of the Mississippi Historical Society* (Oxford, 1901), IV, 418.

24. Garrison, "Annexation of Texas," p. 80.

25. *De Bow's Review*, XXVI (February 1859), 215.

26. After surveying the physiographic features of Kansas, the Southwest, and Latin America, Ramsdell concludes that the natural limits of slavery expansion had almost been reached by 1850. While his arguments on that point are, for the most part, convincing, if one assumes that the character of the plantation was not likely to change, he does not prove with similar persuasiveness that the slaveholders themselves clearly understood that they had almost reached the natural limits of slavery. Charles W. Ramsdell, "The Natural Limits of Slavery Expansion," *Mississippi Valley Historical Review*, XVI (September 1929), 151–171.

27. John Calhoun to Andrew Jackson, January 23, 1820, in *Correspondence of Andrew Jackson*, edited by John Spencer Bassett (Washington, 1928), III, 12.

28. James Jeffrey Roche, *The Story of the Filibusters* (London, 1891), p. 22.

29. Richardson Hardy, *History and Adventures of the Cuban Expedition* (Cincinnati, 1850), p. 3. Lopez is reported to have discussed his scheme with Calhoun while in Washington; but Calhoun, while greatly interested, felt that annexation could not be immediately accomplished and that the only thing that the people of the United States could do was to give assistance in the event of an insurrection on the island. Claiborne, *Quitman*, II, 53–55.

30. Claiborne, *Quitman*, II, 381, 56–57, 385.

31. See page 110.

32. Hardy, *Cuban Expedition*, pp. 3, 31.

33. Robert Granville Caldwell, *The Lopez Expeditions to Cuba, 1848–1851* (Princeton, 1915), p. 59n.

34. Hardy, *Cuban Expedition*, pp. 88–89.

35. Caldwell, *Lopez Expeditions*, p. 78.

36. Claiborne, *Quitman*, II, 75.

37. Chester Stanley Urban, "New Orleans and the Cuban Question during the Lopez Expeditions of 1849–1851," *Louisiana Historical Quarterly*, XXIII (October 1939), 1136–1137.

38. Quoted in Caldwell, *Lopez Expeditions*, p. 78.

39. "The Late Cuba Expedition," *De Bow's Review,* IX (August 1850), 172–173.

40. Caldwell, *Lopez Expeditions,* p. 84.

41. Louis M. Perez, editor, "Lopez's Expeditions to Cuba, 1850–51," *Publications of the Southern History Association,* X (November 1906), 346, 354.

42. Urban, "New Orleans and the Cuban Question," p. 1142.

43. Urban, "New Orleans and the Cuban Question," pp. 1143–1146; and Caldwell, *Lopez Expeditions,* pp. 89–90.

44. Francois Xavier Martin, *The History of Louisiana* (New Orleans, 1882), p. 452.

45. Urban, "New Orleans and the Cuban Question," pp. 1159–1160.

46. Caldwell, *Lopez Expeditions,* pp. 114–115.

47. Claiborne, *Quitman,* II, 194–195.

48. W. W. Holderness, Adams County, Ohio, to Palmerston, September 22, 1854, in Gavin B. Henderson, editor, "Southern Designs on Cuba and Some European Opinions," *Journal of Southern History,* V (August 1939), 375–376.

49. Thrasher was one of the most ardent advocates of Cuban annexation. See his article "Cuba and the United States," *De Bow's Review,* XVII (July 1854), 43–49.

50. Claiborne, *Quitman,* II, 194ff.

51. Amos A. Ettinger, *The Mission to Spain of Pierre Soulé, 1853–1855* (New Haven, 1932), p. 361.

52. *Documents of American History,* edited by Henry Steele Commager (New York, 1942), p. 334.

53. Edward Channing, *History of the United States* (New York, 1927), VI, 141.

54. Ettinger, *Mission of Pierre Soulé,* p. 402.

55. *Ibid.,* p. 402.

56. See John D. P. Fuller, "The Slavery Question and the Movement to Acquire Mexico," *Mississippi Valley Historical Review,* XXI (June 1934), in which the author asserts that slavery was a secondary factor in the South's desire for Mexico during the war.

57. Chauncey S. Boucher and Robert P. Brooks, eds., "Correspondence Addressed to John C. Calhoun, 1837–1849," *Annual Report of the American Historical Association for the Year 1929* (Washington, 1930), pp. 364.

58. Quoted in the *Charleston Mercury,* September 28, 1847.

59. *Niles Register,* LXXVIII.

60. See J. A. Turner, "Annexation of Canada," *De Bow's Review,* IX (October 1850), 412. There were a score of young Southerners in Congress, however, who were vigorous in their demands that the United States should drive England out of Oregon.

61. Fuller, "The Slavery Question," p. 39n.

62. Claiborne, *Quitman*, II, 7–10, 14.

63. Percy L. Rainwater, *Mississippi, Storm Center of Secession* (Baton Rouge, 1938), pp. 70–71.

64. Robert Toombs to W. W. Burwell, March 30, 1857, Phillips, "Correspondence of Toombs, Stephens and Cobb," p. 399.

65. William M. Burwell to Robert M. T. Hunter, August 22, 1848, Charles H. Ambler, ed., "Correspondence of Robert M. T. Hunter, 1826–1876," *Annual Report of the American Historical Association for 1916* (Washington, 1918), II, 263–265.

66. George Fitzhugh, "Acquisition of Mexico — Filibustering," *De Bow's Review*, XXV (December 1858), 620, 625.

67. Walter Prescott Webb, *The Texas Rangers* (Boston, 1935), p. 203.

68. *Ibid.*, pp. 203, 205. See also J. Fred Rippy, *The United States and Mexico* (New York, 1931), pp. 195–196.

69. Webb, *Texas Rangers*, pp. 206–207, 213–214.

70. New Orleans, *Daily Delta*, April 18, 1856.

71. *Ibid.*, November 29, 1856.

72. William Walker, *The War in Nicaragua* (Mobile, 1860), pp. 276–277.

73. William O. Scroggs, *Filibusters and Financiers* (New York, 1916), p. 139n.

74. *Ibid.*, p. 149.

75. William Walker, *War in Nicaragua*, pp. 278–279, 280.

76. Scroggs, *Filibusters and Financiers*, pp. 212, 224.

77. *Daily Delta*, April 18, 1856.

78. *Daily Delta*, November 22, and 29, 1856.

79. Scroggs, *Filibusters and Financiers*, p. 237.

80. *Daily Picayune* (New Orleans), October 24, 1856.

81. Laurence Oliphant, *Patriots and Filibusters* (London, 1860), p. 173.

82. Scroggs, *Filibusters and Financiers*, pp. 278–280.

83. Oliphant, *Patriots and Filibusters*, p. 171.

84. New Orleans *Picayune*, October 23, 1856.

85. *Ibid.*, May 28, 1857.

86. Scroggs, *Filibusters and Financiers*, p. 319.

87. [William Kingsford], *Impressions of the West and South* (Toronto, 1858), p. 61.

88. *Daily Picayune*, January 1, 1858.

89. Scroggs, *Filibusters and Financiers*, p. 334.

90. *Prairie News*, July 1, 1858, quoted in Percy L. Rainwater, "Economic Benefits of Secession: Opinions in Mississippi in the 1850's," *Journal of Southern History*, I (November 1935), 462.

91. *De Bow's Review*, XXVI (February 1859), 230.

92. *An Authentic Exposition of the "K.G.C."* (Indianapolis, 1861).

93. See the account of the Southern Rights group at the University

of South Carolina in Edward Luther Green, *History of the University of South Carolina* (Columbia, 1916), p. 55.

94. C. A. Bridges, "The Knights of the Golden Circle, A Filibustering Fantasy," *Southwestern Historical Quarterly*, XLIV (January 1941), 288.

95. There is a good, brief summary of Bickley's life in Ollinger Crenshaw, "The Knights of the Golden Circle," *American Historical Review*, XLVII (October 1941), 23–50.

96. Bridges, "Knights of the Golden Circle," p. 291.

97. *Authentic Exposition*, p. 15.

98. Crenshaw, "Knights of the Golden Circle," pp. 38, 39.

99. *Ibid.*, p. 38.

100. Edmund Wright, *Narrative of Edmund Wright; His Adventures with and Escape from the Knights of the Golden Circle* (Cincinnati, 1864), p. 55.

101. J. W. Pomfrey, *A True Disclosure and Exposition of the Knights of the Golden Circle* (Cincinnati, 1861), p. iv.

102. Crenshaw, "Knights of the Golden Circle," p. 34.

103. Pomfrey, *A True Disclosure*, pp. 14, 27. The key to the numbers used in the ritual is at the end of the book.

104. *Authentic Exposition*, p. 77.

105. Bridges, "Knights of the Golden Circle," p. 291.

106. Roche, *Story of the Filibusters*, p. 183.

107. Crenshaw, "Knights of the Golden Circle," p. 38.

## 7. *A Little Learning*

1. Joseph Caldwell, "Letters on Popular Education Addressed to the People of North Carolina," in Charles L. Coon, *The Beginnings of Public Education in North Carolina* (Raleigh, 1908), II, 550, 554–555.

2. De Bow, *Industrial Resources*, II, 473.

3. Reported in Olmsted, *Seaboard Slave States*, pp. 293–294.

4. "A Report of the President and Director of the Literary Fund of North Carolina, January 14, 1839," in Coon, *The Beginnings of Public Education*, II, 833.

5. Commonwealth of Virginia, *Journal of the House of Delegates, 1839* (Richmond, 1839), p. 9.

6. J. D. B. De Bow, *Statistical View of the United States . . . Being a Compendium of the Seventh Census* (Washington, 1854), p. 153.

7. See Ellis Merton Coulter, "A Georgia Educational Movement During the Eighteen Hundred Fifties," *Georgia Historical Quarterly*, IX (March 1925), 9–11.

8. Osterweis, *Romanticism and Nationalism*, pp. 95–96, 127–128.

9. Ephraim H. Foster to Dixon F. Allen, May 29, 1831. MS in the David Campbell Papers.

10. James L. Petigru to Hugh S. Legare, October 29, 1832. In James Petigru Carson, *Life, Letters and Speeches of James Louis Petigru. The Union Man of the South* (Washington, 1920), 102–104.

11. Whipple, *Southern Diary*, pp. 22, 23.

12. See page 43.

13. Quoted in Clement Eaton, "Mob Violence in the Old South," pp. 353–354.

14. John Campbell to Mrs. Maria Campbell, July 17, 1807. MS in the David Campbell Papers.

15. See the discussion of strife at Princeton in John Campbell to David Campbell, May 2, 1807, David Campbell Papers. See also Thomas Jefferson Wertenbaker, *Princeton, 1746–1896* (Princeton, 1946), pp. 138–142.

16. Edwin Luther Green, *History of the University of South Carolina* (Columbia, 1916), p. 34.

17. Albea Godbold, *The Church College of the Old South* (Durham, 1944), pp. 173–174.

18. Giles J. Patterson, *Journal of a Southern Student, 1846–1848*, edited with an introduction by Richmond Croom Beatty (Nashville, 1944), 41–42.

19. Godbold, *Church College*, p. 174. The furore arose over the demands of the students for a change in the common system and food service. When their wishes were not granted, many voluntarily withdrew.

20. Edward Ingle, *Southern Sidelights* (New York, 1896), pp. 150–151.

21. Walter Brownlow Posey, *LaGrange — Alabama's Earliest College* (Birmingham, 1933), p. 12.

22. See Ellis Merton Coulter, *College Life in the Old South* (New York, 1928), pp. 91–92, for an account of the student riot at the University of Georgia in 1832.

23. *Ibid.*, pp. 59ff.

24. John Donald Wade, *Augustus Baldwin Longstreet* (New York, 1924), pp. 322–325. See also Alice Felt Tyler, *Freedom's Ferment* (Minneapolis, 1944), p. 523.

25. Garrison, *New Reign of Terror*, p. 132.

26. See Eaton, *Freedom of Thought in the Old South*, pp. 73ff.

27. Edgar W. Knight, *Public Education in the South* (Boston, 1922), pp. 195ff. See also Charles William Dabney, *Universal Education in the South* (Chapel Hill, 1936), I, *passim*.

28. *Southern Literary Messenger*, I (August 1834), 1.

29. Lucian Minor, "An Address on Education," *Southern Literary Messenger*, II (December 1835), 18.

30. *De Bow's Review*, XIII (September 1852), p. 260. For an extensive discussion of the proposed program see John S. Ezell, "A Southern Education for Southrons," *Journal of Southern History*, XVII (August 1951), 303–327.

31. *De Bow's Review*, XV (September 1853), 267. In the following year a similar resolution was adopted at the Charleston convention. *De Bow's Review*, XVI (June 1854), 638, and XVII (November 1854), 509.

32. *De Bow's Review*, XX (January 1856), 67.

33. *De Bow's Review*, XXII (January 1857), 100.

34. William H. Stiles, *Southern Education for Southern Youth* (Savannah, 1858), pp. 4–5, 13, 25.

35. See page 156.

36. Claudius Crozet to Governor D. Campbell, November 21, 1839, in William Cowper, *Claudius Crozet: Soldier — Scholar — Educator — Engineer* (Charlottesville, 1936), p. 210.

37. Edwin Heriot, *The Polytechnic School. The Best System of Practical Education* (Charleston, 1850), p. 11.

38. *Southern Quarterly Review*, X (July 1854), 199.

39. Hill, "Essay on Military Education," p. 112. This address was delivered before a convention of North Carolina teachers, November 14, 1860.

40. Heriot, *The Polytechnic School*, p. 22.

41. L. C. Garland and J. J. Ormond, *University of Alabama Military Department* (Tuscaloosa, 1860), p. 5.

42. George Fitzhugh, "Frederick the Great, by Thomas Carlyle," *De Bow's Review*, XXIX (August 1860), 155.

43. Hill, "Essay on Military Education," p. 113.

44. S. W. Trotti, *Address Delivered before the Calliopean and Polytechnic Societies of the State Military Academy* (Charleston, 1847), p. 19.

45. *Southern Quarterly Review*, X (July 1854), 198.

46. Heriot, *The Polytechnic School*, pp. 13–14.

47. T. Harry Williams, "The Attack Upon West Point During the Civil War," *Mississippi Valley Historical Review*, XXV (March 1939), 491–492.

48. *Southern Advocate* (Huntsville, Alabama), December 21, 1827.

49. *Register of Debates*, 21st Congress, 1st Session, January 22, 1830, pp. 553–554, and February 25, 1830, p. 583.

50. *Register of Debates*, 23rd Congress, 1st Session, June 14, 1834, p. 4483.

51. *Congressional Globe*, 26th Congress, 1st Session, July 20, 1840, p. 554.

52. Andrew Jackson to Andrew J. Donelson, March 5, 1823, in Bassett, *Correspondence*, III, 192; and James D. Richardson, *A Compilation of the Messages and Papers of the Presidents* (New York, 1897), p. 1019.

53. *Congressional Globe*, 28th Congress, 1st Session, March 6, 1844, Appendix, pp. 272–274.

54. *Ibid.*, February 26, 1844, p. 323.

55. *Ibid.*, April 3, 1844, pp. 473–474.

56. The writer was, perhaps, Francis Henny Smith of the class of 1833 at the Military Academy and first superintendent of the Virginia Military Institute.

57. *Southern Literary Messenger*, IX (November 1843), 665–666.

58. *De Bow's Review*, XIII (September 1852), 265–266.

59. *Congressional Globe*, 35th Congress, 1st Session, January 4, 1858, p. 183. See also the *Daily Picayune*, January 29, 1858.

60. John Calhoun to R. M. Johnson, January 15, 1819, in Calhoun, *Works*, V, 56.

61. Percy Gatling Hamlin, *"Old Bald Head" (General R. S. Ewell)*, *The Portrait of a Soldier* (Strasburg, Virginia, 1940), p. 5.

62. Mrs. J. W. Anderson to Edward Willoughby Anderson in Francis P. Sullivan, ed., "Letters of a West Pointer 1860–1861," *American Historical Review*, XXXIII (April 1928), 609.

63. *American State Papers; Military Affairs* (Washington, 1890), IV, 353–355.

64. The figures are compiled from Cullum, *Biographical Register*, I, II, *passim*.

65. William Arba Ellis, *Norwich University, 1819–1911, Her History, Her Graduates, Her Roll of Honor* (Montpelier, Vermont, 1911), I, 7–8.

66. *Ibid.*, I, 395–401.

67. Cullum, *Biographical Register*, I, 70.

## 8. *West Points of the South*

1. *Raleigh Register*, April 6, 1809 quoted in *North Carolina Schools and Academies: A Documentary History, 1790–1840*, edited by Charles Lee Coon (Raleigh, 1915), pp. 415–416.

2. *Raleigh Star*, May 15, 1812, in Coon, *North Carolina Schools*, p. 243.

3. *Raleigh Register*, August 22, 1826, in Coon, *North Carolina Schools*, p. 244.

4. Guion G. Johnson, *Ante-Bellum North Carolina* (Chapel Hill, 1937), p. 289.

5. *Raleigh Star*, December 2, 1830, and *Raleigh Register*, December 2, 1830, in Coon, *North Carolina Schools*, pp. 253–254.

6. *Raleigh Register*, March 12, 1833, and *Wilmington Advertiser*, March 11, 1836, in Coon, *North Carolina Schools*, pp. 261–262.

7. Green, *University of South Carolina*, p. 38.

8. *Citadel Cadets, Journal of Cadet Tom Law, 1858–1859*, John Adger Law (Clinton, 1941), p. 106.

9. Charles S. Sydnor, *A Gentleman of the Old Natchez Region, Ben-*

*jamin L. C. Wailes* (Durham, 1938), p. 205. Wailes was member of the board of trustees.

10. J. K. Morrison, "Early History of Jefferson College," *Publications of the Mississippi Historical Society* (Oxford, 1899), II, 187–188.

11. Sydnor, *Wailes*, p. 205.

12. Ingraham, *Southwest*, II, 211.

13. Edward Mayes, *History of Education in Mississippi*, United States Bureau of Education, Contributions to American Educational History, Number 24 (Washington, 1899), 31–32; and Sydnor, *Wailes*, p. 222.

14. See page 157.

15. *Southern Advocate*, May 14, 1831.

16. Dudley and Lowe were of the West Point class of 1814. Other graduates of the United States Military Academy who worked in Southern military schools were Richard W. Colcock, '26; Albert Miller Lea, '31; Francis Henny Smith, '33; Robert T. P. Allen, '34; Arnoldus V. Brumby and James M. Wells, '35; Bushrod Johnson and William T. Sherman, '40; Daniel Hill, '42; Caleb Huse, '51; and Charles C. Lee, '56.

17. *Southern Advocate*, October 22, 1831.

18. Edward Chambers Betts, *Early History of Huntsville, Alabama* (Montgomery, 1916), p. 79; and *Southern Advocate*, January 21, 1832.

19. Colonel William Couper, *One Hundred Years at V.M.I.* (Richmond, 1939), I, 17–21.

20. Couper, *One Hundred Years*, I, 29ff. See also Couper, *Claudius Crozet, passim.*

21. Couper, *One Hundred Years*, I, 51.

22. Jennings Cropper Wise, *The Military History of Virginia Military Institute* (Lynchburg, 1915), pp. 53–54.

23. Wise, *Virginia Military Institute*, p. 47.

24. *Ibid.*, p. 49.

25. Charles James Faulkner, *Address Delivered to the Graduating Class of the Virginia Military Institute, July 4, 1850* (Lexington, 1850), p. 4.

26. John Peyre Thomas, *The History of the South Carolina Military Academy* (Charleston, 1893), pp. 28–29.

27. *Regulations of the Citadel Academy at Charleston and Arsenal Academy at Columbia* (Columbia, 1849), pp. 5–9.

28. Thomas, *South Carolina Military Academy*, p. 46 and *Regulations*, p. 3.

29. Thomas, *South Carolina Military Academy*, p. 43.

30. Trotti, *Address*, p. 17. See also "Origin of the State Military Academies," *Russell's Magazine*, IV (December 1858), 219–226.

31. Alma Pauline Foerster, "The State University in the Old South — A Study of Social and Intellectual Influences in State University Education," p. 200. Unpublished Ph.D. Dissertation at Duke University.

32. See page 159.

33. Lucius Salisbury Merriam, *Higher Education in Tennessee* (Washington, 1893), p. 66.

34. *Acts Passed at the Annual Session of the General Assembly of the State of Alabama, 1843–44* (Tuscaloosa, 1844), pp. 55, 118.

35. *Acts . . . of the State of Alabama, 1844–45* (Tuscaloosa, 1845), p. 135; and *Acts . . . of the State of Alabama, 1845–46* (Tuscaloosa, 1846), p. 111.

36. *Acts . . . 1845–46*, p. 250.

37. *Southwestern Monthly*, II (September 1852), 131.

38. *De Bow's Review*, XIII (October 1852), 430–431.

39. *Memphis Daily Appeal*, March 23, 1848.

40. Mabel Alstetter and Gladys Watson, "Western Military Institute, 1847–1861," *Filson Club Historical Quarterly*, X (April 1936), 101–105. For several years a monthly school paper, "The Cadet" was published. *Southwestern Monthly*, II (September 1852), 132.

41. Barksdale Hamlett, *History of Education in Kentucky* (Frankfort, 1914), p. 304.

42. *De Bow's Review*, VII (September 1849), 203–204, and VIII (March 1850), 313.

43. *Daily Picayune*, October 6, 1857.

44. *Southern Advocate*, August 25, 1859 and subsequent issues.

45. Cullum, *Biographical Register*, I, 754.

46. *De Bow's Review*, VII (September 1849), 204.

47. See Ingle, *Southern Sidelights*, pp. 153–154.

48. *Self-Instructor* (Charleston), March 1854, quoted in Rosser H. Taylor, *Ante-Bellum South Carolina* (Chapel Hill, 1842), p. 122. See also *The Southern Literary Messenger*, XXIV (April 1857), 247.

49. Sydnor, *Wailes*, pp. 222, 228. See also *De Bow's Review*, X (April 1851), 478. In 1857, the Mississippi Military Institute of Pass Christian was advertising in the New Orleans press, but little else is known of the institution. See the *Daily Picayune*, August 1, 1857.

50. Major Thomas Benton, who served as commandant of cadets and instructor of military tactics, is described as a graduate of West Point in Josiah H. Shinn, *History of Education in Arkansas* (Washington, 1900), p. 27. Cullum, *Biographical Register*, however, does not list any person by that name as a graduate of the Academy.

51. Shinn, *Education in Arkansas*, pp. 27–30.

52. Ellis Merton Coulter, *A Short History of Georgia* (Chapel Hill, 1933), p. 274.

53. George White, *Historical Collection of Georgia* (New York, 1854), pp. 400–401.

54. Charles Edward Jones, *Education in Georgia* (Washington, 1889), pp. 107–109.

55. From the message of Governor Joseph E. Brown to the legislature

of Georgia, November 1860, in Herbert Fielder, *A Sketch of the Life and Times and Speeches of Joseph E. Brown* (Springfield, 1883), p. 166.

56. Alstetter and Watson, "Western Military Institute," p. 109.

57. *Republican Banner and Whig* (Nashville), March 15, 1855, March 18, 1855, and March 22, 1855.

58. Merriam, *Education in Tennessee*, p. 47. See also Henry Carl Witherington, *A History of State Higher Education in Tennessee* (Chicago, 1931), pp. 35–36.

59. The founders were Micah Jenkins and Asbury Coward of the class of 1854. Among other Citadel graduates who worked in Southern military schools were Charles C. Tew, '46; J. M. Robertson, '50; W. W. Armstrong, '51; and T. H. Mangum, '57. See John Peyre Thomas, *Careers and Characters of General Micah Jenkins, C.S.A.* (Columbia, 1903), p. 3.

60. Thomas, *South Carolina Military Academy*, pp. 524–525.

61. *Ibid.*, p. 258.

62. *Acts of the Third Biennial Session of the General Assembly of Alabama* (Montgomery, 1852), pp. 387–390.

63. *Acts of the Fourth Biennial Session* (Montgomery, 1854), p. 187.

64. *Acts of the Fifth Biennial Session* (Montgomery, 1856), pp. 356.

65. *Acts of the Sixth Biennial Session* (Montgomery, 1858), p. 275.

66. *Acts of the Seventh Biennial Session* (Montgomery, 1860), p. 31.

67. Thomas, *South Carolina Military Academy*, p. 258.

68. *Acts of the Fourth Biennial Session*, p. 425.

69. *Acts of the Fifth Biennial Session*, 356; *Journal of the Fifth Biennial Session of the Senate of Alabama, 1855–56* (Montgomery, 1856), p. 290; and *Journal . . . of the House of Representatives, 1855–56* (Montgomery, 1856), p. 543.

70. *Acts of the Seventh Biennial Session*, pp. 130–132.

71. Walter Brownlow Posey, *La Grange — Alabama's Oldest College* (Birmingham, 1933), pp. 5ff.

72. John Allan Wyeth, *History of La Grange Military Academy and the Cadet Corps, 1857–1862* (New York, 1907), pp. 9–10.

73. *Acts of the Seventh Biennial Session*, p. 315.

74. *Southern Advocate*, February 8, 1860.

75. *Acts of the Seventh Biennial Session*, pp. 91–92.

76. *Ibid.*, pp. 31, 90.

77. *Southern Advocate*, February 22, 1860.

78. Basil Manly, *Report on Collegiate Education, Made to the Trustees of the University of Alabama* (Tuscaloosa, 1852), p. 49.

79. L. C. Garland and J. J. Ormond, *University of Alabama, Military Department* (Tuscaloosa, n.d.), pp. 1ff.

80. *Ibid.*, p. 4; Couper, *Virginia Military Instiute*, I, 301–302.

81. *Acts of the Seventh Biennial Session*, p. 25.

82. Willis J. Clark, *History of Education in Alabama* (Washington, 1889), pp. 87–88.

83. Walter L. Fleming, *Louisiana State University, 1860–1896* (Baton Rouge, 1936), pp. 35–36.

84. *Ibid.*, pp. 28–30.

85. *De Bow's Review*, XXVII (October 1859), 486.

86. Fleming, *Louisiana State University*, p. 36.

87. *Ibid.*, p. 38.

88. W. T. Sherman, *Memoirs of General W. T. Sherman, Written by Himself* (New York, 1891), I, 178.

89. Fleming, *Louisiana State University*, p. 96.

90. David French Boyd, "W. T. Sherman as a College President," *The American College*, II (April 1910), 7–8.

91. John J. Lane, *History of Education in Texas* (Washington, 1903), p. 105.

92. *Bastrop Advertiser*, October 9, 1858, quoted in Margaret Belle Jones, *Bastrop* (Bastrop, 1936), p. 33.

93. Jones, *Bastrop*, pp. 35–36.

94. Worth S. Ray, *Austin Colony Pioneers* (Austin, 1949), pp. 324–325.

95. Couper, *Virginia Military Institute*, II, 73.

96. Charles Lee Smith, *The History of Education in North Carolina* (Washington, 1888), p. 138.

97. James H. Lane, "North Carolina Military Institute" in *Histories of the Several Regiments and Battalions from North Carolina in the Great War, 1861–1865*, edited by Walter Clark (Raleigh and Goldsboro, 1901), V, 645–646. See also Alphonso Calhoun Avery, *Memorial Address on the Life and Character of Lt. General D. H. Hill* (Raleigh, 1893), *passim*.

98. Thomas, *South Carolina Military Academy*, p. 526.

99. William Cain, "Hillsboro Military Academy; Its Relation to the War," in Clark, *Regiments and Battalions*, V, 637–641. See also Smith, *Education in North Carolina*, p. 138.

100. Clark, *Regiments and Battalions*, IV, 420, V, 637. See also Jesse Bagby to Bennette Bagby, January 8, 1861, in which Jesse writes his father that the school in which he was teaching at Williamsboro had recently set up a "Military Department." MS in the Bennette Bagby Papers, Luke University Library.

101. See note 16, this chapter.

102. See note 59, this chapter.

103. *Southern Quarterly Review*, X (July 1854), 197.

104. *Southern Advocate*, November 26, 1831.

105. Couper, *Virginia Military Institute*, I, 43; and *Regulations of the Citadel Academy*, p. 12.

106. Fleming, *Louisiana State University*, p. 49.

107. Jones, *Bastrop*, p. 33; and John Allen Wyeth, *With Sabre and Scalpel* (New York, 1914), p. 160.

108. On the role of uniforms in martial society, see Karl Paul A. F. Liebknecht, *Militarism* (New York, 1917), pp. 65–66.

109. Wise, *Virginia Military Institute*, pp. 50–52, 57.

110. Thomas, *South Carolina Military Academy*, pp. 80–81.

111. *Southern Advocate*, September 21, 1859, October 26, 1859, and November 2, 1859.

112. B. J. Barbour, "Address Delivered before the Literary Societies of the Virginia Military Institute, July 4, 1854," *Southern Literary Messenger*, XX (September 1854), 513.

113. Francis Henny Smith, *Introductory Address to the Corps of Cadets of the Virginia Military Institute* (Richmond, 1856), p. 22.

114. Thomas, *South Carolina Military Academy*, p. 283.

115. Fielder, *Joseph E. Brown*, p. 166.

116. Wise, *Virginia Military Institute*, pp. 141ff.

117. Thomas, *South Carolina Military Academy*, pp. 106, 246.

118. Clark, *History of the Several Regiments*, V, 646; Wyeth, *La Grange*, p. 196; and Fleming, *Louisiana State University*, pp. 105–106.

## 9. *The Citizen Soldiery*

1. For a summary of early legislation see Emory Upton, *The Military Policy of the United States* (Washington, 1911), ch. 8.

2. Francis N. Thorpe, *The Federal and State Constitutions* (Washington, 1909), I, 280.

3. *Laws of Tennessee, 1794–1801*, p. 155.

4. *Laws of Tennessee, 1794–1801*, p. 34.

5. *Acts of Tennessee, 1821*, p. 63.

6. *Acts of the Third Biennial Session*, pp. 391–392.

7. *Memphis Daily Appeal*, May 26, 1853.

8. "The History of Richmond," *Southern Literary Messenger*, XVIII (May 1852), 265; and Alfred Hoyt Bill, *The Beleaguered City, Richmond, 1861–1865* (New York, 1946), pp. 4–6.

9. Edward L. Wells, *A Sketch of the Charleston Light Dragoons, From the Earliest Formation of the Corps* (Charleston, 1888), pp. 4–6, *passim*.

10. Charles Gayarré, *History of Louisiana* (New Orleans, 1903), p. 127.

11. In announcing the brigade parade scheduled for December 23, 1853, the *Daily Picayune*, December 21, 1843, carries notices of ten military companies.

12. William F. Gray, *From Virginia to Texas, 1835* (Houston, 1909), p. 26, and the *Daily Picayune*, December 20, 1857.

13. *Memphis Daily Appeal*, August 18, 1853.

14. *Ibid.*, June 4, 1853.

15. Emily Burke, *Reminiscences of Georgia* (Oberlin, 1850), pp. 93–94.

16. For a description of the inelegant uniforms, see Thomas D. Clark, *The Rampaging Frontier* (Indianapolis, 1939), p. 183.

17. *Wilmington Journal*, November 29, 1844.

18. Jane H. Thomas, *Old Days in Nashville, Tennessee* (Nashville, 1897), p. 32.

19. James Battle Avirett, *The Memoirs of General Turner Ashby and His Compeers* (Baltimore, 1867), p. 62.

20. *Daily Picayune*, December 23, 1856. For additional descriptions of colorful uniforms see Reuben Davis, *Recollections of Mississippi and Mississippians* (Boston, 1899), p. 139; *Memphis Daily Appeal*, May 7, 1853; *Southern Advocate*, May 3, 1844; and Alfred T. Vigne, *Six Months in America* (Philadelphia, 1833), pp. 58–59.

21. South Carolina, *The Militia and Patrol Laws of South Carolina to December, 1859*, p. 9. See also *The Militia Law of Virginia* (Richmond, 1858), p. 24; and *Laws of Tennessee, 1794–1801*, p. 223.

22. *Militia and Patrol Laws of South Carolina*, p. 14.

23. Virginia *Militia Law*, p. 24; and *Laws of Tennessee, 1794–1801*, p. 223.

24. See the *Nashville Republican*, April 6, 1830, and succeeding issues.

25. *Daily Picayune*, November 12, 1856.

26. Joseph S. Williams, *Old Times in West Tennessee* (Memphis, 1873), p. 131.

27. Claiborne, *Quitman*, I, 142.

28. See Gerald M. Capers, *The Biography of a River Town; Memphis: Its Heroic Age* (Chapel Hill, 1939), p. 63.

29. H. E. Taliaferro, *Fisher's River (North Carolina) Scenes and Characters* (New York, 1859), pp. 20–25. See also Davis, *Recollections of Mississippi*, pp. 137–141.

30. *Southern Advocate*, August 28, 1830. For other descriptions, see Longstreet, *Georgia Scenes*, pp. 196–206 and Buckingham, *Slave States*, II, 69–70. See also the unfavorable reaction of a New England woman to a Kentucky muster: the militia "whiskey drinking ragamuffins, hardly a decent looking man among them." Caroline Poole's Diary, 1835–1837. MS in the Library of Congress.

31. *Daily Picayune*, November 14, 1856.

32. Davis, *Recollections of Mississippi*, p. 139.

33. William T. Hale, *History of De Kalb County, Tennessee* (Nashville, 1915), p. 42.

34. T. H. Ball, *A Glance Into the Great South-East, or, Clark County, Alabama* (Grove Hill, 1882), p. 206.

35. Williams, *West Tennessee*, p. 131.

36. See Clark, *Rampaging Frontier*, p. 184, for a discussion of the importance of the muster in the rural areas of the ante-bellum South.

37. In Vicksburg, William F. Gray found that the military companies paraded there as frequently as they did in his own Fredericksburg, Virginia. Gray, *From Virginia to Texas*, pp. 26, 30.

38. *Southern Advocate*, May 3, 1844.

39. *Memphis Daily Appeal*, August 1, 1853; August 18, 1853; and September 9, 1853.

40. Powell A. Casey, "Early History of the Washington Artillery of New Orleans," *Louisiana Historical Quarterly*, XXIII (April 1940), 472–473.

41. *Daily Picayune*, April 22, 1857 and April 21, 1858.

42. *Ibid.*, June 6, 1857.

43. *Ibid.*, December 3, 1857 and December 4, 1857.

44. James R. Creecy, *Scenes in the South, And Other Miscellaneous Pieces* (Washington, 1860), p. 34.

45. Gray, *From Virginia to Texas*, pp. 30–32.

46. Casey, "Washington Artillery," p. 474.

47. *Memphis Daily Appeal*, September 16, 1853.

48. *Daily Picayune*, December 13, 1843.

49. *Southern Advocate*, May 26, 1859.

50. See page 203.

51. Margaret Hunter Hall, *The Aristocratic Journey, 1827–1828*, edited by Una Pope-Hennessy (New York, 1931), p. 214.

52. F. Garvin Davenport, *Cultural Life In Nashville on the Eve of the Civil War* (Chapel Hill, 1941), pp. 167–168.

53. *North Carolina Standard* (Raleigh), February 27, 1857.

54. Susan D. Smedes, *Memorials of a Southern Planter* (Baltimore, 1887), p. 41.

55. *Raleigh Star*, September 15, 1831.

56. *Nashville Republican*, October 8, 1831 and November 1, 1831.

57. Capers, *Biography of A River Town*, p. 73.

58. Achille Murat, *A Moral and Political Sketch of the United States of North America* (London, 1833), pp. 262–265.

59. Buckingham, *Slave States*, I, 421.

60. *Daily Picayune*, December 13, 1843.

61. *The Works of Philip Lindsley, D.D.*, edited by LeRoy J. Halsey (Philadelphia, 1866), p. 598.

62. *Southern Advocate*, January 24, 1845. For a similar chastisement in Memphis see the *Memphis Daily Appeal*, September 1, 1853.

63. *De Bow's Review*, X (March 1851), 245–246.

64. *Daily Delta*, December 19, 1856.

65. *Daily Picayune*, February 6, 1857, August 7, 1857, and Casey, "Early History of the Washington Artillery," p. 481.

66. *Journal of the Fifth Biennial Session of the Senate of Alabama, 1855–1856* (Montgomery, 1856), p. 13. See also the *Daily Picayune,* November 15, 1857.

67. Fielder, *Joseph E. Brown,* pp. 163ff.

68. *Richmond Enquirer,* August 10, 1855 and William Ashbury Christian, *Richmond Her Past and Present* (Richmond, 1912), p. 206.

69. *Acts of the Sixth Biennial Session,* pp. 147–152.

70. See, for example, the increase in the membership of the military groups of Mobile. *Daily Picayune,* February 13, 1857.

71. Henry T. Shanks, *The Secession Movement in Virginia, 1847–1861* (Richmond, 1834), pp. 95–96, 126–127; Avirett, *General Turner Ashby,* pp. 55–56; and Christian, *Richmond,* p. 203.

72. Joseph Carlyle Sitterson, *The Secession Movement in North Carolina* (Chapel Hill, 1939), p. 151.

73. *De Bow's Review,* XXVII (October 1859), 466.

74. H. K. Craig to J. B. Floyd, November 20, 1860. MS in "Letters from Ordnance Department to War Department," XIII, 21.

75. For a discussion of the importance of local military organizations at the tme of secession, see Frank L. Owsley, *State Rights in the Confederacy* (Chicago, 1925), pp. 24ff.

76. *De Bow's Review,* XIII (December 1852), 621.

77. Frances Milton Trollope, *Domestic Manners of the Americans* (London, 1832), I, 24.

78. Benjamin Henry Latrobe, *The Journal of Latrobe* (New York, 1905), p. 24.

79. Clark, *The Rampaging Frontier,* pp. 185–186.

80. Buckingham, *Slave States,* I, 126, II, 192–193.

81. Whipple, *Southern Diary,* p. 82. See also the observation in Pulszky, *White, Red, Black,* I, 108–109.

82. P. H. Saunders, "Life of Colonel Felix Lebouve," *Publications of the Mississippi Historical Society* (Oxford, 1903), VII, 133–134.

83. Featherstonhaugh, *Slave States,* I, 83–84.

84. *De Bow's Review,* I (January 1846), 10.

## 10. *Literary and Social Echoes*

1. From the correspondence of the *Portland Daily Advertiser,* April 1, 1833, quoted in *Nile's Weekly Register,* April 27, 1833.

2. Olmsted, *Seaboard Slave States,* p. 404.

3. Buckingham, *Slave States,* I, 355.

4. For a vigorous and convincing criticism of the Twain and Eckenrode thesis, see G. Harrison Orians, "Walter Scott, Mark Twain and the Civil War," *South Atlantic Quarterly,* XL (October 1941), 342–359.

5. Mark Twain, *Life on the Mississippi* (New York, 1917), pp. 375–376.

6. Hamilton James Eckenrode, "Sir Walter Scott and the South," *North American Review,* CCVI (October 1917), 599–602.

7. See the discussion in Grace Warren Landrum, "Sir Walter Scott and His Literary Rivals in the South," *American Literature,* II (November 1930), 258, 265–267.

8. William E. Dodd, "The Social Philosophy of the Old South," *American Journal of Sociology,* XXIII (May 1918), 742.

9. Harold F. Bogner, "Sir Walter Scott in New Orleans, 1818–1832," *Louisiana Historical Quarterly,* XXI (April 1938), 457. See also "The Diary of Rebecca Mandeville, 1848." MS in the Mandeville Collection at Louisiana State University. Here is described the amateur enactment of two scenes from *Ivanhoe.*

10. *Richmond Enquirer,* November 20, 1832.

11. Dodd, "Social Philosophy," p. 742.

12. "Literature in the South," *Russell's Magazine,* V (August 1859), 386.

13. See page 135.

14. This is the only story in *Georgia Scenes* that was not written by Longstreet. Its author was Oliver H. Prince.

15. See page 3.

16. See page 81.

17. Philip Graham, *The Life and Poems of Mirabeau B. Lamar* (Chapel Hill, 1938), p. 169.

18. Buckingham, *Slave States,* I, 217.

19. Alexander Beaufort Meek, *Songs and Poems of the South* (New York, 1857), p. 5.

20. *Ibid.,* p. 57.

21. Buckingham, *Slave States,* II, 79.

22. See page 182.

23. *Southern Advocate,* October 26, 1859.

24. See Esther J. Crooks and Ruth W. Crooks, *The Ring Tournament in the United States* (Richmond, 1936), p. 2; Theodore Jervey, *Elder Brother* (New York, 1905); Thomas A. Ashby, *Life of Turner Ashby* (New York, 1914), pp. 34–36; and *The Richmond Examiner,* August 30, 1845, for descriptions of tournaments.

25. Orians, "Walter Scott," p. 346.

26. G. P. R. James, *The History of Chivalry* (New York, 1857), p. 40.

27. This is convincingly denied in Orians, "Walter Scott," p. 344, and Landrum, "Scott and His Literary Rivals," p. 263.

28. Crooks, *Ring Tournament,* p. 34 and Ashby, *Turner Ashby,* p. 35.

29. Crooks, *Ring Tournament,* pp. 34–40.

30. Orians, "Walter Scott," p. 346.

31. Crooks, *Ring Tournament,* p. 96.

32. Quoted in the *Southern Advocate,* December 31, 1857.

33. Crooks, *Ring Tournament,* pp. 36, 39, 76–77, 100.

34. *Ibid.,* pp. 151, 40, 106.

35. *Southern Literary Messenger,* I (December 1834), 157–159.

36. John Campbell to David Campbell, July 5, 1812. MS in the David Campbell Papers.

37. Williams, *Old Times,* pp. 170–171.

38. William B. Campbell to Maria H. Campbell, July 13, 1830. MS in the David Campbell Papers. Campbell was the orator of the day.

39. Law, *Citadel Cadets,* pp. 35–36.

40. *Southern Advocate,* July 11, 1845.

41. *Ibid.,* July 7, 1859.

42. Minnie C. Boyd, *Alabama in the Fifties* (New York, 1931), pp. 218–219.

43. *Daily Picayune,* July 8, 1857.

44. J. E. Walmsley, "The Presidential Campaign of 1844 in Mississippi," *Publications of the Mississippi Historical Society,* IX (Oxford, 1896), 191.

45. *Daily Picayune,* July 7, 1857, July 10, 1857.

46. *Southern Literary Messenger,* VII (April 1841), 316–320. For descriptions of other celebrations, see Wise, *Virginia Military Institute,* pp. 95–96; Hall, *Aristocratic Journey,* p. 209; and Law, *Citadel Cadets,* p. 9.

47. Buckingham, *Slave States,* I, 126.

48. *Nashville Whig,* February 27, 1822.

49. *Daily Picayune,* February 24, 1857. See also the issues for January 25, February 17, and 20, 1857.

50. *Daily Picayune,* December 30, 1855. The Battle of New Orleans was fought on January 8, 1815.

51. *Southern Advocate,* January 13, 1859.

52. Grace King, *New Orleans, The Place and the People* (New York, 1928), p. 254.

53. Gray, *From Virginia to Texas,* pp. 70–71.

54. *Daily Picayune,* January 8 and 9, 1857.

55. *Ibid.,* January 9, 1858.

56. David Campbell to General Tate, August 24, 1810. MS in the David Campbell Papers.

57. Law, *Citadel Cadets,* pp. 33–34.

58. Robert F. W. Allston to Benjamin Allston, June 25, 1858, quoted in James Harold Easterby, *The South Carolina Rice Plantations as Revealed in the Papers of Robert F. W. Allston* (Chicago, 1945), p. 144.

59. See the *Daily Picayune,* April 11 and 15, 1857, and Crooks, *Ring Tournament,* p. 35.

60. Christian, *Richmond,* p. 102.

61. Murat, *A Moral and Political Sketch,* p. 254.

62. *Nashville Whig*, July 24, 1822.

63. "Diary of Rebecca Mandeville, 1848," MS in the Mandeville Collection.

64. Wilson, *Savannah*, p. 179.

65. *Southern Literary Messenger*, XXIV (June 1857), 462–465.

66. *Southern Literary Messenger*, VIII (September 1842), 603.

67. John N. Norwood, *The Schism in the Methodist Episcopal Church, 1844; A Study of Slavery and Ecclesiastical Politics* (Alfred, New York, 1923), pp. 19–20.

68. See William Warren Sweet, *The Story of Religion in America* (New York, 1939), pp. 428ff.

69. Norwood, *Schism*, pp. 134, 132–133.

70. Whitefoord Smith, *God, the Refuge of His People* (Columbia, 1850), pp. 18–19.

71. From the *Daily Picayune*, quoted in William Jay, *A Review of the Causes and Consequences of the Mexican War* (Boston, 1849), pp. 262, 263.

72. Anthony Toomer Porter, *Led On; Step by Step: Scenes from Clerical, Military, Educational and Plantation Life in the South, 1828–1898* (New York, 1898), p. 121.

73. G. H. Steuckrath, *De Bow's Review*, XXVII (November 1859), 606.

74. Olmsted, *Seaboard Slave States*, p. 404.

75. *Southern Literary Messenger*, XXXI (July 1860), 26.

## 11. *Toward a Unified South*

1. Calhoun, *Works*, V, 133ff; and J. Fred Rippy, *Joel R. Poinsett, Versatile American* (Durham, 1935).

2. *Nashville Whig*, March 14, 1821.

3. Quoted in the *Nashville Whig*, January 31, 1821.

4. *Charleston Courier*, February 2, 1821.

5. *Southern Literary Messenger*, X (April 1844), 251. See also the next five issues.

6. *De Bow's Review*, XII (February 1852), 217.

7. *Daily Picayune*, September 9, 1856.

8. They were George W. Crawford, Georgia, 1849; Charles M. Conrad, Virginia, 1850; Jefferson Davis, Mississippi, 1853; and John B. Floyd, Virginia, 1857.

9. U. B. Phillips, "Georgia and State Rights," American Historical Association *Annual Reports for 1901* (Washington, 1902), II, 159; Sir Charles Lyell, *Travels in North America* (London, 1845), I, 188; and Ingle, *Southern Sidelights*, pp. 158–160.

10. Craven, *Edmund Ruffin*, p. 8.

11. *Daily Picayune*, September 13, 1856.

12. See pages 25–26.

13. *Southern Review*, II (November 1828), 473.

14. William E. Martin, *The South: Its Dangers and Resources* (Charleston, 1850), p. 15.

15. John William DeForest, *A Union Officer in the Reconstruction* (New Haven, 1948), p. 177.

16. *Russell's Magazine*, I (May 1857), 106.

17. *Daily Picayune*, May 2, 1857.

18. Thomas Low Nichols, *Forty Years of American Life, 1821–1861* (New York, 1937), pp. 147–148.

19. "The Difference of Race Between the Northern and Southern People," *Southern Literary Messenger*, XXX (June 1860), 405.

20. Henry W. Hilliard, *Speeches and Addresses* (New York, 1855), p. 48. See also Avery O. Craven, *The Growth of Southern Nationalism* (Baton Rouge, 1953), pp. 1–35, 391–401.

21. *Congressional Globe*, 28th Congress, 2nd Session, Appendix, January 25, 1845, p. 314.

22. *Southern Quarterly Review*, XI (April 1847), iv.

23. See page 135.

24. C. K. Marshall, "Southern Authors — School Books and Presses," *De Bow's Review*, XXI (November 1856), 519–520.

25. *New Orleans Daily Delta*, October 14, 1856.

26. *De Bow's Review*, XXIII (October 1856), 337.

27. *Southern Quarterly Review*, II (September 1850), 179.

28. *Ibid.*, II (September 1850), 25–26.

29. *De Bow's Review*, XXV (November 1858), 590. Northern and Southern sources, however, reveal that Southerners continued to visit the North in large numbers down to 1861.

30. Fitzhugh, *Cannibals All*, p. 88.

31. Du Bose, *Yancey*, I, 362.

32. Carl Russell Fish, *Rise of the Common Man* (New York, 1927), pp. 288–289.

33. *Russell's Magazine*, I (May 1857), 178.

34. Henry C. Carey, *The North and South* (New York, 1854), p. 7.

35. *Russell's Magazine*, I (May 1857), 107.

36. *Southern Literary Messenger*, XXX (June 1860), 401–409.

37. A. Roane, "The South, In the Union or Out of It," *De Bow's Review*, XXIX (October 1860), 448–465.

38. Osterweis, *Romanticism and Nationalism*, p. 93.

39. See Ralph Henry Gabriel, *The Course of American Democratic Thought* (New York, 1940), pp. 89–90.

40. Jesse T. Carpenter, *The South as a Conscious Minority* (New York, 1930), p. 186.

41. *State Documents on Federal Relations*, edited by Herman Vanderburg Ames (Philadelphia, 1906), II, 16.

42. Green, *History of the University of South Carolina*, p. 55.

43. *Proceedings of the Meeting of Delegates from the Southern Rights Associations of South Carolina Held at Charleston, May, 1851* (Columbia, 1851), *passim*.

44. Kibler, *Benjamin Perry*, p. 265.

45. See the *Proceedings of the Southern Rights Convention of the State of Alabama* (Montgomery, 1852).

46. *De Bow's Review*, XVIII (April 1855), 522.

47. See Horace Montgomery, "The Solid South Movement of 1855," *Georgia Historical Quarterly*, XXVI (June 1942), 109ff.

48. Du Bose, *Yancey*, I, 376.

49. Craven, *Edmund Ruffin*, pp. 162–163.

50. Du Bose, *Yancey*, I, 378.

51. *De Bow's Review*, XXVI (March 1859), 346.

52. *Southern Press*, August 22, 1850, quoted in Howard C. Perkins, "A Neglected Phase of the Movement for Southern Unity," *Journal of Southern History*, XII (May 1946), p. 172.

## 12. *Ready to Fight*

1. *Southern Quarterly Review*, III (April 1851), 537.

2. "Rutledge," *Separate State Secession, Practically Discussed* (Edgefield, 1851), p. 7.

3. William Henry Trescott, *The Position and Course of the South* (Charleston, 1850), p. 16.

4. *Daily Picayune*, November 21, 1855.

5. *Ibid.*, November 22, 1857.

6. Herbert Wender, *Southern Commercial Conventions, 1837–1859* (Baltimore, 1930), pp. 220–221.

7. *De Bow's Review*, I (January 1846), 18–20.

8. Lewis Troost, "Military and Naval Resources and Necessities of the South and West," *De Bow's Review*, I (March 1846), 258.

9. Augustus Baldwin Longstreet, *A Voice from the South, Comprising Letters From Georgia to Massachusetts* (Baltimore, 1847), p. 58.

10. Thomas, *South Carolina Military Academy*, pp. 63–65.

11. *Southern Quarterly Review*, II (November 1850), 531–532.

12. Melvin Johnson White, *The Secession Movement in the United States, 1847–1852* (New Orleans, 1916), p. 70.

13. Quoted in the *Southern Literary Messenger*, XIX (October 1853), 645.

14. *New Orleans Daily Delta*, July 17, 1855.

15. *New Orleans Daily Delta*, April 9, 1857.

16. *De Bow's Review,* XXIII (September 1857), 270–271.

17. Perkins, "A Neglected Phase of the Movement for Southern Unity," pp. 153–154.

18. Herbert Collins, "The Southern Industrial Gospel before 1860," *Journal of Southern History,* XII (August 1946), 401.

19. *Southern Literary Messenger,* V (January 1839), 4.

20. *Niles Weekly Register,* April 19, 1845.

21. See Philip G. Davidson, "Industrialism in the Ante-Bellum South," *South Atlantic Quarterly,* XXVII (October 1928), 410–411.

22. William Gregg, *Essays on Domestic Industry* (Charleston, 1845), pp. 29, 31.

23. Broadus Mitchell, *William Gregg, Factory Master of the Old South* (Chapel Hill, 1928), p. 202.

24. William Gregg, "Southern Patronage to Southern Imports and Domestic Industry," *De Bow's Review,* XXX (February 1861), 221.

25. *De Bow's Review,* VIII (January 1850), 1–2.

26. *Austin* (Texas) *Gazette,* quoted in *De Bow's Review,* XX (January 1856), 58.

27. *De Bow's Review,* XXVI (March 1859), 317.

28. Fabian Linden, "Repercussions of Manufacturing in the Ante-Bellum South," *North Carolina Historical Review,* XVII (October 1940), 319.

29. Kathleen Bruce, *Virginia Iron Manufacture in the Slave Era* (New York, 1931), pp. 112–116. See also Claud E. Fuller and Richard D. Steuart, *Firearms of the Confederacy* (Huntington, 1944), p. 45.

30. C. P. Stone to Benjamin Huger, November 22, 1850, MS in the Benjamin Huger Papers, Duke University Library.

31. Bruce, *Virginia Iron Manufacture,* pp. 327–328.

32. *De Bow's Review,* V (April 1848), 379, 380.

33. For example, see the message of Governor Joseph E. Brown in Fielder, *Joseph E. Brown,* p. 165.

34. *De Bow's Review,* XXII (January 1857), 101.

35. *Ibid.,* XXVIII (February 1860), 234.

36. Mark A. Cooper to Howell Cobb, November 20, 1848, in Phillips, "Correspondence of Toombs, Stephens, and Cobb," p. 137.

37. Jere Clemens to George Crawford, January 28, 1850, MS in "War Department, Letters Received," National Archives.

38. James Lyon to John B. Floyd, April 12, 1858, MS in "War Department, Letters Received."

39. *Daily Picayune,* December 22, 1843.

40. *De Bow's Review,* I (March 1846), 266.

41. Wise, *Virginia Military Institute,* p. 30.

42. *Acts of Tennessee, 1823–1824.*

43. Wilson, *Savannah,* p. 177.

44. *Daily Picayune,* February 13, 1857.

45. Casey, "Washington Artillery," p. 472.

46. A. Howard Meneely, *The War Department, 1861* (New York, 1928), pp. 27–28.

47. G. Talcott to C. M. Conrad, February 7, 1851, MS in the Letter Book, Ordnance Office to War Department, X, 85, in the National Archives, hereinafter referred to as Ordnance Office Letters.

48. *Ibid.*, December 9, 1851, Ordnance Office Letters, X, 223.

49. William Maynadier to C. M. Conrad, June 10, 1851, Ordnance Office Letters, X, 127. See also endorsement of H. K. Craig on letter of Samuel Swann, Quartermaster of the Wilmington Light Infantry, April 19, 1853.

50. *De Bow's Review*, XXII (January 1857), 101.

51. H. K. Craig to John B. Floyd, February 1, 1859, Ordnance Office Letters, XII, 242.

52. *Ibid.*, February 8, 1859, Ordnance Office Letters, XII, 243.

53. *Ibid.*, October 25, 1859, Ordnance Office Letters, XII, 314.

54. *Ibid.*, December 13, 1859, Ordnance Office Letters, XII, 336.

55. Fuller, *Firearms of the Confederacy*, p. 3.

56. H. K. Craig to John B. Floyd, November 3, 1860, Ordnance Office Letters, XIII, 13.

57. G. Talcott to C. M. Conrad, February 1, 1851, Ordnance Office Letters, X, 83.

58. H. K. Craig to C. M. Conrad, October 6, 1851, Ordnance Office Letters, X, 170.

59. *Ibid.*, May 14, 1852, Ordnance Office Letters, X, 280.

60. *Ibid.*, March 22, 1853, Ordnance Office Letters, X, 423.

61. H. K. Craig to Jefferson Davis, March 31, 1853, Ordnance Office Letters, X, 425–426.

62. William Maynadier to John B. Floyd, January 4, 1860, Ordnance Office Letters, XII, 343–344.

63. H. K. Craig to John B. Floyd, April 5, 1860, Ordnance Office Letters, XII, 376.

64. *Ibid.*, September 20, 1860, Ordnance Office Letters, XII, 426. See, also, the letter from Craig to Floyd, October 13, 1860, in which Craig reports that the ordnance office had, upon request of the State of Mississippi, provided an inspector to examine the arms that E. Whitney was making for the state but that Whitney refused to permit the inspection. Ordnance Office Letters, XII, 437.

65. John Letcher to John B. Floyd, November 19, 1860, Letters Received, War Department, MS in the National Archives.

66. H. K. Craig to John B. Floyd, November 20, 1860, Ordnance Office Letters, XIII, 21.

67. *Ibid.*, November 20, 1860, Ordnance Office Letters, XIII, 21.

68. William Maynadier's endorsement on letter of G. W. Randolph,

November 12, 1860, and his endorsement on letter of S. Adams, November 26, 1860, Ordnance Office Letters. XIII, 22.

69. William Maynadier's endorsement on letter of Joseph E. Brown, December 1, 1860, Ordnance Office Letters, XIII, 24.

70. H. K. Craig to J. Holt, January 15, 1861, Ordnance Office Letters, XIII, 48.

71. Floyd has been cleared of complicity in this matter by many authors, including Meneely, *War Department*, p. 40; George T. Curtis, *The Life of James Buchanan* (New York, 1883), II, 411; Philip G. Auchampaugh, *James Buchanan and His Cabinet on the Eve of Secession* (Lancaster, 1926), p. 90; and Chauncey F. Black, *Essays and Speeches of Jeremiah S. Black* (New York, 1885), pp. 267–268.

72. Meneely, *War Department*, pp. 47–48.

73. Henry T. Shanks, *The Secession Movement in Virginia, 1847–1861* (Richmond, 1934), pp. 95–96.

74. Christian, *Richmond*, p. 203.

75. Catherine C. Hopley, *Life in the South* (London, 1863), I, 80.

76. Joseph Carlyle Sitterson, *The Secession Movement in North Carolina* (Chapel Hill, 1939), pp. 150–151.

77. Arney Robinson Childs, editor, *The Private Journal of Henry William Ravenel* (Columbia, 1947), p. 4.

78. Avirett, *General Turner Ashby*, p. 66.

79. *The Sherman Letters — Correspondence Between General and Senator Sherman from 1837 to 1891*, edited by Rachel Sherman Thorndike (New York, 1894), p. 80.

80. Hammond, *Letters and Speeches*, p. 85.

81. Edwin Heriot, "Commerce, Naval, and Military Resources of Charleston," *De Bow's Review*, III (June 1847), 518–519.

82. Casey, "Washington Artillery," p. 481.

83. "History of Richmond," *Southern Literary Messenger*, XVIII (May 1852), 265.

84. Martin, *The South: Its Dangers and Resources*, p. 27.

85. *De Bow's Review*, XXIII (September 1857), 236.

86. *De Bow's Review*, XXX (May, June 1861), 677–678.

87. Edson Leone Whitney, *The American Peace Society: A Centennial History* (Washington, 1928), pp. 24–25, 325–334, and Merle Curti, *The American Peace Crusade, 1815–1860* (Durham, 1929), pp. 32, 217.

88. Ellis Merton Coulter, *John Jacobus Flournoy, Champion of the Common Man in the Ante-Bellum South* (Savannah, 1942), pp. 70–71.

89. Alexander B. Meek, *Romantic Passages in Southwestern History* (Mobile, 1857), p. 206.

90. *Congressional Globe*, 30th Congress, 1st Session, Appendix, 380.

91. *Southern Literary Messenger*, XVII (February 1851), 65.

92. Hill, "Military Education," pp. 107–108.

93. *Southern Literary Messenger*, XIII (March 1847), 159.

94. *Ibid.*, XXVI (April 1858), 247–248. "Songs of the South" was a series of poems.

95. *De Bow's Review*, XXVII (March 1860), 303.

96. *Ibid.*, XXIX (August 1860), 185.

97. Joseph I. Greene, *The Living Thoughts of Clausewitz* (Philadelphia, 1943), pp. 20–21.

98. See Karl Liebknecht, *Militarism* (New York, 1917), pp. 72–73, 90.

# Index

# DATE DUE

| | | | |
|---|---|---|---|
| | | | |
| | | | |
| | | | |
| | | | |
| | | | |
| | | | |
| | | | |
| | | | |
| | | | |
| | | | |
| | | | |
| | | | |
| | | | |
| | | | |
| | | | |
| | | | |
| | | | |
| GAYLORD | | | PRINTED IN U.S.A. |